NATURE OF THE
APPALACHIAN TRAIL

2nd Edition

Your Guide to
Wildlife, Plants, and Geology

T0125499

OTHER BOOKS BY LEONARD M. ADKINS

Adventure Guide to Virginia

All About the Appalachian Trail (for ages 9–13)

The Appalachian Trail: A Visitor's Companion (the prior edition of this book)

The Best of the Appalachian Trail: Day Hikes (with Victoria and Frank Logue)

The Best of the Appalachian Trail: Overnight Hikes (with Victoria and Frank Logue)

The Caribbean: A Walking and Hiking Guide

50 Hikes in Maryland: Walks, Hikes, and Backpacks from the Allegheny Plateau to the Atlantic Ocean

50 Hikes in Northern Virginia: Walks, Hikes, and Backpacks from the Allegheny Mountains to the Chesapeake Bay

50 Hikes in Southern Virginia: From the Cumberland Gap to the Atlantic Ocean

50 Hikes in West Virginia: From the Allegheny Mountains to the Ohio River

Hiking and Traveling the Blue Ridge Parkway: The Only Guide You Will Ever Need, Including GPS, Detailed Maps, and More

Images of America: Along the Appalachian Trail: Georgia, North Carolina, and Tennessee

Images of America: Along the Appalachian Trail: Massachusetts, Vermont, and New Hampshire

Images of America: Along the Appalachian Trail: New Jersey, New York, and Connecticut

Images of America: Along the Appalachian Trail: West Virginia, Maryland, and Pennsylvania

Images of America: Along Virginia's Appalachian Trail

Maryland: An Explorer's Guide

Postcards of America: Along Virginia's Appalachian Trail

West Virginia: An Explorer's Guide

Wildflowers of the Appalachian Trail (Joe Cook and Monica Sheppard, photographers)

Wildflowers of the Blue Ridge and Great Smoky Mountains (Joe Cook, photographer)

NATURE OF THE APPALACHIAN TRAIL

2nd Edition

Your Guide to Wildlife, Plants, and Geology

LEONARD M. ADKINS

MENASHA RIDGE PRESS
Your Guide to the Outdoors Since 1982

NATURE OF THE APPALACHIAN TRAIL: Your Guide to Wildlife, Plants, and Geology
Leonard M. Adkins
1st edition 1998
2nd edition 2021, 2nd printing 2021

Copyright © 1998 and 2021 by Leonard M. Adkins
Project editor: Kate Johnson
Cover design: Scott McGrew
Cover photo: The Appalachian Trail as it passes through the Blue Ridge Mountains of western North Carolina.
   © Dave Allen Photography/Shutterstock
Text design: Grant Tatum, with updates by Annie Long
Illustrations: Grant Tatum
Interior photos by Leonard M. Adkins except: pages 2 and 167: Laurie M. Adkins; pages 7 and 9, courtesy
   Appalachian Trail Conservancy; pages 93, 143, 145, 147, 150, and 152 by Ann B. Messicks; page 100 by Brian
   Bardin/Shutterstock; page 136 by Tom Reichner/Shutterstock; page 137 by Jennifer McCallum/Shutterstock;
   pages 138 (bottom) and 139 by FotoRequest/Shutterstock; page 138 (top) by Phaeton Place/Shutterstock;
   page 140 by Agami Photo Agency/Shutterstock; page 141 by RelentlessImages/Shutterstock; page 142 by
   Marc Goldman/Shutterstock; page 143 by Paul Reeves Photography/Shutterstock; page 144 by Cuong Pham/
   Shutterstock; page 149 (bottom) by Tsuguto Hayashi/Shutterstock; page 147 (bottom) by Svoboda Pavel/
   Shutterstock; page 150 by Malachi Jacobs/Shutterstock
Proofreader: Emily Beaumont
Indexer: Rich Carlson

Library of Congress Cataloging-in-Publication Data

Names: Adkins, Leonard M., author.
Title: Nature of the Appalachian trail : your guide to wildlife, plants, and geology / Leonard M. Adkins.
Other titles: Appalachian trail
Description: Second Edition. | Birmingham, AL : Menasha Ridge Press, 2021. | Revised edition of:
   The Appalachian Trail : a visitor's companion, 1998. | Includes bibliographical references and index.
Identifiers: LCCN 2021003057 (print) | LCCN 2021003058 (ebook) | ISBN 9781634043335 (pbk.) |
   ISBN 9781634043342 (ebook)
Subjects: LCSH: Hiking—Appalachian Trail—Guidebooks. | Natural history—Appalachian Trail—Guidebooks.
   | Natural history—Appalachian Trail. | Appalachian Trail—Guidebooks.
Classification: LCC GV199.42.A68 A35 2021 (pbk,) | LCC GV199.42.A68 (ebook) |
   DDC 796.510974—dc23
LC record available at lccn.loc.gov/2021003057
LC ebook record available at lccn.loc.gov/2021003058

Published by Menasha Ridge Press

MENASHA RIDGE PRESS
An imprint of AdventureKEEN
2204 First Ave. S, Ste. 102
Birmingham, Alabama 35233
888-604-4537, fax 205-326-1012

Visit menasharidge.com for a complete listing of our books and for ordering information. Contact us at our website, at
facebook.com/menasharidge, or at twitter.com/menasharidge with questions or comments. To find out more about who
we are and what we're doing, visit blog.menasharidge.com.

TABLE OF CONTENTS

DEDICATION

For Nancy Adkins,

whose inner strength and life wisdom

never cease to amaze me, her son

ACKNOWLEDGMENTS

So MANY PEOPLE provided assistance and encouragement throughout the process of preparing this book for publication that it would be impossible to acknowledge every one of them. However, special thanks must be expressed to Brian King, publisher for the Appalachian Trail Conservancy, for scrutinizing the chapters on the history and route of the Appalachian Trail; Ann Messick, for her amazing knowledge of flowers (and their scientific names); Dan Smith, for looking over several chapters in their early stages of development; V. Collins Chew, author of *Underfoot: A Geologic Guide to the Appalachian Trail,* as the geology chapter would never have been finished without his help, although the final draft may not coincide completely with his opinions; Karen Michaud, for verifying information about Shenandoah National Park; Janet Williams, Robert Williams, and Michael Greenwald, for their generous permission to reprint their bird checklist; and Dr. Stephen Lewis and Caroline Charonko, for the new life I've been granted.

The biggest thank-yous go to Benton MacKaye for having dreamt of the Appalachian Trail in the first place and to every trail volunteer who has ever worked to make and keep that dream a reality.

The final thanks must go to Laurie, for without her, none of my travels, writings, or happiness would be possible.

Nature gives to every time

and every season

some beauties of its own;

and from morning to night,

as from cradle to grave,

it is but a succession of changes

so gentle and easy

that we can scarcely mark their progress.

~ Charles Dickens

NATURE OF THE
APPALACHIAN TRAIL
2nd Edition

Your Guide to
Wildlife, Plants, and Geology

INTRODUCTION

It has been quite a few years now since a friend suggested we hike the entire Appalachian Trail together. My response was, "Sure, let's do it, but what is it?" I had not heard of the trail and, never having backpacked a day in my life, had little idea of the wonderful world to which I was about to be introduced.

About two weeks before the trip was to begin, the instigator of the adventure backed out. Having saved funds for more than a year and obtained the necessary equipment and a leave of absence from work, I began the journey alone. With many adventures and misadventures—some good, some risky, and some downright hilarious—but due mostly to my inexperience, I accomplished only 900 miles that year.

Returning to work, I felt that I'd had my summer of freedom, that it was time to concentrate on the job and get back on the career track. Throughout the winter, though, I kept having mental images of the places I had seen, the people I had met, and the beauty of the mountains I had experienced. The following spring, I returned to the trail and started walking northward from where I had stopped the previous year.

Somehow, during the winter, my experiences on the trail had worked a subtle change inside of me, and I no longer perceived it to be a months-long, 2,000-mile challenge. The uncertainty as to whether I would ever complete the entire trek no longer seemed to matter. The constant, nagging thought that had plagued me the previous year—that no matter how far I had progressed along the way, I was still "here" and Maine was still hundreds and hundreds of miles away "up there"—no longer had me in its defeatist sway. The trip became nothing more than a series of day hikes in the woods, simply walking, and no longer dreading the uphills, cursing every ankle-twisting rock, or fighting every out-of-the-way turn the trail took. I truly began looking at and enjoying my surroundings of the moment—the shapes of the trees, the sunlight filtering through the leaves, the smell of the forest as a summer rain washed over it, the changing color and composition of the soil, the songs of the individual birds, the antics of squirrels and chipmunks, the silent motion of a blacksnake slithering along the woodlands floor. Having come to accept the ways of the trail, I reveled in the muscle-building undulations of the terrain and welcomed each step as an opportunity to see, smell, hear, taste, or feel some new discovery.

Sooner than expected, I had walked the additional 1,200 miles to complete my journey of the Appalachian Trail. Since that time, I have hiked more than 20,000 miles in the United States, Canada, New Zealand, the Caribbean, and Europe. I have followed the Continental Divide from Canada to Mexico along the crest of the Rocky

Author Leonard Adkins at the northern terminus of the Appalachian Trail

Mountains; walked from Glacier National Park to the Pacific Ocean through the mountains of Montana, Idaho, and Washington; traced the Great Divide in Canada for several hundred miles; traversed the glaciers of Iceland; topped the steaming volcanoes of the Caribbean Islands; looked down upon Europe from the crest of the Alps; hiked New Zealand's Milford Track and that country's other Great Walks; and crisscrossed the border of France and Spain along the full length of the Pyrenees.

And yet, the Appalachians, my native mountains, continue to draw me back. I have now hiked the Appalachian Trail in its entirety five times and am within about 600 miles of completing it a sixth time.

While there is no doubt that I enjoy the grandeur of scenery from the higher altitudes of other mountain ranges of the world, I find that the pointed spires of their rough and rocky ridgelines appear like the upraised arms of adversaries, calling me out on a dare to test my mettle, to see if I can survive their soaring elevations, precipitous terrain, or ferocious weather. On the other hand, even though the Appalachian Trail is more physically challenging than any other trail I have hiked, the softer, eroded lines of its mountains, with their gradually descending spur ridges covered in lush vegetation, suggest a compassionate and kindly mother, wanting to encircle me and welcome me with arms cloaked in a shawl of green, reassuring me that everything will be alright.

It was for the love of these Appalachian Mountains that I set out to learn more about them: how they were formed; what makes them what they are; how the individual life-forms make up the whole; and how they can best be appreciated, protected, and preserved.

The one problem I had in putting this book together was deciding not what information to include, but what to exclude. Entire books have been written about just one animal, one plant, one river, one mountain. This book is an overview of more than 2,000 miles worth of these things.

So, I have included as much as was practicable without turning it into an encyclopedia. I have limited the discussion of historical incidents to those that occurred directly on what today is the corridor of land through which the Appalachian Trail passes. This will explain why certain important events that took place adjacent to trail lands, such as some Revolutionary War or Civil War battles, are not discussed.

Where there are competing scientific speculations on topics—such as how the mountains were formed, the origins of the balds in the southern states, or why an animal behaves in a particular manner—I have presented as many of the theories as possible. I have named nearly every mammal inhabiting the mountains and have discussed the hundred or so flowers that are mentioned in the official trail guidebooks available from the Appalachian Trail Conservancy. The same is true for birds.

The longer I study the environment of the trail, the more convinced I become that its greatest importance—much more than the recreational opportunities it provides—is its preservation of the natural world from the encroachments and destructions of the modern world. Because of the Appalachian Trail, rare lungless salamanders may continue to exist, birds still have an unbroken forest from Georgia to Maine in which to rest during their annual migrations, certain flowers and plants have protection and may someday no longer be endangered or threatened, and large mammals—such as bears and moose—now have the extensive tracts of land needed to ensure their survival. I firmly believe that our descendants will look upon such things as the true value and legacy of the Appalachian Trail.

You will note that each time I discuss a particular site I also mention the national park or the state in which it is located. This has been done to make it easier for you to pinpoint each location by consulting the index of the corresponding official trail guidebook available from the Appalachian Trail Conservancy. For example, the chapter on flowers states that diapensia grows near the summit of Mount Lafayette in New Hampshire, so you would consult the Appalachian Trail Guide to New Hampshire–Vermont. Because Virginia contains such a large portion of the trail, four separate guidebooks cover southwest Virginia, central Virginia, Shenandoah National Park, and (Maryland and) northern Virginia.

I also strongly encourage you to make use of the books listed in the Bibliography and Suggested Readings and Field Guides appendix (page 201) to increase your knowledge and enjoyment of the Appalachian Trail and its environs.

May all of your wanderings bring you pleasure, wonder, new discoveries, and an appreciation of the natural world.

Happy trails.

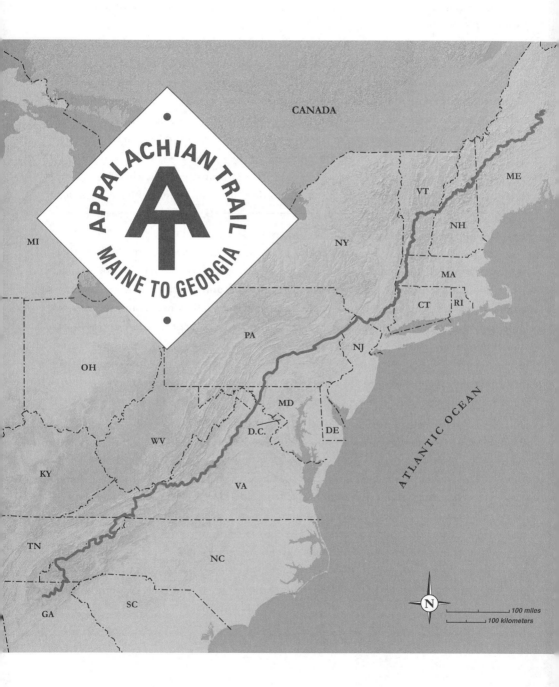

CANADA

ME

VT

NH

MI

NY

MA

CT RI

PA

NJ

OH

ATLANTIC OCEAN

MD

D.C.

DE

WV

KY

VA

TN

NC

N

100 miles

100 kilometers

SC

GA

CHAPTER 1

A Concise History of the Appalachian Trail

The ultimate purpose of the Appalachian Trail?

To walk. To see. And to see what you see.

~ Benton MacKaye

ALTHOUGH OTHER PEOPLE had put forth similar ideas, Benton MacKaye's article "An Appalachian Trail: A Project in Regional Planning," which appeared in the October 1921 issue of the *Journal of the American Institute of Architects,* is generally regarded as having provided the impetus for the Appalachian Trail (AT). A regional planner, MacKaye (pronounced "McKye") saw in the post–World War I era an America that was becoming rapidly urbanized, machine-driven, and far removed from the positive and reinvigorating aspects of the natural world. In addition to providing obvious recreational opportunities, the trail he envisioned would be a connecting line between a series of permanent, self-sustaining camps in which "cooperation replaces antagonism, trust replaces suspicion, emulation replaces competition."

Encouraged and aided by relatives, friends, and like-minded acquaintances, MacKaye set about spreading the idea of an Appalachian Trail to anyone who would listen, including officials of the National Park and U.S. Forest Services. Especially receptive to the trail concept were members and officers of already existing trail organizations such as the Green Mountain Club of Vermont, the New England Trail Conference, and the Appalachian Mountain Club. Not overlooking the publicity power of the press, MacKaye also solicited the support of newspaper reporters and columnists throughout the Northeast. The idea struck a chord, for in October 1923, just two years after publication of his article, the first few miles of trail to be built specifically as a part of the AT were opened to the public in the area of Harriman and Bear Mountain State Parks in New York by the then recently formed New York–New Jersey Trail Conference.

Acting upon a request by MacKaye and others, the Federal Societies on Planning and Parks met in Washington, D.C., in March 1925, for the purpose of furthering action on the AT. There, a constitution establishing the Appalachian Trail Conference (ATC) was adopted, and William A. Welch, of New York's Palisades Interstate Park Commission, was named its chairman. During the meeting, it was decided that the AT would run approximately 1,700 miles from Mount Washington in New Hampshire to Cohutta Mountain in northwestern Georgia. A northern extension was to stretch to Mount Katahdin in Maine, while a southern addition would reach all the way to Birmingham, Alabama. Among various branch routes that were also proposed, one was to follow the Long Trail in Vermont, another would extend into the Catskills, and another was to run along the Tennessee River into Kentucky.

With the establishment of the Potomac Appalachian Trail Club (PATC) in 1927, and the appointments of Arthur Perkins and Myron H. Avery as ATC chairman and assistant chairman in 1928, construction of the AT began to rapidly accelerate. Avery, a founding member of the PATC whose indefatigable energies have been likened to those of Bob Marshall (a founder of the Wilderness Society), took it upon himself to recruit volunteers and to spread the word about the AT. Perhaps more important, he went out into the field scouting practical routes for the trail and building and blazing multiple miles of the pathway. With his help, and within four years of its formation, the PATC constructed more than 250 miles of trail and solicited enough volunteers to create trail clubs that would reach all the way to Georgia.

With more than 1,200 miles of the AT completed, Avery became ATC chairman in 1931. During his tenure, construction of the trail throughout its entire north–south route continued to accelerate, and more than 1,900 miles of trail were completed by the end of 1934.

Sadly, during this time, it was becoming obvious that the two most avid proponents of the AT had different visions of what the trail should be. MacKaye continued to iterate that the pathway was more or less a means for regional planning, a way to establish workers' communities along its route. His hope was that those communities would help to foster an America that would question the continued expansion of its cities and the increasing enslavement to mechanized work and commercialism. Avery, on the other hand, saw the trail as a footpath through the mountains for those who wished to enjoy the benefits of outdoor recreational opportunities.

Construction of the Skyline Drive through Shenandoah National Park drove the final wedge between the two men. Avery accepted the venture, seeing it as a means of acquiring further federal governmental support for the AT, thereby aiding his agenda of completing the trail as quickly as possible. In some ways he was correct; at the very least, the portion of the AT that was displaced by the Skyline Drive project was relocated and reconstructed by the government-funded Civilian Conservation Corps (CCC). Having set a precedent, other divisions of the CCC ended up constructing somewhat limited, but significant portions of the trail throughout its entire route. It is a lasting tribute to these hardworking men that most of the trail sections they built in the 1930s are still in use today, requiring little maintenance or repair.

MacKaye, in direct contrast to Avery, despised the building of skyline drives anywhere. He felt they were not only intrusions on the natural world, but also, in reality, conspiracies by businessmen determined to make a monetary profit off the wilderness. This fundamental difference between the two men was so great that MacKaye more or less turned his back on the AT, putting his time and efforts into the Wilderness Society, which he helped form in 1935.

By 1936, the entire route of the Appalachian Trail had been constructed or laid out on paper. In the same year, Avery became its first 2,000-miler, having hiked and measured every mile of the trail—whether it had been built or not. On August 14, 1937, the final section of the trail was constructed on a ridgeline connecting Sugarloaf and Spaulding Mountains in central Maine. So, in less than 16 years from the publication of MacKaye's original article, the AT was a reality, a continuously marked, 2,045-mile footpath from Maine to Georgia. This feat is even more remarkable as most of the work on the trail was done by volunteers whose only real motivation was a love of the outdoors and whose sole compensation was the satisfaction of having contributed to the successful completion of such a noble project.

Barely a year later, the AT's continuous route was broken. In 1938, a major hurricane swept through the Northeast, killing an estimated 700 people, leaving 60,000 people homeless and toppling millions of trees. So many miles of trail were destroyed in New England that it overwhelmed the best efforts of volunteer trail crews. Soon afterward, construction of the Blue Ridge Parkway displaced so much of the AT in Virginia and North Carolina that more than 110 miles of the trail would eventually have to be relocated and rebuilt. Americans focused their attention on their

Benton MacKaye set about spreading the idea of an Appalachian Trail.

country's efforts abroad during World War II, and more and more miles of the trail fell into disrepair. With so much of the trail in need of attention after the war, many people (including Avery) began to doubt the AT would ever again be one continuous route.

Recognizing the fragility of the route, Daniel Koch (a member of the ATC board of managers, president of the Blue Mountain Eagle Climbing Club of Pennsylvania, and, most important, a member of the US Congress) introduced legislation in the House of Representatives in 1945 to establish a system of federally protected footways. Unfortunately, the bill never made it out of committee. The same was true for similar legislation introduced in 1948.

Yet, as often seems to be the case throughout human history, just when things are looking their bleakest, a popular hero arises whose exploits inspire people to take the necessary actions. In 1948, Earl V. Shaffer became the trail's first "thru-hiker" by walking the entire 2,050-mile route from Georgia to Maine in a continuous four-month trek. Shaffer, an unassuming man from Pennsylvania, undertook the journey not to set any records, but merely to enjoy some time in the mountains and to put his memories of service in World War II in perspective. Armed with just road maps and no guidebooks, Shaffer found an Appalachian Trail with few blazes and signs, its way blocked by hundreds, if not thousands, of blowdowns and its route forced onto many roadways because of timbering operations or disputes with landowners. To protect himself from the overgrowth, Shaffer always clad himself in long pants, and in order to toughen his feet, he walked with sand in his boots but wore no socks.

Many people in the trail community, including both MacKaye and Avery, initially doubted that Shaffer had actually walked the entire length of the trail. Only after he presented a detailed daily account of his trip, showed hundreds of slides he had taken along the way, and submitted to hours of grueling questioning was Shaffer proclaimed the first thru-hiker by the Appalachian Trail Conference.

An article carried by the Associated Press about Shaffer's exploits soon appeared in many newspapers nationwide, piquing the public's curiosity about the trail. Ensuing articles in *Reader's Digest* and *National Geographic* brought more publicity to the pathway and an upsurge in the number of trail volunteers. Through the efforts of these volunteers, the AT once again would be a continuous 2,000-mile trail by the end of 1951. That same year, 24-year-old Gene Espy of Georgia became the second man to thru-hike the AT, duplicating Shaffer's hike in the same amount of time, four months. The following year, as far as records can tell, Mildred Norman Ryder became the first woman to hike the entire trail, hiking initially northward with a male companion to the Susquehanna River and then, after taking motorized transportation to Mount Katahdin, walking southward back to Pennsylvania.

In June 1952, Avery stepped down as chairman of the Appalachian Trail Conference after 20 years. Murray H. Stevens, a former chairman of the New York–New Jersey

Trail Conference and an active supporter of the AT for more than two decades, was elected the new chairman. Just eight weeks later, Avery collapsed and died while on a trip to Canada.

In 1955, Emma "Grandma" Gatewood, who walked in sneakers and carried her gear in a duffel bag slung over her shoulders, became the first woman to thru-hike the trail alone. (She would make history again by eventually becoming the first person to hike the entire length of the AT three times.)

The 1950s turned out to be a decade spent fine-tuning the trail. Many clubs undertook the task of relocating large portions of the trail to more optimal locations—off roads, along scenic streams, over additional peaks, and out to better viewpoints. Because of increased development on and around Mount Oglethorpe, the southern terminus of the AT was moved to Springer Mountain in 1958.

The trail was, in fact, being threatened by numerous developments along the whole of its length. Mining and logging operations, ski resorts, housing projects, communication and utility towers and lines, and new roadways were encroaching on the trailway and detracting from the general nature of its wilderness experience. Additionally, federal plans to construct several new scenic parkways would severely impact the AT in a number of states.

In response to these threats (and the crusading efforts of trail volunteers and supporters), Senator Gaylord Nelson introduced a bill in 1964 to federally protect the AT.

Myron H. Avery became the first 2,000-miler, having hiked and measured every mile of the trail—whether it had been built or not.

As with much legislation, the bill went through several revisions and its original scope was expanded. Finally, Senator Nelson's intentions became reality when the National Trails System Act was passed and signed into law by President Lyndon Johnson on October 2, 1968. The Appalachian Trail and the Pacific Crest Trail (which runs from Mexico to Canada through California, Oregon, and Washington) were designated the country's first two national scenic trails. The act gave the National Park Service (through the Interior Department) the primary responsibility for administering the AT and authorized the agency to protect the pathway through easements; cooperative agreements; land exchanges, donations, or purchases; and, as a final resort, acquisition of land through eminent domain. Five million dollars of public funds were appropriated for the purchase of trail lands. Additionally, the act authorized agreements between the Interior Department and nonfederal agencies—in effect, the ATC and its affiliated clubs—to "operate, develop, and maintain" the trail.

Recognizing that the task of managing the AT was becoming too complex for volunteers alone to handle, the ATC hired Lester L. Holmes in 1968 as a part-time administrative officer, soon upgrading his position to full-time executive director. In 1972, the conference moved out of Washington, D.C. (where it had been sharing facilities with PATC), and relocated just a short walk from the AT in Harpers Ferry, West Virginia.

The backpacking boom of the late 1960s and early 1970s necessitated the hiring of more full-time employees, primarily to keep up with requests for information about the trail (and to educate people about proper trail etiquette). From 1936 to 1969, just 50 people had walked the entire AT. Yet, by the end of 1974, the number of 2,000-milers had increased to nearly 300.

The year 1975 saw several administrative changes as George M. Zoebelein was elected ATC chairman to succeed Stan A. Murray, who retired after 14 years in the position. Another retirement, that of Lester L. Holmes, led to the hiring of Paul Pritchard as executive director. Pritchard relinquished his position in 1977 when he was appointed to the Interior Department, and he was replaced by Henry W. Lautz.

Benton MacKaye, the man whose efforts not only bore fruit on the AT, but also helped shape the way Americans view their responsibilities toward the wilderness, died on December 11, 1975, at the age of 96.

Although an AT Project Office was opened by the National Park Service in 1976, disappointment and apprehension remained high concerning the service's general lack of progress procuring lands for the AT. Eventually, trail supporters influenced Congress to make amendments to the National Trails System Act, and these were signed into law on March 21, 1978, by President Jimmy Carter. At that time, less than 1,250 miles of the trail were in the public trust. The act appropriated $90 million in federal funds to purchase—over several years—the acreage needed to move the other 900 or so miles of trail off roadways and private property.

To coordinate efforts more efficiently with the ATC, the National Park Service moved its AT Project Office from its original location to Harpers Ferry and the office's manager, David T. Ritchie, began an aggressive campaign to acquire the thousands of acres that were needed to bring the full length of the AT into the public domain. The office was so successful in completing its mission that its name was changed to the Appalachian Trail Park Office to reflect the fact that, by the end of 1996, less than 35 miles of trail remained in private hands; the land-purchase "project" was coming to an end, and management of the AT as a true component of the national park system was beginning.

In 1979, Charles L. Pugh was elected ATC chairman but decided to resign early in 1980. After a short period in which cochairs presided over the board of managers, Ruth Blackburn was elected to fill the position until Pugh's term expired. Soon afterward, Henry Lautz resigned as executive director, and Lawrence Van Meter of the Green Mountain Club was named his successor.

Although federal funding was available for the continued acquisition of AT lands, there was a growing fear among the trail's supporters that the funding would be cut or eliminated. Under the guise of helping to balance the federal budget, Secretary of the Interior James Watt and others in the administration of President Ronald Reagan were putting forth the idea of abolishing or cutting land-acquisition programs. In response, the Trust for Appalachian Trail Lands, which was funded privately for the most part, was established in 1982.

Although federal funding has not been eliminated, it has not been available at times to purchase important pieces of property: Either the federal government couldn't react quickly enough or the funds appropriated for a particular year were already exhausted. It has been at these times that the trust has proved to be a valuable resource for the AT, not only by obtaining bits and pieces of the trail route itself but also by purchasing tracts of land outside the actual AT corridor, thereby protecting important viewsheds and the wilderness nature of the trail. The trust was eventually phased out, but today the Appalachian Trail Landscape Partnership, a cooperative effort of the ATC, NPS, and scores of other organizations, works to identify high-priority lands that are in need of protection.

Elected as ATC chairman in 1983, Raymond F. Hunt helped lead the conference into an amazingly unprecedented collaboration with the US government. Showing its faith in the capabilities of the volunteers and members of ATC, the National Park Service delegated most of its responsibility for managing the Appalachian Trail to the ATC in January 1984. This meant that, even though federal monies were being used to purchase land for the trail, its day-to-day affairs would be overseen by those most closely associated with it.

Because of the makeup of its organization, the ATC in turn has relegated the vast majority of its responsibility for care of the footpath to the volunteers of the local trail clubs. Volunteers have always been the backbone of the AT, and, in many ways, may be even more valuable to the trail than the ATC. To this day, it is volunteers who undertake the bulk of trail maintenance, devoting weekends and other spare time to relocating and rebuilding the pathway and keeping it clear of undergrowth and blowdowns. When a major hurricane ripped through the Southern states in 1995, the National Park Service predicted the trail in North Carolina and Georgia would be closed for months; yet so many volunteers rose to the challenge that the AT was open again in just a few weeks. (In recent years, more than 6,000 volunteers have been contributing well in excess of 200,000 hours of trail-related labor annually!)

Sometimes volunteer efforts don't involve weed whacking or local club functions. Oftentimes individuals' simple love of the AT causes them to respond publicly or politically to situations that threaten to destroy the integrity of the trail. A perfect example of this is that the Virginia Department of Transportation canceled plans in 1996 to build a four-lane highway across the AT in the Mount Rogers National Recreation Area after having received hundreds of letters in protest.

Volunteers also make up the boards of most of the local trail clubs, devoting numerous evenings and days sitting through meetings to ensure that their sections of trail remain in the best shape possible.

Under the 1984 ATC/NPS agreement, volunteers took on new responsibilities, which included monitoring the trail lands for any problems, such as encroachment, development, timbering and the like, or illegal use by motorized vehicles or bicycles.

In 1986, Dave Startzell, who had been on the ATC's staff since 1978, was named executive director, and in 1989, Margaret Drummond took over as chair of the board of managers. Under their guidance, there was speedy growth in the conference's general membership; it stood at about 24,000 by the end of 1996.

David B. Field, who took his first hike on the AT in 1955 and went on to become a trail maintainer, officer in the Maine Appalachian Trail Club, and member of the ATC board of managers, was named ATC chair at the conference's biennial meeting in 1995.

In 2005, to reflect the increasing need to protect the AT and the land around it, the Appalachian Trail Conference was renamed the Appalachian Trail Conservancy.

Today, the job of bringing the entire length of the AT under public protection is nearly complete. But, in the words of Myron Avery, "the trail, as such, will never be completed." There will always be the need to safeguard the pathway from the encroachments of modern civilization, such as new highway construction, increasing communications and utility-line towers, and nearby housing developments.

In many ways, the AT is being threatened by its own successes. Increasingly, the Appalachian Trail Conservancy, the National Park Service, the local maintaining clubs, and other managing agencies must focus on ways to manage and minimize the impact of the rapidly rising number of people who come to hike on the trail. It took from the inception of the AT in the 1920s to the early 1980s for the first 1,000 people to hike the entire trail. Now, in the span of just four decades, the number of officially certified 2,000-milers has risen to well over 20,000.

It is not only thru-hikers who are on the increase. The conservancy estimates that millions of people make use of some portion of the AT annually. The challenge in the coming years will be not only to protect the actual physical aspects of the trail from such numbers, but also to preserve the quality of trail experiences for those who come in search of the tranquil beauty the trail can provide.

CHAPTER 2

From Georgia to Maine:
The Route of the Appalachian Trail

Every part of this soil is sacred. Every hillside,

every valley, every plain and grove has been hallowed

by some sad or happy event in days long vanished.

~ Chief Seattle

THE SOUTHERN STATES

From its southern terminus atop Springer Mountain, the Appalachian Trail winds its way through Georgia in a northeasterly direction for more than 75 miles. Staying close to the crest of the Blue Ridge Mountains, it rarely drops below 3,000 feet in elevation and it attains the 4,000-foot mark on Blood, Blue, Rocky, and Tray Mountains and Kelly Knob. Soon after entering North Carolina, it turns to the northwest, crosses the ridgelines of several transverse mountain ranges, tops the summits of numerous mountains above 5,000 feet, and enters Great Smoky Mountains National Park. Once it attains the height of the land, the trail straddles the North Carolina–Tennessee border through the Smokies, over Snowbird Mountain, and across the Bald and Unaka Mountain ranges. It then makes a bit of a swing westward into Tennessee to drop into Laurel Fork Gorge, go by Watauga Lake, and cross the Iron Mountains to arrive at the Virginia border.

THE APPALACHIAN TRAIL follows the crest of the Blue Ridge Mountains for nearly half its length, that is, from Georgia to central Pennsylvania. In order to have an appreciation of the trail's route, it is necessary to understand the makeup of these mountains. The Blue Ridge Mountains have their southern roots in northern Georgia, but immediately they split into two arms. The eastern arm swings out toward the flatter lands of Georgia, North Carolina, and Virginia to form the western boundary of the Piedmont. The western arm, as it is traced northward, is known respectively as the Cohutta, Ellijay, Frog, Unicoi, Great Smoky, Unaka, Iron, and Stone Mountains. It is generally at a higher elevation than the eastern prong and is crossed by numerous rivers, which cut it into several segments.

Forming a large oval, the two arms come back together near the Roanoke River in Virginia. A number of ranges stretch from east to west between the two main ridges, creating a patchwork of additional high-mountain country. Known variously as the Black, Balsam, Cheoah, Nantahala, and other mountains, these transverse ranges contain mountains that are actually higher than the main backbone of the Blue Ridge. In fact, the highest summit of the eastern United States, Mount Mitchell (6,684'), towers above its Black Mountain neighbors quite a few miles east of the AT.

In the early days of the trail, when Cohutta Mountain in the western part of northern Georgia was still being contemplated as its southern terminus, volunteers and planners (especially those in North Carolina) envisioned the pathway working its way southward from the Great Smokies along the western arm of the Blue Ridge. Eventually those who would have to construct the AT in Georgia were able to convince the others that, due to easier accessibility and the chance to use existing pathways on the lands of the Chattahoochee National Forest, the trail could be more readily built along the Blue Ridge's eastern rim.

Once that agreement was reached, volunteer members of the Georgia Appalachian Trail Club (GATC) were able to construct the AT from its original southern terminus on the summit of Mount Oglethorpe in the Amicalola Range to the Georgia–North Carolina border by the spring of 1931. Other than one major relocation—moving the trail's southern terminus to Springer Mountain in 1958 when development on Oglethorpe became incompatible with the trail's wilderness character—the AT has changed little from its original route through Georgia. This means that those who hike here are, without a doubt, walking on some of the very same ground that was trod by such AT pioneers and legends as Myron Avery, Earl Shaffer, Gene Espy, Mildred Norman Ryder, Grandma Gatewood, and Dorothy Laker.

Today, with the summit of Springer Mountain inaccessible to motorized vehicles, a large percentage of hikers begin their AT trip by taking the Approach Trail from Amicalola Falls State Park. (In part, the State of Georgia established this more-than-200-acre park in 1948 to protect the area around one of its most impressive waterfalls. In a series of cascades, Amicalola Creek descends nearly 500 feet down the face of Amicalola Mountain in only 0.3 mile.)

Rough and steep with many ups and downs, the 8-plus miles of the Approach Trail are so strenuous that it convinces many would-be thru-hikers to abandon their dream of walking from Georgia to Maine. Almost every year there are stories of people who never even make it to Springer Mountain before deciding that, if the Appalachian Trail is anything like the Approach Trail, they would rather go home than face the rigors of the 2,000-mile journey.

Unbeknownst to most people who hike the Approach Trail, they are walking upon a historically significant pathway. Portions of this trail follow the original route of the AT that, prior to the 1958 relocation, wound its way through the Amicalola Range from Mount Oglethorpe to Springer Mountain.

The 3,782-foot summit of Springer Mountain overlooks the western arm of the Blue Ridge Mountains and out to the Cohutta Mountains in northwest Georgia. A plaque, originally placed on Oglethorpe in 1933 and moved to Springer Mountain in 1959, provides a simple but succinct definition of the AT: APPALACHIAN TRAIL, GEORGIA TO MAINE, A FOOTPATH FOR THOSE WHO SEEK FELLOWSHIP WITH THE WILDERNESS.

Initially making use of the western arm of the Blue Ridge, the AT crosses Stover Creek amid what is believed to be a stand of virgin hemlock and moves on to the first of many waterfalls passed on its northward journey. Long Creek Falls is striking, especially during heavy spring rains, and it is surrounded by dense thickets of rhododendron. Skirting the side of Hawk Mountain, the AT ascends to the eastern arm of the Blue Ridge Mountains, which it follows closely the rest of the way through Georgia except for a short 4- to 5-mile stretch between Cooper Gap and Gooch Gap.

Twenty miles north of Springer, the trail crosses its first paved road in Woody Gap. It also traverses the first of many congressionally designated wildernesses through which the AT passes. In a farsighted move, the United States achieved permanent protection for certain tracts of land with the passage of the Wilderness Act in 1964. Within a few years, more than 11 million acres had been brought into the National

Wilderness Preservation System. But it soon became apparent that the system was not as far-reaching as its supporters had hoped; all but four of the wilderness areas were west of central Kansas. The law's definition of wilderness, with phrases such as "the area generally appears to have been affected primarily by the forces of nature, with the imprints of man's work substantially unnoticeable," prohibited most areas in the eastern United States from being included in the system. Recognizing that the East, with its earlier settlement and heavier concentrations of population, had more disturbed land than the West, another law was passed in 1975. This one permitted places where the evidence of human activity was gradually being replaced by natural processes to fit into the definition of wilderness. That law (and hard work by wilderness advocates) has enabled more than 800 sites and more than 111 million acres of land throughout the United States to be preserved.

But while the Wilderness Act does protect the land, it contains a provision that makes it harder for trail volunteers to maintain the AT: to preserve the wilderness atmosphere, the act prohibits the use of power tools, such as chainsaws and motorized weed whips. Therefore, all trail maintenance must be done with manual tools, such as handsaws, weed whackers, and hand clippers. With a large percentage of the AT in Georgia traversing designated wilderness areas, GATC volunteers put forth stupendous efforts to keep the trail clear of blowdowns and entangling vegetation, especially after natural disasters, such as hurricanes or heavy ice storms, bring down hundreds of trees and large branches across the trail.

Climbing to 4,000 feet above sea level for the first time, the AT comes to its highest point in Georgia on Blood Mountain (4,461'). The mountain's name can be traced to a battle that, according to Native American legend, occurred on its slopes some 400 years ago. The fight between Cherokee and Creek Indians was so ferocious that the mountain was said to have run red with blood. From that time on, lichens growing upon the rocks have displayed traces of red stains.

Today, the mountain provides an Olympian view of the Blue Ridge Mountains in all directions, with the southward vista extending to Springer Mountain and beyond. On some places on the summit, gneiss, the rock of which the top of the mountain is composed, has been laid bare in a sloping surface almost as smooth as ice. Exfoliation, the process that caused this, has a tendency to crack deeply buried rock parallel to the surface after weathering has eroded the uppermost layer and relieved the pressure bearing down on the rock.

The two-room stone shelter on top of Blood Mountain was constructed by the Civilian Conservation Corps in the 1930s and is of such significance that it has been placed on the National Register of Historic Places. Thanks to an effort among GATC, the U.S. Forest Service, the U.S. Army Rangers, and other volunteers, the shelter has been renovated several times throughout the years. Don't expect to be alone here, as

Hurricane damage on the trail requires much work to clear.

the area on and around Blood Mountain receives more visitors than any other spot on the AT in Georgia. On a weekend when the weather is nice, it is not uncommon to encounter a steady stream of day hikers and overnighters as the trail descends more than 1,300 feet to Neel's Gap.

From the gap, the AT follows broad ridges with names such as Levelland Mountain, Corbin Horse Stamp, and Wolf Laurel Top to come into Tesnatee Gap. The barely discernible roadbed descending southward from the gap is all that remains of what was once a toll road dating from the first half of the 1800s. At the time, it was the only viable transportation route for people and supplies moving between Dahlonega on the eastern side of the mountain and Blairsville on the western side.

North of Tesnatee Gap, the AT makes a steep climb over Wildcat Mountain, but prior to 1966 and the construction of the Richard B. Russell Scenic Highway, the trail swung around the western side of the mountain for a gradual climb to Hogpen Gap. North of here, the AT makes a wide arch, first heading northward and then eastward to follow ridges around the headwaters of the Chattahoochee River. In Chattahoochee Gap, it's possible to drop a few feet off the trail to take a sip from Chattahoochee Spring, the source of the river that supplies drinking water to millions of people as it descends from the mountains; flows through Atlanta, Georgia; and eventually empties into the Gulf of Mexico. Chattahoochee Gap also affords a view of Brasstown Bald (4,784'), the highest mountain in Georgia.

Several more ups and downs and one long ascent bring the AT to its second summit above 4,000 feet, Tray Mountain. Mica, which is prevalent here, is a silicate mineral that splits into wafer-thin, almost plastic-looking, translucent sheets. Because it has a tendency to weather and deteriorate irregularly, Tray Mountain has a wild, rugged, and ragged look. Its summit provides an extensive view of the surrounding Blue Ridge Mountains, Brasstown Bald, Rabun Mountain (the second-highest peak in Georgia), and on clear days it is even possible to look southward for nearly 100 miles to Stone Mountain just outside of Atlanta.

Dropping from this lofty perch to the Swag of the Blue Ridge, the AT follows a broad ridge for approximately 3 miles, neither gaining nor losing much in the way of elevation. The easy walking does not last and the trail soon climbs to Kelly Knob, the last point above 4,000 feet in Georgia. The AT then drops to Dicks Creek Gap and makes the final ascent in its southernmost state to leave Chattahoochee National Forest and enter Nantahala National Forest and North Carolina just before coming into Bly Gap.

Barely across the state line, the trail attains an altitude of more than 4,000 feet, staying above that height for the next 26 miles. Zigzagging in several directions, it first swings around the headwaters of the Tallulah River and then those of the Nantahala River. In the process, it climbs above 5,000 feet for the first time on the bald summit of Standing Indian Mountain (5,498'), whose viewpoint has earned it the nickname "Grandstand of the Southern Appalachians." Catawba rhododendron dots the mountaintop with purple during June, while the paler blossoms of great rhododendron burst forth in July.

The AT takes its leave of the Blue Ridge's eastern arm and, on Ridgepole Mountain, turns to the northwest, necessitating an arduous 70-mile journey across a series of jumbled transverse ridges—the Nantahala, Stecoah, Cheoah, and Yellow Creek Mountains. Those who have hiked the trail in New England often refer to this stretch, especially the steep, almost rock-scramble ascent of 5,280-foot Albert Mountain, as a training ground for hiking in New Hampshire and Maine.

Passing through Wallace Gap, the AT climbs over Siler, Wayah, and Wesser Balds, each providing views of the surrounding countryside. Dropping quickly past aptly named Jump-Up Lookout, the trail steeply drops nearly 3,000 feet to the Nantahala River.

The deep and narrow gorge the river cuts through the mountains easily explains the Cherokee name of Nantahala: "Land of the Noonday Sun." The hills and valleys of this land (and Great Smoky Mountains National Park) were once the farmlands and hunting grounds of the Cherokee, the only nation of Native Americans to actually live upon the heights of any mountain ranges in the eastern United States. Their first contact with Europeans came around 1540 as Hernando de Soto crossed the Nantahalas (scholars believe it was around Wallace Gap) in search of gold. The mistreatment and torture suffered by the Cherokee at the hands of de Soto established the pattern of contact between the Indians and other arrivals from the Old World, which culminated in the natives' expulsion in 1838. Driven by soldiers of the U.S. Army, 17,000 Cherokee were forced to march the Trail of Tears to Oklahoma—4,000 of them perishing along the way. About 1,000 Cherokee managed to escape into the mountains, and after many years of hiding out, they were permitted to establish the Qualla Reservation (also called Qualla Boundary) along the eastern edge of the Great Smokies.

The AT leaves the Nantahala Gorge in an ascent that gains more than 3,000 feet in just over 8 miles to the summit of Cheoah Bald, which has a view that is among the best in the Southern Appalachians. Some hikers used to speculate that there were more steep ascents and descents per mile between Cheoah Bald and Fontana Dam than on any other stretch of the AT, but hard work by volunteers working on relocations has helped moderate those ups and downs.

Constructed during the 1940s, 480-foot-high Fontana Dam (the tallest in the eastern United States) impounds the Little Tennessee River to create the 29-mile-long Fontana Lake. Crossing the dam, the AT enters Great Smoky Mountains National Park, surely one of the highlights along the trail's entire route. Within a day-and-a-half's drive of more than 50% of America's population, the park has been receiving more than 12 million visitors a year—the highest visitation of any national park. Yet, surviving this onslaught, within park boundaries are found 1,570 species of flowering plants (including almost 130 native trees), more than 200 species of birds, 48 freshwater fish, 60 mammals, and 2,000 fungi. Included in the park's 78 kinds of amphibians and reptiles are more than 25 salamander species, giving the park the distinction of having the greatest diversity of salamanders in the world.

Much of this disparate life owes its existence to the height of this grand mountain range referred to by early explorer Arnold Guyot as "the master chain." Known to meteorologists as the orographic effect, the elevation and the shape or terrain of the mountains combine to influence local weather patterns—in other words, the mountains make their own weather. As moisture-laden air arrives from the west, the high mountains form a sort of barrier, slowing the movement of the air and receiving an increased amount of precipitation. In addition, higher elevations have cooler temperatures, and colder air is not able to absorb as much moisture as the warmer air of the lower elevations. No longer capable of hanging onto the water, the skies release even more of their moisture onto the mountains. This effect is illustrated by the fact that Gatlinburg, Tennessee, which is located in a valley on the western boundary of the park, receives an annual rainfall of approximately 50 inches; yet Clingmans Dome, about 5,000 feet higher in the heart of the Smokies, receives more than 80 inches of precipitation.

The special conditions created by the weather patterns directly affect the types of plants that grow and the communities they form. A forest of spruce and fir, more typically found in New England and Canada, can grow in the Smokies at elevations above 4,500 feet. Adjoining these trees near the summits of the mountains are northern hardwoods such as American beech and yellow birch, more common to Michigan than the Southern Appalachians. These stands found in the Smokies are the highest broad-leaved forests in the East. Bluets, violets, trilliums, and trout lilies cover the forest floor.

Below 4,500 feet, tall and mighty eastern hemlocks provide such deep shade that the air underneath their canopy can be 10°–12° cooler than that of the surrounding woods. These venerable giants are reminders that more than 100,000 acres of these mountains have never been timbered, which means the Smokies embrace the largest expanse of virgin forest east of the Mississippi River.

Unfortunately, the hemlocks are under attack throughout the eastern United States by the invasive hemlock woolly adelgid. First appearing on the West Coast in the 1920s, the insects had minimal effect on western hemlocks, but by the 1950s, eastern hemlock trees began to suffer. Apparently having no resistance to the insects, which suck the sap from the base of the trees' needles, eastern hemlocks have been dying at an alarming rate. Sadly, many of the trees may be dead by the time you hike here and along much of the AT. (It is estimated that more than 90% of the eastern hemlock trees in Shenandoah National Park have succumbed.)

Black and scarlet oaks and white, pitch, and shortleaf pines dominate below 3,000 feet on the drier eastern and southern slopes of the mountains. Also included in this forest are yellow poplar, dogwood, hickory, and thickets of rhododendron and mountain laurel.

Covering sheltered slopes and extending into low-elevation coves and valleys, the Southern Appalachians' famous cove hardwood forests are encountered at elevations of approximately 4,000 feet and lower. Here is the most diverse forest of all. While other trees can be present, some of the most prevalent species are hickory, beech, basswood, poplar, sugar maple, yellow birch, buckeye, magnolia, Carolina silverbell, eastern hem-lock, and white ash. Before the leafy canopy blocks out most of the sunlight in mid-spring, the floor of this forest will be dotted with luxuriant growths of trillium, fringed phacelia, bloodroot, hepatica, rue anemone, squirrel corn, Solomon's seal, bellwort, and lady's slipper. Existing within one-quarter of an acre of cove hardwood forest will be anywhere from 40 to 60 species of vascular plants, while an equal area of a spruce-fir forest will contain only 7 or 8 species.

This national park might never have been. When Horace Kephart, a librarian from St. Louis, arrived in the Great Smoky Mountains region in 1904, hoping to cure himself of alcoholism, he encountered an area that was being devastated by America's demand for lumber and wood products. He soon became fascinated with the area's nat-ural and human history. Wanting to protect the forested slopes, he promoted the idea of preserving the Smokies by means of a national park. By the 1920s, though, logging operations grew so extensive that the mountain people were abandoning their farms for lives in company towns and the regular paychecks that came from felling trees. Within a decade, the lumber companies had managed to log all but the most inaccessible areas, leaving only the steepest slopes and highest peaks in virgin timber.

However, Kephart's dream was not lost. In the 1920s, groups of concerned citizens from North Carolina and Tennessee formed an organization to promote his idea. The National Park Service, seeking to build upon the public support it had received from establishing national parks in the Western states, sought to create a park closer to a larger percentage of the country's population. The thought of a national park aroused the public's interest, and private citizens, along with the states of North Carolina and Tennessee, donated millions of dollars to purchase land. Even schoolchildren in the two states held "penny drives" to help the effort. These contributions, along with a multimillion-dollar gift from the Laura Spellman Rockefeller Memorial Fund and a $2 million appropriation from the federal government, made it possible to purchase the thousands of tracts of private land from which the park was created. (Kephart, an early supporter of the AT who helped arbitrate route controversies in the Southern states, went on to become the author of *Our Southern Highlanders,* still recognized as one of the most authoritative works on the lifestyles of early-20th-century Southern Appalachian inhabitants.)

Finally, on June 15, 1934, Great Smoky Mountains National Park was officially established. It was formally dedicated by President Franklin D. Roosevelt in 1940. Today the park encompasses 522,427 acres.

From Fontana Dam, the Appalachian Trail rises to an impressive view (via a short side trail) from the Shuckstack Mountain fire tower, taking in much of the southern portion of the Smokies, the Nantahala Mountains to the south, and Fontana Lake directly below. The trail turns to follow the Smokies' main crest along the North Carolina–Tennessee border and crosses Ekaneetlee Gap, where a Cherokee pathway once passed, leading from valley settlements to overhill villages. The AT alternately passes through mature hardwood forests and crosses the open, grassy meadows of Devils Tater Patch, Russell Field, Little Bald, Spence Field, Rockytop, Thunderhead Mountain, Chestnut Bald, and Silers Bald.

Clingmans Dome is the highest point of the Appalachian Trail at 6,643 feet, but obtaining a view from the wooded summit requires ascending the lookout tower. Even then you're not assured of seeing much, as the vista is often obscured by clouds and fog. Once known as Smoky Dome, the peak is named after Civil War general, US senator, and early Smokies explorer Thomas L. Clingman, reputed to be the first person to measure the height of the mountain during the 1850s.

Making use of a pathway constructed by the Civilian Conservation Corps (CCC) in 1939–1940, the trail arrives in Indian Gap, the site of the Tuckaleechee and Southeastern Trail that once connected Cherokee villages to British traders in Charleston, South Carolina. During the Civil War, Confederate general Will Thomas upgraded the path to a roadway with the labor of his "Legion of Indians and Highlanders," a contingent of Cherokee and mountaineers. Having mined saltpeter for gunpowder from nearby Alum Cave Bluff, Thomas's men hauled it back over the roadway to soldiers in North Carolina.

After crossing the highway in Newfound Gap, the AT, in mostly spruce-fir forests, ascends or passes just below summits named for Horace Kephart; Sequoyah, the creator of the Cherokee alphabet; David C. Chapman, a strong proponent for establishment of the national park; Arnold Guyot, a mountain explorer and mapmaker prior to the Civil War; and Arno B. Cammerer (an early National Park Service director).

Dropping more than 4,000 feet on switchbacks whose well-constructed rock cribbing has needed little maintenance since the 1930s, the AT leaves Great Smoky Mountains National Park in Davenport Gap, crosses the Pigeon River, and climbs nearly 4,000 feet to traverse Snowbird Mountain.

Just beyond Snowbird is Max Patch Mountain, whose broad, open, grassy meadow has been used as an airplane landing strip and for grazing sheep and cattle. Its heights furnish a view of some of the East's most formidable peaks, including Mount Mitchell. Following a pathway constructed by the CCC in 1936, more ups and downs are encountered—notably over Walnut and Bluff Mountains—then the AT eventually drops to the French Broad River at Hot Springs, North Carolina.

In 1778, two men on a search for lost horses stumbled upon warm springs bubbling up from the river. Within four years a hotel had been constructed. A road built

View of the Nolichucky River in Tennessee

from Tennessee in 1795 facilitated access to the area, and its fame as a healing center began to spread. The extensive and elegant Mountain Park Hotel, which could accommodate close to 1,000 guests, opened in the 1890s, and for the next two decades visitors soaked themselves in the hotel's bathhouse (built on the springs) or sipped the bubbling, healing waters. More than 2,000 German prisoners were incarcerated in the hotel during World War I, and they enjoyed themselves so much that, upon hearing a rumor they were to be moved, the prisoners poisoned the drinking water in the hopes that they would become too ill to be relocated.

Once the medical profession determined that the same health benefits could be derived from hydrotherapy (which can be administered anywhere), the popularity of Hot Springs declined. The hotel eventually shut down, and hikers of the 1960s, 1970s, and 1980s who went to visit the site saw only ruins. Thanks in part to efforts by the ATC's Trust for Appalachian Trail Lands and the city government, the springs are once more a commercial enterprise so that those passing through town may again "take the waters."

North of Hot Springs, the AT looks back down upon the town and the French Broad River from Lover's Leap, named by the Cherokee when Mist-of-the-Mountain jumped to her death after her sweetheart, Magwa, was murdered by an envious rival, Lone Wolf. Following the ridges of the Bald Mountains, the trail ascends to the Rich Mountain fire tower for views of the Smokies to the south, the Black Mountains to the east, and the valleys of Tennessee to the west.

Twin tombstones on Coldspring Mountain mark the graves of David and William Shelton, an uncle and nephew who fought for the Union during the Civil War. Their loyalties to the Northern cause were typical of those who inhabited the mountains along the Tennessee–North Carolina border. On a per capita basis, the area furnished more volunteers to the Union army than did many states above the Mason-Dixon Line. Returning home for a family reunion, the Sheltons (and a young friend) were waylaid and killed by the Confederates, whose sympathizers were most often the townspeople and farmers of the lowlands. (Photos taken by Earl Shaffer on his 1948 thru-hike show the gravestones to be in an open farm meadow. Today the gravestones rest within the confines of a healthy forest, testimony to nature's regenerative abilities.)

Hillsides thick with rhododendron and mountain laurel bring northbound hikers over the Nolichucky River near Erwin, Tennessee, and onto the Unaka Mountains for a most enjoyable stretch. Just north of Erwin is beauty spot with views east onto Roan Mountain, south to the Black Mountains, and west back to the Bald Mountains and the Nolichucky River.

With its spruce and fir trees—holdovers from an ancient time—the summit of Unaka Mountain feels more like Maine than Tennessee. The Ice Age's cooler temperatures permitted these trees to begin to compete with, and even gain a foothold against, the traditional southern hardwoods such as oaks and hickories. Once the glaciers receded and warmer temperatures returned, most of the northern plants died out, unable to tolerate a southern climate. However, the cooler temperatures on the higher peaks and ridges, such as those in the Smokies and on Unaka Mountain, have allowed the spruces and firs to remain, separated from their relatives several hundred miles to the north.

Rising above 6,000 feet for the last time until New England, the AT ascends Roan Mountain and crosses the open meadows of Round Bald, Jane Bald, Little Hump, and Hump Mountains. The long-distance Overmountain Victory Trail crosses the AT between Jane Bald and Little Hump Mountain. Built mostly with volunteer labor in the 1970s and 1980s, this National Historic Trail commemorates the route that mountaineers from Virginia, Tennessee, and North Carolina followed on their way from Sycamore Shoals, Tennessee, to Kings Mountain in South Carolina. Their October 7, 1780, defeat of a Tory army under the command of Colonel Pat Ferguson (who was killed during the battle) was a turning point in the Revolutionary War.

Dropping from the heights of Hump Mountain, the AT crosses a series of low mountains and knobs in a section that, prior to the 1980s, was located generally on roadways through farmlands and isolated mountain settlements. The trail then enters Laurel Fork Gorge, whose volume of rushing water, 40-foot cascades, and sheer cliffs covered in rhododendron and mountain laurel make this a highlight of the AT's southern portion. Several bridges, constructed by volunteers, enable the trail to snake its way through the gorge and across the stream, but occasionally one or another must be rebuilt, as floods have a tendency to wash them away. (The author watched as a wall of floodwaters crashed into and destroyed one of these bridges, just moments before he was going to cross it.)

Skirting Watauga Lake, the trail passes by a monument on Iron Mountain inscribed "Uncle Nick Grindstaff, born Dec. 26, 1851, died July 22, 1923, lived alone, suffered alone, and died alone." On a trip to the West to seek his fortune at the age of 26, Nick was beaten and robbed. He returned home only to find his sweetheart married to another. Disillusioned, Nick ascended Iron Mountain to live out the rest of his days with only a dog or two for companionship.

Crossing over to Holston Mountain, the AT enters the mid-Atlantic states via Damascus, Virginia. (Although many of us think of Virginia as a Southern state, geographers consider it to be part of the mid-Atlantic grouping.)

THE MID-ATLANTIC STATES

From Damascus, Virginia, the AT rises to open meadowlands just below the summit of Mount Rogers, the state's highest point. Continuing its swing westward, the trail crosses I-81 and the Great Valley of Virginia to ascend Garden Mountain overlooking isolated Burkes Garden. Once over the New River in Pearisburg, it follows the Virginia–West Virginia border atop Peters Mountain before turning eastward and cutting across several parallel ridges to begin following the main crest of the Blue Ridge Mountains. With the mountains barely more than a single, narrow ridgeline north of Roanoke, Virginia, the AT is forced to closely parallel the Blue Ridge Parkway and then the Skyline Drive through Shenandoah National Park.

After several quick miles in West Virginia, the trail enters Maryland, where it attains the crest of South Mountain for views from Weverton Cliffs, White Rocks, Annapolis Rocks, Black Rock Cliffs, Buzzard Knob, and High Rock. The South Mountain ridgeline continues to provide the trail with a route as it passes through the southern portion of Pennsylvania. Here the AT is forced to leave the Blue Ridge Mountains it has been following since Georgia, as the mighty mountain range finally comes to an end.

After the trail spans the wide and fertile Cumberland Valley, it crosses the Susquehanna River at Duncannon and turns eastward, ascending, crossing, and following a series of parallel mountains to Port Clinton and going by sites of long-abandoned villages and old iron furnaces. Continuing to follow long ridgelines with little change in elevation, rock outcroppings—Pulpit Rock, The Pinnacle, Dan's Pulpit, Bear Rocks, and Bake Oven Knob—provide viewpoints across the Pennsylvania countryside. Attaining the heights of Kittatinny Mountain, the trail then drops off Mount Minsi to cross the Delaware River and enter New Jersey.

The AT rises to regain the northward-running ridgeline of Kittatinny Mountain, where Sunfish Pond gives an indication of what the glacial lakes and ponds are like farther north in New

England. Following this same mountain for more than 40 miles, hikers report great views, red sunrises and sunsets, and more sightings of deer than in any place other than Shenandoah National Park. At High Point, the AT again turns eastward, closely following the New Jersey–New York border.

Above Greenwood Lake, the trail enters New York in earnest and soon comes to Harriman and Bear Mountain State Parks, where the first few miles of the AT were blazed in the 1920s. Crossing the Hudson River less than 50 miles north of New York City, the AT continues eastward through one of its most heavily populated stretches by way of public lands in Fahnstock State Park, along the Taconic State Parkway, and along narrow corridors purchased with federal and state appropriations. A relocation over Schaghticoke Mountain brings the trail into New England.

BILLING ITSELF AS The Friendliest Town on the Trail, Damascus, Virginia, plays host for Trail Days every year in May. Conceived in 1987 by Dan "Wingfoot" Bruce as a way to celebrate the 50th anniversary of the AT's completion, the event now attracts multitudes of hikers, locals, and visitors for a series of events focusing on the trail. The town had its beginnings in 1821, when a settler from North Carolina arrived to establish Mock's Mill. In 1886, John D. Imboden promoted a rail line from Abingdon and began extracting the area's timber and mineral wealth. Because of the abundance of manganese, iron ore, coal, water, and timber, he named the area (so folklore says) for Damascus, the ancient capital of Syria.

Climbing to 5,000 feet for the last time until New England, the trail crosses over the slopes of Whitetop Mountain and enters the Mount Rogers National Recreation Area. Established by an act of Congress in 1966, the more-than-100,000-acre area is so full of natural and scenic wonders that it has become one of the most popular hiking destinations in Virginia. Below spruce- and fir-covered Mount Rogers are hundreds of acres of open grasslands reminiscent of the Continental Divide in Montana and Wyoming. Adding to the feel of being in the West are the abundant wild ponies of Grayson Highlands State Park. Roaming free most of the year, they are rounded up in the fall, when some are auctioned. A portion of the money raised goes toward local efforts to keep the rest of the herd healthy and running wild. Also plentiful are the more than 150 birds that have been sighted here. In addition, bears, deer, foxes, bobcats, raccoons, red squirrels, chipmunks, and woodchucks all make homes within the recreation area.

Prior to the 1950s, the AT headed eastward from the Mount Rogers area, worked its way to Galax, Virginia, and turned north along the eastern rim of the Blue Ridge Mountains. Many of the highlights of that route—Puckett Cabin, Pinnacles of Dan, Mabry Mill, Rocky Knob, and Smarts View—can still be seen or accessed from the Blue Ridge Parkway. Construction of the scenic highway displaced much of the AT and prompted Tom Campbell, Jim Denton, additional members of the Roanoke Appalachian Trail Club, and others to relocate the trail farther west onto lands that had been recently acquired by the Jefferson National Forest.

North of the Mount Rogers National Recreation Area, the trail of today swings westward, making use of old roads and railroad grades left behind by logging activities in the early 20th century and manganese strip-mine operations during World War II. Crossing the Great Valley of Virginia and I-81, the AT enters Crawfish Valley. Extensively farmed and logged from the 1880s to the 1920s, the spot is now a quiet, isolated valley located far from any signs of civilization.

Having left the Blue Ridge for the Allegheny Mountains, the trail goes over Big Walker Mountain (whose ridgeline the trail followed for miles prior to the 1980s) and attains Garden Mountain. Besides overlooking beautiful Burkes Garden, the trail along

The wild ponies of Grayson Highlands State Park in Virginia

this section provides a chance to search for trace fossils dating from more than 400 million years ago. Tracks in the rock show where animals, probably wormlike creatures, burrowed along sand-bed surfaces, leaving labyrinths several inches long and nearly 1 inch wide.

Descending Garden Mountain, northbound hikers may encounter evidence of beavers in isolated Hunting Camp valley before arriving in Lickskillet Hollow. Like their predecessors of generations ago who worked hard to relocate the AT away from the Blue Ridge Parkway, many present members of the Roanoke Appalachian Trail Club have toiled to move the trail to optimal locations. Under the skillful direction of its trails supervisors, Charles Parry, Mike Vaughn, and others, the club has relocated the majority of its more than 120 miles since the late 1970s, much of it onto land purchased through the National Park Service acquisition program. The new pathways have not only taken the trail off roads and into more scenic areas, but have been well constructed with switchbacks to reduce erosion and eliminate steep ascents.

From Lickskillet Hollow, the AT traverses Pearis Mountain, crosses the New River, and follows the Virginia–West Virginia border for more than 10 miles along Peters Mountain. A junction with an excellent long-distance pathway is encountered just before the AT drops down to Pine Swamp Branch. The Allegheny Trail, constructed by the West Virginia Scenic Trails Association, winds northward through the best part of The Mountain State for nearly 300 miles to the Pennsylvania border.

Heading eastward, the AT goes by what was named by Laurie Messick on one of her thru-hikes as Virginia's Triple Crown of viewpoints. The monolith of 3,050-foot Dragon's Tooth gazes out upon Catawba Valley, Big Tinker Mountain, and Peaks of Otter, while the view from McAfee Knob on Catawba Mountain is considered by many to be the best vista in all of Virginia. Overlooking both the Catawba and Roanoke Valleys, the knob permits hikers to gaze northward, tracing the route of the trail for more than 80 miles. Just 6 miles north is Tinker Cliffs, a half-mile-long precipice with views into Catawba Valley, out across North and Potts Mountains, and back onto McAfee Knob.

Recrossing the Great Valley of Virginia and I-81, the trail returns to the Blue Ridge Mountains on Fullhardt Knob and turns northward along the Blue Ridge Parkway at Black Horse Gap.

Meandering along the crest of the mountains for more than 469 miles, the parkway provides a motorized link between Great Smoky Mountains and Shenandoah National Parks. In 1933, President Franklin Roosevelt inspected the first Civilian Conservation Corps camp to be established in Virginia. He not only enjoyed the beauty of Shenandoah National Park, but was also pleased with the progress and potential of the Skyline Drive. Prodded by local politicians (who realized the economic benefits) and naturalists from Virginia, North Carolina, and Tennessee, Roosevelt approved the idea of the parkway, and development began on September 11, 1935. With the construction of the Linn Cove Viaduct on the eastern flank of Grandfather Mountain in North

Carolina in 1983 and the subsequent connection of several "missing link" sections, the task was accomplished. On September 11, 1987, a ceremony on the viaduct declared the completion of the parkway, exactly 52 years after the project was started.

Passing through Bearwallow Gap, thought by some scholars to be one of the major buffalo crossings of the mountains until the 1700s, when the animals disappeared, the trail crosses over Bryant Ridge and Floyd Mountain, where once stood some of the mighty chestnut trees that formerly dominated the Appalachian forests.

Thanks in large part to the efforts of Natural Bridge Appalachian Trail Club member (and later president) Bill Foot, the AT was brought back onto its historical route over Apple Orchard Mountain in the 1990s. For more than 20 years the trail had crossed the summit until it was forced off by the establishment of a radar station operated by the Strategic Air Command from 1954 to 1975. After that, the Federal Aviation Administration continued to use the radar to monitor domestic flights.

From the top of Apple Orchard Mountain, the last time the AT rises above 4,200 feet until New England, the trail descends to cross the James River, the largest waterway in Virginia, and climbs to a monument for "Little" Ottie Cline Powell. In November 1891, 4-year-old Ottie apparently became disoriented after being separated from classmates gathering wood for the stove of the Tower Hill School. Hundreds of people searched for several weeks but failed to find him. Five months later, his body was discovered atop 3,372-foot Bluff Mountain, a distance of more than 3.5 miles (as the crow flies) from the schoolhouse. A plaque (bearing the wrong date) was placed on the mountain in 1968 in honor of the child.

The trail descends from Bluff Mountain, crosses over to the eastern side of the Blue Ridge, and climbs steadily to the crest of Cole Mountain, where the meadows, kept open by burning and other methods, provide views reminiscent of the ones from balds farther south. Steadily gaining in altitude, the AT rises over The Priest at 4,063 feet in elevation, only to plunge 3,100 feet to cross the Tye River. In August 1969, Hurricane Camille, in combination with another storm front, dropped somewhere between 2 and 3 feet of rain onto the Tye River valley in less than 6 hours. Swollen streams uprooted trees and sent house-size boulders crashing down the mountainsides, destroying homes, bridges, and roadways and taking a large toll in human life. Enough soil was stripped away to reveal granite rock that had been hidden for hundreds of millions of years.

Regaining the heights of the Blue Ridge, the trail passes through Rockfish Gap. Millions of years ago, the present Rockfish River began west of the Blue Ridge and flowed through the gap toward the Atlantic Ocean. At the same time, the Shenandoah River was gradually cutting through the softer limestone of the Shenandoah Valley, and it eventually captured and diverted the headwaters of the Rockfish River, drying out the gap the stream had once used to cross the mountain. The Shenandoah River

Foamflower lines the trail in Shenandoah National Park.

created other wind gaps, as such places are known, at Manassas, Ashby, Snickers, and Keys Gaps in northern Virginia.

North of Rockfish Gap, the AT enters a land of gently graded pathways, abundant wildflowers, and herds and herds of deer. Encompassing a large section of the crest of the Blue Ridge Mountains and hundreds of attendant spur ridges spreading in all directions, Shenandoah National Park stretches from Rockfish Gap to Front Royal, a distance of almost 75 miles, and covers an area of nearly 200,000 acres. Congress authorized the establishment of the park in 1926 but provided no funds for land acquisition. The Commonwealth of Virginia can be thanked for making the idea a reality. The Virginia Assembly appropriated $1 million, and another $1.2 million in donations from various sources (much of it from individual citizens) made it possible to purchase nearly 4,000 tracts of private land, which were deeded to the federal government in 1935.

Some of this land was not sold willingly, and there is still deep-seated resentment of the government by some of the families who were relocated from their ancestral homes. While the loss experienced by these people should not be minimized, the many benefits that accrued from establishing the park cannot be denied.

As the 20th century began, second- or third-growth forests, logged since the early 1800s, covered much of what is now the park. Today, any signs left by lumbering, as well as by grazing and farming, have been largely erased by the growth of the forests. First came shrubs, pines, and black locusts; now 95% of the park is nearing a climax forest of oak, hickory, yellow poplars, and other hardwoods. This forest growth is so complete that nearly half of the park was designated a wilderness area in 1976.

President Franklin Roosevelt officially dedicated the park in 1936, as men of the Civilian Conservation Corps busily built trails, shelters, fire roads, and various visitor facilities. The 105-mile Skyline Drive was completed in 1939. Through the years, countless millions of Americans and foreign visitors have been able to enjoy these parklands that—based upon what has happened to other mountain areas of the East— would probably have been turned into housing developments or high-priced resorts if they had remained in private hands. Today, through law, the park cannot spend any funds to acquire new lands; sadly, shortsighted groups have spearheaded a movement to limit even its ability to accept additional lands given as a gift.

There are many legends and stories about the origin of the word Shenandoah, but perhaps the most romantic and beautiful is that it is a derivative of a Native American word meaning "daughter of the stars." When applied to Shenandoah National Park, those words seem more than appropriate, for the park is truly a stellar treasure in the system of public lands. More than a dozen waterfalls tumble down the slopes, 200 species of birds—including 35 kinds of warblers—have been identified in the park, and more than 1,100 species of flowering plants can be found within its borders. Turkeys, bobcats, raccoons, and skunks inhabit the region in significant numbers, and there is a very real chance of seeing black bears in the backcountry. There are so many deer that it has become common knowledge in Virginia that if you want to see a deer, you simply go to Shenandoah.

Displaced by Skyline Drive, the AT now weaves back and forth across it, coming into contact with the roadway more than 40 times. Although it seems this would be an intrusion, the natural beauty of the park still comes through. Rising from Rockfish Gap, the trail crosses the open talus slopes of Blackrock. Millions of years ago, when erosion exposed this Hampton quartzite, it was already cracked from pressure and cycles of heating and cooling. Rainwater seeping into the cracks and fissures froze and cracked the rock further, turning it into the large boulders over which the trail crosses. The area may have received its name from the dark-brown rock tripe that covers most of the rock.

Skirting Loft Mountain Campground, the AT drops into a narrow mountain valley created by Ivy Creek, where hikers may see a few trout in the ripples of the stream or a crayfish or two crawling from one submerged crevice to another. Tiny, harmless ring-necked snakes sometimes take advantage of the flat rocks to warm themselves in the bit of sunshine that makes it through the lush forest canopy.

In Swift Run Gap, monuments beside the highway commemorate the Knights of the Golden Horseshoe. In 1716, Governor Alexander Spotswood led the first organized body of English knights across the Blue Ridge. The diaries of these gentleman farmers and businessmen paint the excursion as more of a lark than an exploration. At each meal they drank to the health of the king and his children. Upon reaching the mountain crest, they paused to toast the king and the governor. Finding the Shenandoah River (which they named the Euphrates), they drank to the health of the king and took possession of the land in the name of George I. At dinner that evening they used champagne, Burgundy, claret, and other spirits to toast the king, other members of the royal family, the governor, and themselves. After returning home, Governor Spotswood presented each expedition member with a small golden horseshoe. Although monuments to the knights are in Swift Run Gap, research seems to suggest the expedition crossed the mountains a few miles to the north in Milam Gap, through which the AT passes before skirting the park's two lodges, Big Meadows and Skyland.

George Freeman Pollock opened his mountain resort, Skyland, in 1894. A carriage road from Luray wound up the western slope of the Blue Ridge, carrying his guests to the lodge situated below Stony Man Mountain. The resort was almost an immediate success, as the flatlanders and high society of politicians and business leaders found it to be a congenial place to enjoy the beauties of the mountains and escape the heat of summer in the cities, valleys, and Piedmont.

A supporter who worked hard for the establishment of Shenandoah National Park, Pollock had originally come to the mountains on a scientific expedition to study mammals for the Smithsonian Institution and to observe the copper-mining operations, of which his father owned part interest, on Stony Man. The mining had begun around the turn of the 19th century, but the ore proved hard to work, and operations ceased by the mid-1800s.

The land has had well over a century to heal, so hikers will find little, if any, evidence of mining as the AT climbs to its highest point in the park (3,837') on the side of Stony Man. The spruce and fir trees here provide a chance to learn how to tell the two trees apart. The easiest way is to shake hands with their branches. The balsam fir will feel soft and welcoming to the touch, and while the red spruce's needles won't puncture your skin, you will certainly not want to give it a firm handshake. Another way to distinguish the two is that the spruce's needles extend out from all sides of the branches, while the fir's needles, with two white stripes on the bottom, grow with only one row on two sides of the branch.

Going over Marys Rock, a favorite birders' perch for watching the fall hawk migration, the AT passes by its junction with the long-distance Tuscarora Trail, which rejoins the AT south of Duncannon, Pennsylvania. The AT stays close to 3,000 feet when it crosses over Hogback, South Marshall, and North Marshall Mountains before leaving the national park near Compton Gap.

Following a fenceline along an easement next to land belonging to the National Zoological Park, hikers might see a number of exotic birds or animals, such as African donkeys. Crossing Manassas Gap, the AT passes through an area ablaze with trillium in the spring in G. Richard Thompson Wildlife Management Area and Sky Meadows State Park. North of Ashby Gap, the AT used to follow a paved roadway through a development of Northern Virginia suburban homes (with fencelines plastered with NO TRESPASSING signs) for more than 10 miles. Hikers often complain about the seemingly senseless and frequent ups and downs of the trail relocation, but the narrow corridor of land through which the AT now passes is in public hands, away from roads and houses, and free from the threat of further development.

Once the trail passes through Snickers Gap, only a minor variation in elevation at Keys Gap brings the AT to a descent to cross the Shenandoah River and arrive in Harpers Ferry, West Virginia, home of the Appalachian Trail Conservancy. Membership dues are minimal, and all of those who hike or have an interest in the AT owe it to themselves to join this effective organization. The site of John Brown's raid on a federal arsenal in 1859, a portion of the small town is now a National Historical Park.

Leaving West Virginia and entering Maryland after crossing the Potomac River, the AT turns eastward along the level route of the C&O Canal towpath. Maryland's 40 miles of trail may have more historical documentation than any other AT section of similar length. From the late 1700s, individual canals in the eastern United States provided water routes through the mountains and around falls and rapids. By the 1830s, the C&O Canal linked Harpers Ferry with Washington, D.C. Operations came to an end in 1924 when a major flood damaged many of the canal's structures. Today, the towpath is part of the C&O National Historical Park and the Potomac Heritage National Scenic Trail. Its more than 180 miles can be hiked from the nation's capital to Cumberland, Maryland (where the canal extended by 1850).

Switchbacking up to Weverton Cliffs for a view of the Potomac River and Harpers Ferry, the AT heads northward, following the ridgeline of South Mountain. Folklore states that the mountain was used by escaped slaves on their flight to freedom as part of the Underground Railroad, and by some of John Brown's men following the failed raid on Harpers Ferry. While the mountain could have furnished a passageway, its heavily wooded slopes would have been excellent cover for bounty hunters. More than likely, the valleys on either side of the mountain provided the preferred escape routes.

Traversing the mountain with little change in elevation, the trail comes into Crampton Gap, site of Gathland State Park and, as far as can be determined, the only monument in the world to war correspondents. Planned and built by George Alfred "Gath" Townsend, a journalist and columnist from 1866 to 1910, it memorializes more than 150 reporters and artists who covered the Civil War from both sides of the conflict. The off-balance monument contains a large Moorish arch below three smaller ones of Roman design. Taking the time to peruse the dozens of inscriptions and mythological figures could take up much of an afternoon.

The site of the monument is quite appropriate. On September 14, 1862, the Battle of South Mountain—where Union forces under General George McClellan met Confederate troops commanded by General Robert E. Lee—raged from Crampton Gap to Fox Gap (where Union General Jesse Reno was killed and future president Rutherford B. Hayes was wounded) to Turners Gap. The Union prevailed as Lee retreated west to Antietam Creek. About 72 hours later, the two sides fought at that site during the single bloodiest day of the war.

Just a few miles north of Crampton Gap and more than a century earlier, British forces under General Edward Braddock (accompanied by George Washington) built a rudimentary road through Turners Gap to facilitate their march westward, where they were ambushed (and Braddock was killed) by French and Indian troops near present-day Uniontown, Pennsylvania. Improved with funds provided by the state of Maryland, the route became part of the National Road and is said to have carried such luminaries as Daniel Webster; Henry Clay; and Presidents Abraham Lincoln, Andrew Jackson, William Henry Harrison, James Knox Polk, Zachary Taylor, and Martin Van Buren.

North of Turners Gap, the AT passes below the original Washington Monument, built by citizens of Boonsboro, Maryland, and dedicated to America's first president in 1827. Passing by viewpoints from Annapolis Rocks, Black Rock Cliffs, and High Rock, the trail enters Pen Mar Park. Though it appears to be not much more than a community picnic ground today, the spot was an amazingly popular resort between 1890 and 1920. Seven hotels and close to 100 guest cottages were located nearby to cater to the daily crowds of 5,000 or more that were drawn to the amusement park. Gas rationing during World War II forced the park to close in 1943.

The border with Pennsylvania provides one last bit of history before the trail leaves Maryland. To settle a dispute between the followers of William Penn and the descendants of George Calvert, the first Lord of Baltimore, British astronomers and surveyors Charles Mason and Jeremiah Dixon were commissioned in 1765 to firmly establish the boundary between the two colonies. Because the Mason-Dixon line later became the dividing point between slave-holding and free states, many people believe it was the impetus for calling the South "Dixie." The name actually came from $10 bills printed by a bank in Louisiana; much of the population in that state traces its ancestry back to France, and they referred to the money as dix, French for "10." The bills became so extensively distributed that the South became known as Dixie. The term became even more widely used when a minstrel from Ohio wrote and popularized the song "Dixie."

The mountains throughout Pennsylvania, which arch from the southwest to the northeast, are long, parallel ridgelines that, for the most part, stay well below 2,000 feet with little change in elevation. Continuing along the crest of South Mountain, the trail passes by short side paths to viewpoints from Chimney Rocks and Snowy Mountain.

Along the trail in Pennsylvania are many reminders of the state's iron and steel industry. Large deposits of iron ore, an abundance of trees perfect for converting into charcoal, and plenty of streams to harness for power enabled Pennsylvania to supply more than half of America's raw iron during the late 1700s and throughout most of the 1800s. The trail passes by disturbed areas, 30–50 feet in diameter, where wood was burned to produce charcoal used to fuel the iron furnaces. The ruins of the Caledonia Iron Works furnace, built in 1837, can be seen near the AT as it passes through Caledonia State Park, while a few miles north in Pine Grove Furnace State Park, the trail goes by another historic furnace that is still standing. The park's swimming lake was originally a 90-foot-deep ore hole. Also along the AT is the 1827 Iron Master's Mansion, which was used as a stop on the Underground Railroad.

Today, the park has a somewhat less noble claim to fame, as the general store next door is the home of the infamous Half Gallon Club. Hikers join this dubious society by consuming a half gallon of ice cream each in one sitting. (The author's half gallon was toasted almond, a flavor never eaten again.) The state park is also the home of the Appalachian Trail Museum, the country's only museum dedicated to hiking.

Near this point, the Blue Ridge, the group of mountains the AT has been following almost all the way from Georgia, comes to an end. Here the AT encounters the Cumberland Valley, part of the Great Valley that stretches from Alabama to Canada and through which the trail crossed in southwest and central Virginia. Prior to land acquisitions by the National Park Service during the 1980s, the trail was mostly a road walk through the valley. Today, the more than 14 miles are a pleasant mix of walking along a low ridge, into open fields, and through the small village of Boiling Springs. Listed on the National Register of Historic Places, the springs are some of the largest in Pennsylvania, pouring forth 24 million gallons of water a day.

Going over Blue and Cove Mountains, the AT crosses the Susquehanna River at Duncannon and climbs to the crest of Peters Mountain, part of the same bed of sandstone and conglomerate rock it followed on Cove Mountain. Soon entering Saint Anthony's Wilderness, the largest roadless tract in southeastern Pennsylvania, the trail follows the bed of an old stage route through deep woods and passes crumbling, vegetation-covered foundations that mark the site of Yellow Springs Village, a long-abandoned coal-mining community. A few miles to the north along the trail, disturbed and eroding land, an old railroad grade, and a family cemetery are all that remain of Rausch Gap Village.

With little change in elevation, except to cross the Schuylkill River at Port Clinton and the Lehigh River near Palmerton, the trail follows Blue Mountain nearly 100 miles to Wind Gap. Although much of the treadway in the northern portion of Pennsylvania is on rocky terrain, it is here that the famous rocks Pennsylvania hikers seem to love to describe in horrifying detail begin to appear in great numbers. Until

A lofty view of the Lehigh River in Pennsylvania

now, the grapefruit-size stones that twist ankles and scrape shins have not been so abundant as to keep hikers from putting their feet flat on the ground, but for the next 15 or so miles, only bits of boot soles touch the soil. The AT crosses over to Kittatinny Mountain and descends more than 1,000 feet into the Delaware Water Gap along the Pennsylvania–New Jersey border.

Rising out of the gap and entering New Jersey, the trail quickly arrives at Sunfish Pond, which sits in an idyllic hollow created when glaciers slid along Kittatinny Mountain. The pond was once threatened with becoming nothing more than a reservoir for a power plant, but public outcry has preserved the sanctity of the pond and the thousands upon thousands of tasty swamp blueberries that surround it during the summer months. More than 20 varieties of blueberries grow east of the Mississippi, ranging in size from the 6-inch plants in Shenandoah National Park to these bushes in New Jersey that attain heights of 10 feet or so.

North of the pond and from the eastern escarpment of Kittatinny Mountain, it is possible to watch children swimming in backyard pools as parents mow the lawn and barbecue lunch. Catfish and Culver fire towers provide 360-degree views of the surrounding countryside.

The vistas from the observation platform in High Point State Park are even more impressive: just below the platform is Lake Marcia, northwest is the Catskill Plateau; west are the Pocono Mountains in Pennsylvania; to the south the Kittatinny ridgeline slopes down into Delaware Water Gap; east are Wawayanda and Pochuck Mountains;

and to the southeast, some people claim the skyline of New York City is visible on clear days. A side path from the platform leads to a monument to "New Jersey's heroes by land, sea, and air in all wars in our country," which sits atop the state's highest point at 1,803 feet.

Dropping down to a walk through the Vernon Valley at less than 500 feet in elevation, relocations from paved roadways in the 1980s permit northbound hikers to encounter the boggy wetlands that will become more prevalent as the trail works its way into New England. In the 1990s, a 110-foot-long, 14-foot-high suspension bridge was built across a creek in the Pochuck Swamp, the result of an amazing effort by the combined forces of the ATC and its volunteers; the National Park Service; New York–New Jersey Trail Conference members; local community members, including students, engineers, and bankers; an electric power company; several corporations; the U.S. Forest Service; and the State of New Jersey. An engineering feat that had to be built not on bedrock or solid soils but on a base of organic muck, the bridge not only enables hikers to get across without getting their feet wet but also protects the fragile environment.

Atop Bearfort Mountain overlooking Greenwood Lake, the AT enters New York, where it soon turns eastward to cross Bellvale Mountain, Mombasha High Point, and Buchanan and Arden Mountains along a narrow strip of public land obtained by the National Park Service in the 1970s. During the 1800s, the hills in this area, named Sterling Forest after Revolutionary War general Lord Stirling (yes, someone misspelled the forest's name), were denuded to supply charcoal to the iron industry; hikers can still see depressions in the forest floor that are the remains of charcoal pits.

In the late 1800s, Sterling Forest came into the hands of the Harriman family, who offered it to New York in the 1950s to be used as a park. In a remarkably shortsighted move, the state refused the offer, saying the property contained too many wetlands and other problem areas and that the state already had all the parklands it would ever need. The land was soon sold to private landowners. Their plans in the 1980s to build extensive subdivisions, malls, and communities dismayed large segments of the population. A variety of groups and organizations banded together, not just to protect the AT and its corridor but also to preserve this last large, undeveloped green space along the New York–New Jersey border, barely an hour's drive from New York City. Prodded by these concerned citizens, New Jersey was able to obtain 2,100 acres of Sterling Forest by condemnation and, in 1996, after years of negotiations at local, state, and federal levels, the owners agreed to sell the bulk of the 20,000-acre forest at a cost of multiple millions of dollars in federal, state, and private funds. It took an act of Congress, literally, to save this property, which could have been obtained for a pittance when it was originally offered. It's a hard but important lesson to all concerned with preserving the beauty of open spaces.

From Sterling Forest, the trail passes through the area of Harriman and Bear Mountain State Parks, where the first section of the Appalachian Trail was opened on October 7, 1923. With a series of more ups and downs than the trail has seen since entering Maryland, the AT reaches the 1,305-foot summit of Bear Mountain for superb views across the Hudson Highlands and the New York City skyline. A zoo through which the AT passes at the base of the mountain ensures that thru-hikers will see at least one bear on their journey. The bears' den is important for another reason: at about 120 feet above sea level, it is the lowest point of the entire AT.

Crossing the Hudson River on the Bear Mountain Bridge just a scant 44 miles upstream from New York City, the AT climbs steeply past Anthony's Nose. It rarely tops 1,000 feet in elevation as it twists eastward over a series of low ridges, sometimes making use of old railroad grades and sometimes on hillsides just a few yards above traffic along the Taconic State Parkway. Although much of the trail in this part of New York is along extremely narrow strips of public land, it must be remembered that those who hiked this section prior to the late 1980s did so on many miles of paved roadway. Entering Connecticut to cross Ten Mile River, the trail deviates back into New York just long enough to traverse Schaghticoke Mountain before returning to Connecticut for good.

NEW ENGLAND

Staying fairly close to the New York state line, the AT in Connecticut follows the Housatonic River before ascending the Taconic Mountains at Lions Head, crossing over Bear Mountain, and leaving the state in Sages Ravine. After the trail enters Massachusetts, it continues to be quite close to the New York border, crossing over Everett and Race Mountains to swing eastward through the Housatonic Valley. Rising into the Berkshire Hills, the trail makes use of public lands in state forests to swing by numerous ponds and climb over Mount Greylock, the highest point in Massachusetts.

At the Massachusetts–Vermont border, the AT joins the Long Trail to share the same route for more than 100 miles through the Green Mountains. Numerous ponds, plenty of trail-side shelters, and a well-built trail make for pleasant walking in this section. Just north of Sherburne Pass (near Rutland), the AT turns east, following a rough up-and-down route to cross the Connecticut River, and enters New Hampshire.

The mountains of New Hampshire are younger than those in Connecticut, Massachusetts, and Vermont, which means they are taller and much more rugged—especially the White Mountains, which the AT enters on Mount Moosilauke. Dropping thousands of feet into deep notches and gaining thousands to reach the height of the land, the trail traverses the Kinsman, Franconia, Presidential, and Carter-Moriah ranges to enter Maine near Gorham, New Hampshire.

For 280 miles in Maine, the AT crosses its most rugged and isolated landscape, climbing over the nearly vertical sides of the Mahoosuc Range, going above treeline on Baldpate, Bemis, Saddleback, Bigelow, and Moxie Bald Mountains, and skirting dozens of ponds and lakes. For more than 100 miles, the AT traverses rugged forestland so isolated that only an occasional logging road is encountered. Inside Baxter State Park, it finally arrives at its northern terminus atop the "greatest mountain," Mount Katahdin.

ENTERING CONNECTICUT, the AT briefly passes through the Schaghticoke Indian Reservation, the only Native American lands the trail traverses. Zigzagging over Mount Algo and Calebs Peak, the trail drops down St. Johns Ledges to begin one of its longest level stretches, a walk of nearly 5 miles along the Housatonic River.

Until recently, the trail north of here crossed the river to make a traverse of the forests through the Litchfield Hills. Due to concerns over increased development, the trail was relocated in 1988 to stay on the western side of the river and pass through the highlands of the Housatonic State Forest for views of the Taconic Mountains to the west and the Housatonic Valley to the east. The original route is now part of the

Connecticut Blue Trail System, and it reconnects with the AT where the AT recrosses the Housatonic River to hook up with a nature trail south of Falls Village. The stone ruins along this pathway were part of a canal system built in 1851 to bring water to a hydroelectric plant that was to provide the power to turn Falls Village into a huge industrial center. In what today would surely have been grounds for a lawsuit, the plan failed because the builders of the canal neglected to use mortar to hold the rock walls of the canal together.

At Great Falls, the trail again crosses the Housatonic River and ascends to grand vistas of the Housatonic Valley; the Taconic Mountains; and, on clear days, Mount Greylock, 50 miles north. The trail gains the heights of the Taconic Range as it crosses over barefaced Lions Head and, for the first time since Maryland, rises above 2,000 feet atop Bear Mountain (2,316'), the highest mountain located entirely in Connecticut.

The AT enters Massachusetts along deep, dark, and beautiful Sages Ravine, which is full of tall trees, neon-green mosses and ferns, and scores of tumbling cascades. Just beyond, early mornings at Bear Rock Falls can be quite spectacular as the scarlet rays of a rising sun are reflected by water somersaulting 30 feet down the mountain. A number of acres around the stream were purchased and donated to the Appalachian Trail in memory of three hikers who died in 1990—Molly LaRue and Geoffrey Hood were murdered while on a thru-hike, and Susan Hanson was killed in an airplane accident.

Following the escarpment and crossing the summit of Race Mountain, the trail swings by high-elevation Guilder Pond, then drops more than 1,000 feet and leaves the

Housatonic River

Taconic Mountains. On its way to once again cross the Housatonic River, the trail passes through a wide and flat valley that was the site of the last skirmish in Shays' Rebellion.

In nearby Hatfield, representatives of western Massachusetts villages met in 1786 to formulate their 25 grievances against the state and federal governments following the War of Independence. Soon afterward, about 1,000 farmers, led by Daniel Shays, marched on Springfield to emphasize their frustration with what they perceived to be unfair taxes, overpaid bureaucrats, and a lack of a soundly established currency. Incidents began to escalate, and it was only after 5,000 federal troops clashed with the rebels and chased them for 10 days through the Massachusetts countryside that peace was restored. Sentenced to hang, Shays and most of his followers were eventually pardoned in response to public opinion.

The trail rises into the Berkshire Hills and passes by Ice Gulch, a geological oddity whose narrow depths may keep ice well into summer. Once they've taken a dip in glacially made Benedict Pond, northbound hikers will be able to enjoy a swim on an almost-daily basis as the trail continues through New England.

From Cobble Hill, the AT overlooks quiet Tyringham Valley and its surrounding hills, which were home to a community of Shakers throughout most of the 19th century. To escape persecution in England, members of this offshoot of Quakerism arrived in North America in 1774. Known for a while as Shaking Quakers because dances during religious services made their bodies shake and tremble, they held fast to four principles of belief—common property, confession of sins, separation from the outside world, and celibacy (with complete separation of the sexes). Bowing to the material world as little as possible, their homes, barns, furniture, and utensils were practical and unadorned, but so simple and well made that today they are seen as works of art.

Providing additional chances for a swim, the trail swings past Upper Goose and Finerty Ponds before crossing the Housatonic River in Dalton to rise to another spot called the Cobbles. The view from here is of the quintessential New England village. Surrounded by lush green mountains, the pure-white spire of the church in Cheshire rises above streets of manicured lawns and well-kept homes.

Beyond Cheshire, the trail climbs over Saddleball Mountain (the first peak above 3,000 feet since Shenandoah National Park in Virginia) to attain the 3,491-foot summit of Mount Greylock. The view from the top of the war memorial's 89 steps is impressive, taking in the Catskills in New York, the Taconics and Berkshires in Massachusetts, and the Green Mountains of Vermont. The spruce-fir forest of the higher elevations on Greylock and the northern hardwoods on the surrounding slopes leave no doubt that the trail is now within the northern reaches of its length. Dropping to cross the Hoosac River, the AT climbs into Vermont.

From the Massachusetts–Vermont border, the AT and the Long Trail, the country's oldest long-distance pathway, share the same route for more than 100 miles. The idea for the footpath occurred to James P. Taylor, associate principal of the Vermont Academy, after a 1909 hike with his students was hampered by thick brush. Resolving to make Vermont's heights accessible, Taylor began to advocate a pathway through the Green Mountains. Volunteers rallied around the idea, and in September 1931, the Long Trail from the Massachusetts–Vermont border to the Vermont–Canada border was completed (with its southern portion already having been adopted into the route of the AT).

Following the joint pathway almost due north, the AT rises and falls over numerous knobs and summits whose higher elevations are covered almost exclusively with spruce and fir, while the trees of the lower slopes are northern hardwoods. Hikers on Harmon Hill can look down upon the city of Bennington and the 306-foot blue limestone obelisk of its battle monument.

Soon after the signing of the Declaration of Independence, British general John Burgoyne was making a rapid march southward through Vermont on his way to the Hudson River. He badly needed supplies and munitions and knew they could be obtained in Bennington, which was guarded by just a small militia. Upon hearing of Burgoyne's movements, New Hampshire general John Stark led a force of 1,000 across the Molly Stark Trail (now highway VT 9, which the AT crosses) and joined Vermont's Green Mountain Boys under the leadership of Seth Warner. In a 3-hour clash, they soundly defeated the British, who, deprived of supplies, lost the subsequent Battle of Saratoga.

North of VT 9, the AT rises over Maple Hill and Little Pond Mountain to the fire tower on Glastenbury Mountain, where it seems to many thru-hikers that the sunrises, sunsets, and stargazing are better than anywhere else along the trail. A $3 million purchase has permitted the trail to be rerouted back over Stratton Mountain, which was bypassed by the AT for several years because of private-land concerns. Although he sometimes presented conflicting stories, Benton MacKaye says he first envisioned a long-distance trail along the crest of the Appalachian Mountains while gazing at the countryside from Stratton's 3,936-foot summit.

After passing by the apparatus of a ski resort on Bromley Mountain and climbing over Styles and Peru Peaks, the trail enters one of its most pleasurable stretches in Vermont with little change in elevation as it skirts Griffith Lake and Little Rock Pond to come to Clarendon Gorge, a popular recreation spot with local residents. Swiftly moving waters create a delightful whirlpool effect among the boulders as Mill River flows into a narrow cleft eroded through light-gray crystalline rock.

For the first time since Virginia, the AT reaches 4,000 feet in elevation just below the summit of Killington Peak. It was on top of Killington, in 1763, that a Vermont circuit-riding preacher, the Reverend Samuel Peters, claimed he broke a bottle of whiskey across a rock to christen the state Verd-Mont. Many people dispute Peters's claim, pointing out he also asserted he had a degree from the nonexistent University of Cortona in Tuscany.

Killington and Pico Peak—the next mountain to the north—are two of the most popular ski areas in the northeast, and their plans for expansion had threatened the integrity of the AT and the Long Trail. After many years of intense (and bitter) negotiations, an agreement was reached to relocate the trail, allowing the resorts to expand to the east but keeping them from developing onto the western slopes.

Coming to the Maine Junction north of Sherburne Pass, the AT leaves the Long Trail and turns eastward, passing through 114-acre Gifford Woods State Park. Established in 1931, the park not only preserves a 12-acre stand of virgin timber (mostly sugar maple), but also helps protect an important rest area used by a variety of birds during the spring and fall migrations.

Land acquisitions of the 1980s and 1990s rerouted the AT from the dirt and paved roads that it once followed for the next 40 miles. A more scenic route, albeit one with additional steep ups and downs, now crosses fields, meadows, and Northern Hardwood Forests as the trail goes through eastern Vermont to cross the Connecticut River and enter New Hampshire at Hanover.

Life in Hanover is dominated by Dartmouth College, which was chartered in 1769 for the education of Native American children. The school started out as a single log building amid a small agricultural community of about 20 people; the 6,600 students of today attend classes in a number of buildings of Colonial, Federal, and Georgian design. The school's outing club, founded in 1909, is the oldest such college organization in the country, and maintains about 53 miles of the AT in New Hampshire. As a diversion from the trail, the college and the town have numerous epicurean and cultural attractions. However, with overnight accommodations limited to two hotels, and one of them charging well over $200 a night, many hikers find a stay in Hanover to be beyond their means.

Leaving Hanover, the trail passes through a moist wood festooned with lichens, mosses, and ferns and climbs steeply over Moose Mountain, Holts Ledge, and Smarts and Cube Mountains. The area is well known for the quality of its maple syrup, and, until the trail was relocated off private property, hikers used to pass under hundreds of feet of plastic tubing connecting one tree to another.

The trees, primarily sugar maples, are tapped during late winter and early spring when freezing and thawing causes the sap to rise. Elaborate arrays of tubing channel the sap into storage tanks and evaporator plants, which have pretty much replaced collection buckets and individual sugar houses. Colorless and low in sugar content, the sap is boiled to concentrate the sugar and obtain the color and flavor of maple syrup. A mature tree can yield up to 8 gallons of sap, but it takes 30–50 gallons of sap to produce 1 gallon of syrup.

Although it has crossed over many mountains with open viewpoints since leaving Georgia, the trail's entrance into the White Mountains on the 4,802-foot summit of Mount Moosilauke is the first time it rises above treeline. The AT is now in the land of alpine and subalpine plants, including dwarfed spruce and fir trees, known as krummholz. The stunted, almost horizontal growth is a result of windblown snow and ice crystals, which remove living tissues from the trees. In addition, critical water loss occurs when the trees' cells are exposed to sunlight and warmed above a snowpack.

A hotel built in 1860 on Moosilauke's summit turned the mountain into a popular tourist destination served by a 5-mile carriage road. The Prospect House burned down in 1942, but the spectacular views remain. To the east is Franconia Ridge and the Presidential Range, while westward are the Green Mountains of Vermont.

An exciting descent of nearly 3,000 feet along the cascades of Beaver Brook drops the trail into Kinsman Notch, where it immediately begins the steep and rugged climb over the nearly 4,000-foot summits of the Kinsman Range. At Lonesome Lake the AT goes by the first in a string of huts operated by the Appalachian Mountain Club. The huts, some of which date back to the 1800s, permit American hikers to emulate trekkers of the Alps by enabling them to enjoy the traverse of high elevations without having to carry fully loaded backpacks, and to have evening and morning meals served to them while observing the alpine scenery from inside warm accommodations.

After descending another 3,000 feet into Franconia Notch, the AT climbs more than 3,500 feet to rise above 5,000 feet in elevation for the first time since the Mount Rogers National Recreation Area in southwest Virginia. There are 2 miles of grand and glorious hiking above treeline as the trail traverses narrow Franconia Ridge with its continuous 360-degree views; then wild fluctuations in terrain bring the northbound hiker past Zealand Falls and Ethan Pond, and into Crawford Notch.

In the 1770s, Timothy Nash, while hunting moose on Cherry Mountain, spied a narrow defile through the White Mountains. After following the Saco River through the notch, Nash informed the governor of New Hampshire of his important discovery. A skeptical Governor Benning Wentworth told Nash that if he could bring a horse through the pass from Jefferson to Portsmouth, he would be rewarded with a large land grant at the notch's mouth. Assisted by a friend and making use of ropes, Nash transported his horse up and over boulders of the gorge, gaining his property of more than 2,000 acres from the governor.

In 1825, the Samuel Willey family opened a hostel in the notch about a mile south of where the trail now crosses. A year later, in a bizarre incident recounted in "The Ambitious Guest," one of Nathaniel Hawthorne's *Twice-Told Tales,* the family perished when they rushed out to avoid an avalanche that appeared to be heading for their home. The slide was diverted into two streams by a huge boulder, swept around the house, and then flowed back together, crushing its unlucky victims beneath the rubble.

Along the Presidential Range in New Hampshire

From Crawford Notch, the trail begins its traverse of the Presidential Range, a stretch many hikers consider the most spectacular in New Hampshire, if not on the entire AT. Once it reaches the heights of 4,310-foot Mount Pierce, the trail joins the Crawford Path, built in 1819 as the first pathway to provide access to Mount Washington. The AT winds its way among the clouds, almost always above treeline, for more than 12 miles. Alpine flowers and lichens, which are really more at home in the tundra of the Arctic, grow upon the boulders or in the small bits of soil between cracks and spaces in the rock. Situated at about 5,000 feet in elevation, the glacially created Lakes of the Clouds are the highest freshwater ponds in the northeast.

On April 12, 1934, atop the 6,288-foot summit of Mount Washington (the highest the trail has been since the North Carolina–Tennessee border), a weather observatory anemometer registered a wind speed of 231 miles per hour, a world record at the time. Wind speeds of 100 miles per hour or more occur on the mountain close to 45 days each year, sometimes even in the height of summer. The first full-scale scientific expedition onto Mount Washington was made in 1784 as a band of scientists, historians, and explorers climbed up the mountain's east slope in heavy fog and clouds. Laden with muskets, pistols, compasses, thermometers, barometers, a sextant, and a telescope, the group was forced by bad weather to spend an evening in Tuckerman Ravine. Upon preparing a manuscript of the trip later in the year, Reverend Cutler made mention of Mount Washington, the first recorded use of the name for the mountain.

Accessed by a cog railway and a toll road in addition to the AT and other pathways, the summit provides views of four states and the Atlantic Ocean on clear days. Most days visitors have to be content with the knowledge of what they would be seeing if the fog wasn't swirling around the mountaintop.

The AT continues above treeline on a pathway of rocks and boulders that have been broken apart by water that froze in cracks. This type of rock debris, called felsenmeer, which means "rock sea" in German, is characteristic of areas that have temperatures close to freezing throughout the year. With views into the Great Gulf Wilderness, across to the Carter-Moriah Range, onto the Mahoosuc Mountains along the New Hampshire–Maine border, and westward to the White Mountains beyond Crawford Notch, the trail crosses Mount Madison, tops the Osgood Ridge, and descends into the trees before crossing Pinkham Notch.

The strenuous climb to the heights of the Carter-Moriah Range is made only slightly easier by a few steps blasted out of the rocky cliffs. For approximately 20 miles, the AT alternately rises and dips in a spruce and fir forest, through krummholz and a subalpine environment, and onto open ridges above treeline. Descending from nearly 5,000 feet to less than 1,000 feet, the AT crosses the Androscoggin River to enter its northernmost state.

Maine greets the AT visitor with the most rough, rugged, and seemingly wild and isolated terrain of the trail's entire route. Although they average well below 4,000 feet in elevation, the wildly fluctuating ups and downs of the mountains within the first

Lakes of the Clouds in New Hampshire

48 miles of the state force the northbound traveler to face an overall elevation gain of close to 19,000 feet—about 400 feet of climbing for each mile hiked!

From the New Hampshire–Maine border, the trail rises into the Mahoosuc Range for views of the Presidential Mountains back south and of the rigors to come farther north. Soon, the AT drops steeply into what has been called its most rugged mile, Mahoosuc Notch. The extremely narrow and steep valley was created as glaciers quarried rocks from the mountainsides; after the glaciers receded, freezing water continued to cause giant blocks of rock to break off and tumble into the valley, clogging the pathway of the trail. For a full mile, hikers must crawl over, around, between, and even under house-size boulders. Receiving very little direct sunlight, temperatures in the notch are cool year-round, with chunks of ice lingering well into late summer.

After this exhaustive effort, northbound hikers must sometimes use both hands and feet to ascend the nearly vertical side of Mahoosuc Arm, a climb of close to 1,500 feet in a little over 1 mile. Glacially created Spec Pond, the highest body of water in the state, provides a relaxation point before the trail resumes climbing over the north shoulder of Old Speck, only to leave the Mahoosuc Range by descending 2,500 feet into Grafton Notch.

The process of exfoliation, which has also taken place on the summit of Blood Mountain in Georgia, has created wide, bare areas of smooth, flat rock, and gently rounded domes and slopes along the Baldpate Mountain ridgeline. In some spots the rock has broken into large, steplike rises. Miles of trail above treeline bring the AT over Surplus Mountain and into Dunn Notch. The present route is the result of a 1980s relocation to put the trail onto a more scenic and secure pathway. Like the Roanoke Appalachian Trail Club far to the south, the Maine Appalachian Trail Club has done a herculean job of relocating the AT onto a more protected route. Largely under the leadership of Dave Field, the club relocated more than 170 miles of the 280 miles under its jurisdiction and built 20 new shelters and close to 35 privies between 1973 and 1992.

Traversing subalpine bogs, the trail comes into a stand of virgin red spruce on Elephant Mountain. The forest here is at the end of its natural cycle, but it is still sad to watch this grove of 300- to 400-year-old trees pass into memory; however, seedlings sprouting from the forest floor show that a new cycle has already begun.

Once over the Bemis Range, whose glacially smoothed bare rock affords views of the Rangeley chain of lakes, the trail, in quick succession, skirts glacially created Moxie, Long, Little Swift River, and South Ponds—all providing the possibility of spotting a moose or two. On Saddleback Mountain, the longest stretch of AT above timberline offers miles of delightful hiking on exposed bedrock dotted with glacial erratics (rounded boulders randomly left behind as the iceflows began to melt). Expansion plans by a ski resort have led to a hostile conflict over the protection of the trail on Saddleback.

A plaque on a shoulder of Spaulding Mountain commemorates the 1937 completion of the AT; then the trail skirts the summit of Sugarloaf Mountain, the second-highest point in Maine. The trail once went over its summit but was relocated in the 1970s to avoid ski resort development. Rising to more than 4,000 feet in elevation, the AT crosses the heavily wooded Crocker Mountains before traversing the rugged Bigelow Range. This grand, wild, and rugged area, with its magnificent above-treeline views, could have suffered the same fate as Sugarloaf Mountain. Entrepreneurs of the 1960s and 1970s had plans to build one of the largest ski resorts in the northeast on and around the Bigelow Range but were thwarted when a petition drive forced a reluctant state government to hold a referendum. By a 3,000-vote margin, the sagacious citizens of Maine directed the state to purchase land and create a 33,000-acre wilderness preserve, protecting 17 miles of the AT in the process.

Dropping to skirt the eastern edge of Flagstaff Lake, the AT is now in a region of lakes and ponds, and from here to Mount Katahdin, northbound hikers have the opportunity to camp each evening upon the shore of some lake, pond, or stream. Between Middle and West Carry Ponds, the AT follows the route of the Arnold Trail.

Appointed in 1775 by George Washington to lead 1,150 men across Maine to mount a surprise attack on British troops in Quebec City, Benedict Arnold followed the Kennebec River north to the Carry Ponds area. Here the Colonial forces turned to follow a portage trail around rapids in the Dead River to continue the march into Canada. Plagued by miserable New England winter weather, the forces dwindled to less than 800 men as they spent six weeks slogging through the icy rivers, swamps, and bogs of Maine. Weakened by such an ordeal, they still attacked Quebec City (during a blizzard!), but were soundly defeated.

For many years hikers had to bravely ford the 70-yard-wide Kennebec River, made especially dangerous due to releases of water from hydro facilities upstream, which caused the depth and current strength of the river to rise quickly and unpredictably. Partially in response to a drowning in the 1980s, the ATC and the Maine Appalachian Trail Club have returned to the original means of crossing the river when the AT was first blazed in Maine by providing a free canoe ferry service during the height of the hiking season. (When the trail route was declared officially complete in 1937, it contained four canoe ferries in Maine—at Moxie Pond, the Kennebec River, Rainbow Lake, and the West Branch of the Penobscot River.)

The trail makes a short, steep climb over Pleasant Pond Mountain, whose smooth, rounded knobs are the result of the abrasive action of rock and debris underneath a glacier as it slid over the summit. Moxie Bald's heights are those of a classic *roche moutonnée*. As glaciers slid over the northwest, or upslope, side of the mountain, pressure melting caused the combination of rock debris and water to act as a type of liquid sandpaper, polishing the rock into smooth slopes. When the water topped the mountain, the pressure was relieved and refreezing occurred, pulling large pieces of rock off the downslope and creating a jagged, nearly vertical cliff on the southeast face of the mountain.

In a lowland of ponds and streams, the trail follows the West Branch of the Piscataquis River for 5 miles before skirting the north side of Lake Hebron and entering the 100 Mile Wilderness, the longest stretch of trail between easily accessible resupply points.

The trail here follows a lowland landscape past several ponds and waterways, including 60-foot Little Wilson Falls (one of the highest cascades on the AT) before fording Long Pond Stream and making the steep climb onto the Barren-Chairback Range. The five peaks along this 15-mile stretch are all below 3,000 feet, but the ruggedness of terrain makes it a rough route going by mountain tarns, bogs, and cliffs and ledges with frequent views out across the Northern Forest.

After fording the West Branch of the Pleasant River, the trail ascends along Gulf Hagas Brook to the summit of White Cap Mountain with an imposing view of Mount Katahdin thrusting up into the northern sky. Another ford, this one of the East Branch of the Pleasant River, brings the AT into lowlands dotted by isolated, crystal-clear lakes and ponds. To camp next to one of these, to watch a grazing moose silhouetted by the glow of a setting sun, and to wake to the cry of a loon is to experience the essential nature and lure of the Maine woods.

Along Cooper Brook, the AT follows portions of an old tote road that was built to accommodate the Lombard log hauler, a steam engine that was used near the beginning of the 20th century to pull sled trains of logs and pulpwood out of the forest. The lagged tracks on which it was mounted were similar to those used for military tanks.

A designated campsite on lower Jo-Mary Lake (named after an Abenaki Indian chief noted for his hunting abilities) was once the site of Potter's Antlers Camp, one of the dozens of sporting camps that were popular in this area from the late 1800s to about the 1950s. Patronized by sportsmen and families of means, the camps provided comfortable accommodations from which to enjoy the recreational and scenic opportunities of the Maine wilderness. Making use of their primitive roadways, the AT originally went by, or came close to, quite a number of these camps. The trail has since been relocated away from the few that are still in operation.

Rising from Nahmakanta Lake, which is large enough to create small waves when a strong wind blows, the AT (now farther north than Montreal) crosses Nesuntabunt Mountain (Abenaki Indian for "three heads" or "three summits") and parallels Rainbow Stream and Lake to emerge from the 100 Mile Wilderness at Abol Bridge on the West Branch of the Penobscot River. By trail, the northern end of the AT on Mount Katahdin is only 15 miles away, inside Baxter State Park.

During his years as a member of the legislative branch, and then as governor of Maine, George Percival P. Baxter was unable to convince the state legislature to act

Rainbow Ledges in Maine

upon his dream of setting aside great tracts of land in central Maine as a nature pre-serve. A man of considerable wealth, he purchased and donated nearly 6,000 acres, including most of Mount Katahdin, to the state after his governorship ended in 1931. Continuing throughout his life to purchase and consolidate additional tracts, he even-tually deeded more than 200,000 acres to Maine. A condition of the gift was that the area "shall forever be used for public park and recreational purposes, shall forever be left in the natural wild state, shall forever be kept as a sanctuary for wild beasts and birds, and that no roads or ways for motor vehicles shall hereafter be constructed therein or hereon." An additional purchase of several thousand acres was made in 1992 and 1993 with funds he had left to the park authority. The park is now the largest area in the East maintained primarily for wilderness, with recreation as just an incidental use.

Just like the AT (and so many of our natural areas), the park is being loved to death. Trying to follow Baxter's mandate to keep it wild, the park authority has so far resisted pressure from captious groups to build more campsites, cabins, and roads simply so that more people can gain access to the park during the busy season. May the gov-ernor's vision and wisdom prevail.

From Abol Bridge, the AT parallels the West Branch of the Penobscot River and Nesowadnehunk Stream (Abenaki for "swift stream between mountains") and passes by Big and Little Niagara Falls and Daicey, Elbow, and Tracy Ponds to arrive at the base of its final mountain. To the Abenaki Indians, Mount Katahdin was the "greatest mountain," and for those hikers who have come all the way from Georgia, there is no doubt in their minds that they were right. A monadnock (a mountain which stands alone and is not part of a range), Katahdin towers over smaller peaks and ridges, hundreds of ponds and lakes, and the flat coastal plain of spruce and fir that stretches out to the Atlantic Ocean.

Climbing nearly 4,000 feet in 5 miles, the trail quickly goes past Katahdin Stream Falls, climbs above treeline, and scrambles over huge rocks and cliff facings, necessitating the use of handholds. The trail levels out some at the Tableland and Thoreau Spring. Henry David Thoreau never drank from this watering spot (named for him in the 1930s) and, in fact, failed by about a mile to reach the mountain's summit in 1846 when he turned back due to bad weather and reluctant companions. Often amid the clouds, the trail's final mile winds among boulders to 5,276-foot Baxter Peak, the northern terminus of America's premier long-distance footpath. A frequently quoted phrase, often erroneously attributed to Thoreau but actually the words of journalist J. K. Laski, which appeared in the *Bangor Courier* in 1847, beautifully summarizes the peak's view of dozens of Maine lakes, ponds, and streams: "The scene reminded me of that represented by a splendid mirror broken into a thousand fragments and widely scattered over the grass, reflecting the full blaze of the sun."

CHAPTER 3
Mountains Rise, Mountains Fall

Mountains are earth's undecaying monuments.

~ Nathaniel Hawthorne

Like other mountain ranges in the world, the Appalachian Mountains, at various times through the ages, have risen to great heights from the sea or have been continental rock covered by shallow oceans. For millions of years the land, along with the rest of the North American continent, has alternately been subjected to the effects of the movements of the earth's crustal plates, rising and falling seas, erosion from wind and water, and advancing and receding glaciers. Each time the crustal plates collide, North America takes on a new face. Giant land masses grind into each other, causing the earth's surface to break, crack, and fold upward, creating mountains. At the same time, large slabs of the lower portion of the crust slide underneath one another, raising the surface even higher.

Remember that even though geologists study something as solid as rock, theirs is a continually developing science and nothing is set in stone. Theories are always changing, evolving, or being replaced by new theories. Time frames are constantly being revised and new information steadily unearthed. The following information is what is presently considered by geologists to be the general story of the formation of the Appalachian Mountains. Exact dates may be in dispute, but the order of events is commonly acknowledged.

In the late 1960s and early 1970s, the theory of plate tectonics came to be accepted as an explanation for many of the surface features of the earth. The theory states that the earth's outer crust is not one solid mass, but rather is made up of several large plates and numerous smaller ones that ride upon the hot, more plastic matter of the mantle below them. Floating along on their semiliquid bed, the plates drift about, away from, into, or past each other. Vast oceans are created when they pull apart, but when two plates collide, they buckle, heave, and fold, pushing masses of rock high into the air and creating towering and mighty mountain ranges. Although plate tectonics goes a long way in explaining how the continents came to look the way they do, the theory still leaves many questions unanswered. One such quandary involves the distribution of various species on the plates. Why do the Appalachian Mountains and a region in China share many of the same types of plants when the two areas have, as far as we know, never come close to each other and don't have common geological backgrounds? Recent paleontological evidence out of northern Africa is beginning to raise some doubt about the sequence of events in the movements of the plates. Many geologists will even acknowledge that it is unknown just how many times the plates have repeated the process of collision and regression over the ages.

Geologists tend to agree, however, that at one time—during what is known as the Taconic Orogeny—the land masses that were to become Australia, South America, Africa, Antarctica, and a portion of Asia were part of one giant continent called Gondwana. An ancient sea, the Iapetus Ocean, separated Gondwana from Laurentia, another large chunk of land containing what would one day become North America, Greenland, and a portion of the British Isles. East of this was Baltica, which would become a part of Europe.

Close to 500 million years ago, the Iapetus Ocean shrank in size, pulling Baltica's plate toward and under the Laurentian plate. This force created immense amounts of sedimentary rock from the erosion of the land masses and caused major eruptions of lava to surface near the line where the two plates met, raising a range of tall volcanic mountains. (This process, known as subduction, is happening today as the Gorda and Juan de Fuca Plates slide underneath the North American plate in the Pacific Northwest. The chain of volcanoes found in the mountains of northern California, Washington, and Oregon is a result of that subduction.) Although the volcanic and other mountains created during the Taconic Orogeny were no doubt over 10,000 feet high, 100 million years of weathering erosion reduced them to nothing more than a small, rocky rubble.

About 380 million years ago, during the Acadian Orogeny, Laurentia and Baltica fused together into one. A range called the Caledonide Mountains rose and formed where the two plates met. The remnants of these mountains, which probably resembled the present-day Alps, are today's northern Appalachian Mountains. In addition, because the opening up of the Atlantic Ocean caused these two plates to eventually split apart, the highlands of England, Greenland, Scotland, and Scandinavia also had their origins in the Caledonide Mountains. (Recent theories suggest the formation of the Caledonides to be more nearly related to the Taconic Orogeny than to the Acadian.)

At about this time, changes also started to take place in the animal and plant worlds. Insects began to fly through the air, and some aquatic life-forms left their watery homes to become amphibians and spread across the land. Ferns and club mosses, growing as much as 50 feet or more in height, covered the continents in far-reaching forests of luxuriant green vegetation. For millions of years this giant foliage grew, died, and fell to the earth, decomposing into a peatlike soil. Additional millions of years and layer upon layer of sediments eventually compressed the peat into the coal found throughout the eastern United States and Canada.

It is interesting to note that several diminutive plants commonly found along the length of the AT can trace their ancestry back to this colossal vegetation. Unlike dinosaurs, which were evidently too big for their own good, running cedar, ground pine, and several of their relatives in the Lycopodiacae family have, through evolution, shrunk in size in response to changing climatic and geological conditions. With several means of reproduction, including spores and running vines, these plants can carpet large portions of the forest floor. You'll easily be able to recognize them as you walk along the trail; they grow only 6–12 inches tall and look like clusters of tiny evergreen Christmas trees.

As the great coal-making episode came to an end, the two large continental masses, Gondwana and Laurentia/Baltica, began to drift toward each other, closing the Iapetus Ocean. During the Alleghenian Orogeny, the part of Gondwana that was to become western Africa crashed—over the course of 50 million years—into Laurentia/Baltica. The rise of the Southern Appalachian Mountains was the result.

The force of the Alleghenian Orogeny crash of continental plates was so severe that it uprooted older deposits of rock along Laurentia/Baltica's eastern shore, shoving these deposits more than 100 miles to the west, up and over younger deposits.

All of Earth's land masses had now joined together into a single supercontinent, Pangaea, which was encircled by one continuous ocean, Panthalassa. Yet, as they had done before, the individual continental masses did not stay in one place. The European and African plates pulled away from the North American Plate, creating the Atlantic Ocean in between. The other land masses began drifting off in their own individual directions. These latest movements have continued to the present, giving us the make-up and position of the continents as we know them today.

So, it was about 200 million years ago that the great forces that had compressed and crushed the Appalachians came to an end. But that doesn't mean the mountains then looked like the mountains upon which we now hike. Many geologists believe they more closely resembled today's Rocky Mountains or the Andes in South America. In the ensuing years, the lofty peaks of those early Appalachian Mountains have been shaped by two great and irresistible powers—glaciers and erosion.

Earth has experienced dozens of glacial episodes throughout its history. The latest, known as the Wisconsin glaciation, began about 75,000 years ago and lasted approximately 65,000 years. Advancing slowly from the north, sheets of ice slid their way up, over, and through the northern Appalachians, eventually halting their southern movement about midway through Pennsylvania. The ice masses were so thick that they swept over the surface and the summits of all or most of the mountains.

As they moved southward, the glaciers made dramatic alterations in the landscape. Hikers climbing out of the White Mountains' Crawford and Franconia Notches can observe these changes firsthand. Like huge routers, the glaciers forced their way through the mountains, turning the once narrow river gorges into the U-shaped valleys seen today.

In one place the glaciers went beyond just scouring out simple valleys. In the Hudson River Valley the glaciers created the only fjord crossed by the AT. It is also the only spot along the trail with salt water (actually a brackish mix of fresh and salt water). The glaciers have done such a good job of deeply scouring the land that the river is at sea level here, meaning that it experiences the rise and fall of the tides as they bring in water from the Atlantic Ocean to mix with the fresh water flowing down from the mountains.

Sometimes, especially on the higher ridgelines, the ice flows performed an action more akin to a woodworker's plane, creating an amazingly smooth appearance on the rock. The rounded-rock hilltops and even-surfaced stone in the Harriman and Bear Mountain State Park area of New York; the flat rock ridges of central Vermont; the large, open, and bare slabs of stone in the southern Mahoosuc Range on the New Hampshire–Maine border; and the smoothed-out summit of Bemis Mountain in southern Maine are all evidence that glaciers have passed over these areas. In other places, such as The Cobbles in northern Massachusetts, stones and boulders that had been captured in the bellies of the glaciers scored the surface of the rock with tracks that are still easily discernible.

Glaciers not only smoothed out rock plateaus, but also scraped out large depressions that filled with water as the glacial period ended and the ice sheets liquefied. Sunfish Pond near the Delaware Water Gap in New Jersey is the southernmost glacial pond on the AT. By the time a northbound hiker reaches Benedict, Upper Goose, and Finerty Ponds in Massachusetts, such bodies of water are quite common and are passed in rapid succession. Gore Pond in Massachusetts; Stratton and Little Rock Ponds and Griffith Lake in Vermont; Lonesome Lake and Moss and Gentian Ponds in New Hampshire; and Speck, Horns, and Crawford Ponds in Maine are some of the more scenic and well-known glacier-carved water basins.

Even in their retreat, as the climate grew warmer and the ice sheets withdrew to the far north, glaciers had an impact on the land. The bogs of New England, mostly found in Maine along the AT, are one result. Whereas advancing glaciers might gouge out places in rock to form ponds, receding glaciers often leave large deposits of boulders and sand, forming dams that slow and impede the flow of water. With the passing

Franconia Ridge in New Hampshire

of years, plant growth, most notably sphagnum moss, would slowly expand, first near the edges of the dammed water and then eventually all the way across the surface of the water. Hundreds of years of rotting vegetation from the moss and other plants put down a continually thickening layer of muck in the watery soil, eventually becoming a full-fledged bog of mucky, peatlike soil.

In some places—especially in New Hampshire and Maine—as alpine glaciers (formed when snow accumulated and turned to flowing ice) slid down the mountainsides, they created what are known as cirques, bowl-shaped valleys open on one side and bounded by high, nearly vertical walls on the others. The slopes of Mount Moosilauke in New Hampshire contain the southernmost cirques found on the AT, though these formations can be more easily discerned as hikers gaze into Tuckerman's Ravine from the top of Mount Washington or stare out across the expanse of the Great Gulf Wilderness from the high ridges of the Presidential Range.

Erosion is the major force that has changed the face of the Appalachian Mountains. Much more than the ice of the glaciers, it has been erosion that has converted the mountains from jagged, rocky peaks of 10,000 feet or higher to the rounded and more gently sloping hillsides of today. Both mechanical and chemical actions come into play during the erosion process, with mechanical action probably being the easiest to observe and comprehend.

Glacially created pond along the Appalachian Trail

All of us have seen how even the tiniest clump of grass can crack a thick slab of concrete on the sidewalk in front of our homes. In the same way, as tree and shrub roots grow and expand, they will actually pry apart large rocks, breaking them into smaller pieces that then become more susceptible to other types of weathering.

Wind also plays a part in the mechanical process of erosion. Just as sandblasting will clean away the outer surface of dirt and grime on stone buildings, so too will wind-blown particles of sand eat away at surface rock, wearing it down and sometimes etching intricate patterns on the rock face or creating interesting rock outcropping formations.

It is water, though, that plays the largest role by far in the process of eroding the mountains and sculpting them into the shapes we see today. During colder weather, water that has seeped into the small cracks and openings of exposed rock will freeze and expand, splitting the rock apart in the same manner that roots do. Sometimes this process will take place over a large surface area, creating long, rough cliff facings such as those the AT follows near the ridgeline of Peters Mountain in Pennsylvania.

In fact, the ridgelines of the central Appalachians are the result of a combination of continental uplift and erosion. The uplift caused the rainwaters and streams to flow and wash over the land at an increasing rate, eroding the softer shale rock and creating valleys nestled among mountains composed of the harder and more erosion-resistant deposits of sandstone.

This process is still going on today, and as you stand upon the summit of just about any mountain on the AT, you can see it in action. You'll notice that there are spur ridges emanating like knobby-knuckled fingers from the main ridgeline and descending into the valleys below. In between these spurs (which, like the main ridgeline, are composed of harder, more erosion-resistant rock) are the indentations of narrow hollows and valleys where water has run off the mountain, perhaps along cracks, joints, or faults. If you walk downhill into one of these hollows, you will more than likely come across a small stream that continues to carry away bits of the mountain.

Many of the largest rivers in the East that cut through the crest of the Appalachian Mountains were already flowing before the mountains formed. As the mountains rose, the rivers eroded the rock that lay under their course, creating gaps in the mountains, known as water gaps. Water gaps are quite common along the central portion of the AT. Among some of the most well known are the James River in central Virginia; the Potomac River at Harpers Ferry, West Virginia; the Susquehanna River near Duncannon, Pennsylvania; and the Delaware River on the Pennsylvania–New Jersey border.

Besides mechanically eroding the rock by breaking it apart or wearing it down, water is involved in chemical erosion processes. Some of the minerals found in rock are actually water-soluble, so when the rains or streams wash over them, they more or less dissolve into the water and are carried away downstream.

The cirque of the Great Gulf Wilderness

We've all heard about the modern-world problem of acid rain, but rain falling from the sky has always mixed with atmospheric chemicals to form a mild acid. (The problem today is that this acidic rain now falls in a more concentrated form.) The acid in the rain dissolves elements in the rock, which then has a tendency to crumble and fall apart, much like the way rust eats through the metal body of your car.

Lichens, those stalwart little plants that are able to grow and survive in some of the most unlikely and harshest of environments, erode rock both mechanically and chemically. They are actually two living entities, algae and fungus, which have combined into one organism to overcome adversity. Algae produce food for the fungus, which is unable make its own nourishment. The fungus, in turn, absorbs and holds water, at times even from moist air or fog, keeping the algae alive during hot, dry spells. Spreading across the surface of a rock, the lichen anchors itself using minute, rootlike holdfasts that pry loose small bits of the rock. In addition, a weak acid emitted by these plants chemically dissolves minerals in the rock, hastening wear.

So, what happens to all this rock that has been broken, chipped, cracked, and dissolved? The larger pieces of rock continue to break apart into smaller and smaller pieces until those pieces become tiny particles that are swept away in a spring thaw, a violent

Exposed rock in the mountains of Maine

summer thunderstorm, or a gentle fall rain. Carried by the waters, the coarse particles then sand away the streambeds, making them deeper and wider. Traveling farther from the mountains, the particles might be deposited in the valleys; they might move on to add substance to the rich soil of the Piedmont or help create the sands and clays of the Coastal Plain; or they might even be carried all the way out to sea. Thus, some of the material that a child uses to build a sand castle on Virginia Beach could well have once been an outcropping on the crest of the Blue Ridge Mountains or a rocky ridgeline in the hills of Pennsylvania. The matter that makes up part of St. George Island off the Florida Gulf Coast may have been carried from the North Georgia mountains by the Chattahoochee and Apalachicola Rivers.

Erosion of rock and soil occurs naturally, but sometimes it is intensified by the works of human beings. Although Charlies Bunion in the Great Smoky Mountains may look like an ancient geological feature, it has only recently been exposed. Before the area was established as a national park, heavy logging had disturbed and exposed so much of the soil that it all washed away in a heavy rainstorm in 1925, laying bare the rock. But you don't have to go to the Smoky Mountains to see how humans aid the erosion process. A large majority of the ridges the AT follows or crosses have old logging, mining, or carriage roads on them, and their deeply channeled surfaces are evidence enough that the mountains are wearing away faster than they would if left undisturbed.

GEOLOGIC TIME

ERA	PERIOD	AGE IN YEARS
CENOZOIC Age of Mammals	Quaternary	— 10,000
		— 2 million
	Tertiary	— 5 million
		— 24 million
		— 37–38 million
		— 55–57 million
		— 36–66 million
MESOZOIC Age of Reptiles	Cretaceous	— 138–144 million
	Jurassic	— 205–208 million
	Triassic	— 240–245 million
PALEOZOIC Age of Fishes	Permian	— 286–290 million
	Pennsylvanian	— 320–330 million
	Mississippian	— 360–365 million
	Devonian	— 408–410 million
	Silurian	— 435–438 million
	Ordovician	— 500–505 million
	Cambrian	— 570 million
PRECAMBRIAN	Origin of Life	— 3.77–4.28 billion
	Origin of Earth	— 4.6 billion

CHAPTER 4

The Long Green Tunnel

Amidst the greens and the blues of the forest is where I belong,

and am at the height of my contentment with life.

~ Leonard M. Adkins

MANY PEOPLE WHO LIVE in the eastern part of the United States have no idea that they live in one of the most environmentally diverse areas on Earth. For almost nowhere else in the world is there the lushness and variety of trees, flowers, shrubs, and other plants that are to be found in the mountains through which the Appalachian Trail passes. More species of trees grow in the Great Smoky Mountains than in all of northern Europe. Only in the rainforests of South America is it possible to find a larger number of species of plants per acre than can be found within the Appalachians.

Sometimes, visitors from the wide-open spaces of the western United States complain about the lack of views along the Appalachian Trail, referring to it as "the long green tunnel." Yet those who come to the trail looking only for the far-off vistas miss the bigger picture of the world around them and of the true beauty to be discovered and appreciated in the Appalachian Mountains.

At one time this great wooded area was not limited to just the mountains of the East. When the explorers from Europe first arrived in North America, the forest spread out along the coastal area from Florida to Canada, went inland over the Piedmont to cover the ridges and valleys of the Appalachian Mountains, and stretched as far as the banks of the Mississippi River and a bit beyond.

Some botanists theorize that farther back in time this forest covered even more land. About 200 million years ago, when the Appalachian Mountains were experiencing their final upward thrust, all of the continents of the world had joined together into one supercontinent, Pangaea. Around the mid-Mesozoic period, Pangaea split in two, with North America and Eurasia united as the northernmost of the two resulting masses. Eventually, those two large continents began to drift apart, but North America continued to be joined to Asia by a land bridge between Alaska and Siberia, and, with the earth experiencing a rather mild climate—even into the Arctic regions—a single, vast deciduous forest stretched from North America's eastern coast to the mountain regions of Asia. When the land bridge became covered by the ocean, the forest was split in two. Although the bridge reemerged during the Ice Age, frigid northern temperatures prevented the two halves of the forest from reuniting.

Much of this is just theory, but how else can the similarities between the two forests today be explained? Including sassafras, witch hazel, tuliptree, catalpa, fringe tree, yellowwood, silverbell, tupelo, hickory, and magnolia, there are more than 60 genera of trees that grow only in the eastern parts of Asia and in eastern North America and nowhere else in the world. Some species, such as the red maple and its counterpart found in Japan, are nearly identical.

Varying this theory a bit, other scientists say information based upon the dating of fossil evidence shows that, long before the land bridge connection, all of the northern hemisphere was covered by the same type of forest. The trees of Europe, however, were subjected to and destroyed by extensive glaciation, while those in North America and Asia were not. In conjunction with this, North America and Asia have enjoyed similar climates since then, conducive to the continued growth of the same kinds of trees.

Even though most of us recognize a tree when we see one, it is hard to define what exactly constitutes a tree. A dictionary will describe a tree as being a woody perennial plant usually having a single main stem with few or no branches on its lower part. Yet trees are not a group of plants related to each other, but rather to other types of plants. For example, the black locust is a legume, a member of the pea family. Apple, cherry, and hawthorn trees are roses, and tulip trees and magnolias are related to buttercups and anemones. Hackberries and elms are linked to nettles and marijuana, while buckeyes, hollies, and maples are closely related to jewelweed and poison ivy.

TYPES OF FORESTS ALONG THE AT

THE PRESENT FORESTS of the Appalachian Mountains consist of various communities or associations of trees known as forest types. The Society of American Foresters defines and recognizes close to 100 forest types in the eastern United States, but there is usually no clear boundary from one forest type to another. Rather, as various environmental changes occur (such as moisture, elevation, and temperature), the trees of one will grad- ually begin to change, blend in with, and then yield to the trees of another forest type. Also, a particular tree might be found not in just one forest type, but in many different types and locations. Additionally, ever since the early settlers arrived from Europe, the woodlands of the eastern United States have been manipulated and changed to meet human needs and purposes. Forest types have been cut down and replanted with trees from a different forest type or with just a single species of tree. Other trees have been planted and grown outside of their natural environment purely for ornamental or scenic value. Keeping all this in mind, it is still possible to discuss the various forest types commonly found along the AT.

Most of the forests covering the Appalachian Mountains are deciduous, meaning the trees lose their leaves each year. Of the deciduous forests, the **southern hardwood forest,** dominated by the various species of oaks and hickories, is probably the most extensive forest type along the AT. Found along the drier slopes and ridges, it stretches from Georgia to the mid-Atlantic states and even into bits of New England.

At one time, chestnuts were the predominant trees in this forest, making up 25% of the woods in some areas. However, the chestnut blight, a fungal disease accidentally introduced into North America from Asia, removed the trees from the landscape by the end of the 1930s. The chestnut had played an important role in the daily life of Appala- chian Mountain residents. Being plentiful, the nuts were gathered in the fall, providing a supplement to people's diet and a source of cash when sold by the bushel. The tree's timber was used to build log homes and durable fences to keep livestock from roaming too far. Its bark, rich in tannin, was stripped and sold for the processing of hides. The inner bark, the cambium, also contains a large amount of tannin, which makes the wood resistant to decay and explains why much of it has yet to rot away. In fact, there are some places along the AT, such as near Stony Man Mountain in Shenandoah National Park, where you might still find the silvery-gray logs of the once-mighty chestnuts, but as time goes on, more and more of them are yielding to rot. The roots and stumps of these fallen trees still produce sprouts that grow for a while before they become fungus-infested and die. The hope is that someday the sprouts will be able to resist the disease or scientists will develop a strain of tree that will not succumb to the blight.

Although the southern hardwood forest is dominated today by oaks and hickories, it is a highly variable forest populated by numerous species of trees. More than any- thing else, moisture and temperature (controlled in large part by elevation) determine which trees grow where. Because of this, it is possible to encounter many species of trees on just one ridgeline as you ascend from lower to higher elevations.

Due to hotter summer temperatures and less rainfall, the forest below 2,000 feet tends to produce trees of only average or less than average height. Here cucumber tree, white ash, buckeye, sourwood, holly, and an evergreen, the eastern white pine are found.

EASTERN WHITE PINE

LATIN NAME *Pinus strobus*

AVERAGE MATURE HEIGHT 80–100 feet

LEAVES The soft evergreen needles are bluish green, 3–5 inches long, and arranged in bundles of 5.

BARK The bark of young eastern white pines is greenish brown and smooth, but as the tree ages it turns more of a dark gray and becomes thicker, developing deep vertical furrows.

RANGE IN APPALACHIAN TRAIL STATES Georgia to Maine

MOST LIKELY LOCATIONS Just south of Spivey Gap in North Carolina; Turkeypen Gap in Tennessee; near Little Irish Creek (a virgin stand) in central Virginia; about 0.5 mile north of Jug End Road in Massachusetts; along the West Branch of the Piscataquis River north of Horseshoe Canyon Lean-To in Maine

The largest percentage of Appalachian trees probably occurs between 2,000 feet and 3,500 feet in elevation (with some local variations up to 4,000 feet). A huge variety of trees, ranging close to 50 in number, are native to these elevations. On mountains that receive ample rainfall, there will be black cherry, Fraser magnolia, mountain silverbell, sugar maple, basswood, black walnut, pitch pine, striped maple, rhododendron, and mountain laurel.

FRASER MAGNOLIA *(Mountain Magnolia)*

LATIN NAME *Magnolia fraseri*

AVERAGE MATURE HEIGHT 30–40 feet

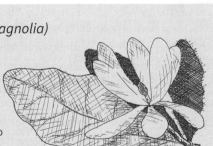

LEAVES The deciduous leaves of the Fraser magnolia are 8–12 inches long and 5–8 inches wide, are a bright green above and rather whitish underneath, and are the only magnolia leaves whose bases are lobed into almost a heart shape.

BARK The bark is smooth to scaly, thin, and gray to brown in color.

RANGE IN APPALACHIAN TRAIL STATES Georgia to Virginia/West Virginia; most often found in swampy areas and along mountain streams

MOST LIKELY LOCATIONS Between Big Pine Mountain and Laurel Fork in Tennessee

In late spring and early summer, basswood trees produce long-stalked, fragrant clusters of yellowish white flowers that seem to be irresistible to honeybees—you may actually be able to locate one of these trees by the very audible hum produced by the

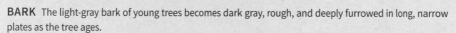

SUGAR MAPLE *(Rock Maple)*

LATIN NAME *Acer saccharum*

AVERAGE MATURE HEIGHT 60–100 feet

LEAVES The opposite, 3- to 5-inch-long (and about as wide) leaves usually have 5 long-pointed lobes; are irregularly and slightly toothed; and possess long, slender, and sometimes hairy petioles. The leaves may appear thin but are strong and firm and dark green on top, with the bottoms being paler and often with hairy veins.

BARK The light-gray bark of young trees becomes dark gray, rough, and deeply furrowed in long, narrow plates as the tree ages.

RANGE IN APPALACHIAN TRAIL STATES Georgia to Maine

MOST LIKELY LOCATIONS Sugar Tree Gap in Great Smoky Mountains National Park; 0.5 mile south of VA 606 in southwest Virginia; around Black Rock and the headwaters of Cornelius Creek (a virgin stand) in central Virginia; Mount Greylock in Massachusetts; between Lottery Road and the summit of Beacon Hill in Vermont; and near and along the Sandy River in Maine

hundreds of bees attracted to it. The light-colored honey has a distinctive flavor and is sought by honey enthusiasts. Native Americans used the fibers of basswood's inner bark (known as bast) to make rope and woven mats.

The mountain silverbell is another tree known for the flowers it produces in early to midspring. The 1-inch, bell-shaped white flowers (sometimes tinged with pink) drape themselves in clusters of two to five. Although mountain silverbell trees range from Georgia to West Virginia, they are most abundant in the Great Smokies, turning entire hillsides a snowy white. Usually a small tree compared to others, the mountain silverbell attains its largest proportions in the Smokies, with some trees recorded to have grown over 3 feet thick and nearly 100 feet tall.

On the hillsides where precipitation is abundant, melted snow and rainfall come rushing down into mountain valleys, bringing soil, bits of wood, and stone that has eroded from higher up on the ridge. When the slope becomes less steep, the running water begins to slow and deposits much of the debris, which, after thousands of years and an accumulation of deposits, creates a deep and rich soil. Protected from wind and other harsh elements, such places develop into the Appalachian's most diverse and vibrant woodlands, the **cove hardwood forest.** Nowhere else in the world at midlatitudes, except maybe China, will be found a deciduous forest so intricate and productive. A single cove may harbor scores of wildflowers and more than 40 species of trees, mingling some found far to the north with those of decidedly southern environments. Where conditions are optimal for this type of forest, such as in the Smokies, the number of tree species can be almost twice that many.

The cove hardwood forest is the lumberman's dream not only because of its great diversity, but also because the trees often reach near-record size. It is hard to determine which tree is dominant here; abundant are basswood, black cherry, yellow birch, sugar maple, American beech, yellow buckeye, yellow poplar, northern red oak, white ash, mountain silverbell, red maple, and cucumber magnolia.

YELLOW POPLAR *(Tuliptree)*

LATIN NAME *Liriodendron tulipifera*

AVERAGE MATURE HEIGHT 80–100 feet

LEAVES The shiny, hairless, dark-green leaves are paler underneath and measure 3–6 inches long and wide. Their unmistakable square shape has 4 (sometimes 6) short-pointed lobes, a broad base, and an indentation at the summit.

BARK The nearly smooth, ashy-gray bark of a young tree becomes thicker and develops interlacing deep furrows as the tree ages.

RANGE IN APPALACHIAN TRAIL STATES Georgia to southern New England

MOST LIKELY LOCATIONS Liss Gap in Georgia; about a half mile south of US 522 in northern Virginia

Although some of these forests may have succumbed to America's demand for timber, many still exist within the confines of the Southern Appalachians. Probably the most famous is Cades Cove on the west side of Great Smoky Mountains National Park, but a number can be found right along the AT, such as the forest around the headwaters of Cornelius Creek in central Virginia, which contains virgin sugar maple and hemlock trees.

Hemlocks often grow in such extensive stands, especially along streams and on slopes up to 5,000 feet in elevation, that they establish their own **hemlock forest.** Hemlocks are very tolerant of shade from taller trees or from those standing higher up on the mountainside. As a result, the sun is blocked by both the overstory trees and the spreading branches of the hemlocks, creating temperatures 10° cooler than the surrounding woods and making these groves favorite places for hikers on hot, humid days. In winter, the thickets provide cover and food for wildlife, with deer browsing on the foliage and red squirrels and birds cutting open the small cones to obtain the seeds. As discussed in the previous chapter, a very large percentage of eastern hemlock trees are, sadly, succumbing to the infestation of the hemlock woolly adelgid.

Growing beneath the canopies of southern and cove hardwood forests are mountain laurel, rhododendron, and a plant that has played an important role in the lives of Southern Appalachian inhabitants: ramps. It was not that long ago that preserving vegetables by canning or freezing was unknown; by the time winter ended, people were craving fresh green foods. To the rescue came ramps, which appear in early spring as

EASTERN HEMLOCK
(Canada Hemlock)

LATIN NAME *Tsuga canadensis*

AVERAGE MATURE HEIGHT 60–70 feet

LEAVES The flat, linear, evergreen needles about 0.5 inch long are a shiny dark green above with two narrow stripes of white underneath. Attached to the twigs by minute leafstalks, the needles are arranged spirally but appear to grow in twos. They can be slightly toothed, and the rounded tips may be notched.

BARK The tannin-rich bark is brown and deeply furrowed.

RANGE IN APPALACHIAN TRAIL STATES Georgia to Maine

MOST LIKELY LOCATIONS Along Stover Creek in Georgia; between Big Pine Mountain and Laurel Fork in Tennessee; just north of Max Patch Mountain in North Carolina; near Little Irish Creek (a virgin stand) and along Cornelius Creek in central Virginia; Rattlesnake Den in Connecticut; close to Kay Wood Lean-To and on Mount Prospect in Massachusetts

ADDITIONAL NOTE A relative, the Carolina hemlock (*Tsuga caroliniana*), ranges from Georgia to Virginia and may be seen in Tennessee just north of the Nolichucky River and in Virginia at Thunder Ridge Overlook; Petite's Gap; and, at its northern limit, near the James River.

a pair of lilylike leaves growing in the rich cove soils, often beside creeks and small streams. Sometimes referred to as a wild leek, the underground portion of a ramp is a small onion containing allyl sulfate, the ingredient that gives garlic its taste. Gathered when the plants are young, the strong-tasting ramps have a loyal following to this day, with ramp festivals held annually, such as the one near Whitetop Mountain in southwest Virginia. If permitted to grow, the ramp's leaves eventually wither away, and a cluster of white flowers blooms on top of the stem.

Providing a source of income, ginseng is another southern and cove hardwood forest inhabitant that was, and is, a valuable plant. It is gathered for its roots, not for its flowers and foliage. Many Chinese people have faith in the "doctrine of signatures," that is, that a plant can cure whatever ails the body part it resembles. For example, it is believed that members of the snapdragon family are useful in treating throat sicknesses because of the mouth-and-throat form of the blossoms. The forked roots of the ginseng resemble the trunk and legs of a man. (The word *ginseng* is taken from the Chinese *jin-chen,* which means "manlike" or "trouser-shaped.") For this reason, the roots have been revered in China for hundreds of years as an overall health remedy and aphrodisiac. Even in the United States there is ongoing research into the medicinal value of ginseng. A few preliminary reports say it is of some aid to the endocrine glands, which help regulate the flow of hormones. The greatest benefits seem to be to the aged and those under stress.

Ginseng has been gathered so extensively through the years that it has become an endangered or threatened plant in numerous states. Now under strict guidelines, the roots are still gathered and brought to buyers who travel the southern mountains, setting up temporary markets during the fall. In Georgia alone it is estimated that ginseng brings in more than $3 million each year.

Prevailing weather patterns in the Appalachians bring in storms from the west, dropping the bulk of precipitation on that side of the mountain. This is why cove hardwood forests, which thrive on moisture, are most often found on the western side of a ridge or mountain range. Often, as you hike the trail and swing from the western face of a ridge to the eastern flank, you'll notice that lush foliage gives way to an **oak forest** whose canopy is thinner and undergrowth less dense—even though you have gained little or no elevation. On these hillsides, or on ridgelines exposed to the strong southwestern sun, tuliptree, hemlock, cherry birch, and mountain magnolia become scarce or nonexistent. In this harsher growing environment, the oaks—black, white, scarlet, chestnut, and others—become the dominant trees. A number of factors have come together to make them some of the most prevalent trees throughout the Appalachian forests.

Thriving on open sunshine, oak trees are some of the first to establish themselves (from both seeds and stump sprouts) after a woodland has been destroyed by fire or cut logging. Some, such as northern red oak, chestnut oak, and white oak, are also quite shade-tolerant. So, even if a sapling sprouts beneath a larger tree, it will probably survive long enough to take the place of the larger tree when that tree dies. The leaves

NORTHERN RED OAK *(Gray Oak)*

LATIN NAME *Quercus rubra*

AVERAGE MATURE HEIGHT 70–90 feet, but occasionally up to 150 feet

LEAVES The leaves are smooth and dark green above, paler below, and have barely noticeable tufts of hairs where the veins join the midrib. They have 7–11 lobes whose points are tipped in bristles. Four to eight inches long and 3–6 inches wide, the somewhat oval-shaped leaves are connected to the twigs by sturdy 1- to 2-inch petioles (leaf stalks).

BARK The bark of young northern red oaks is smooth and greenish brown to gray. Older trunks are dark and rough near the base, while the upper portions are fissured into narrow ridges. The inner bark is light red, giving the tree its name.

RANGE IN APPALACHIAN TRAIL STATES Georgia to Maine

MOST LIKELY LOCATIONS On the summit of Apple Orchard Mountain, at Thunder Ridge Overlook, and between Humpback Mountain and Humpback Rocks in central Virginia; Stony Man Mountain in Shenandoah National Park; Mount Greylock in Massachusetts; and along the West Branch of the Piscataquis River in Maine

of a sapling are larger and less indented than those of mature oaks, which provides the younger tree with more surface area from which to gather nourishment from the sun.

Deep taproots and/or a large system of branching roots permit oaks to soak up subterranean moisture that is unavailable to most other trees. Additionally, the oaks seem to be more efficient in their retention of that water. The pores in their wood are confined to the annual rings, while other trees, such as the mountain magnolia and cherry birch, have pores distributed throughout, causing them to have a higher rate of transpiration (the plant world's equivalent to perspiring). Though no one knows why, chestnut oaks and scarlet oaks grow even better in drier years than in wetter ones.

In many ways it was the blight of the American chestnut that permitted oaks to gain such dominance in the Appalachian Mountains (amazingly, oaks make up an estimated 70% of the forests in some areas). Yet the oaks are now themselves under attack. While the gypsy moth does prey on other trees and plants, oaks appear to be its preferred food. The gypsy moth was brought to Massachusetts from France in 1868 for experimental crossbreeding with silkworms. Some escaped, and the moth, having no natural predators in the New World, has now spread across much of North America, having been found as far away as California and Washington.

It is when they are in the larval, or caterpillar, stage that they feed upon the leaves of trees and other foliage, sometimes completely defoliating vast acreages. A healthy tree can withstand one or two consecutive years of defoliation, but much more than that and the tree will die. In the 1980s, there were quite a few places along the AT, such

In Bears Den Rocks, Virginia, dead trees (on the left) show gypsy moth damage.

as ridges in Shenandoah National Park and much of the woods between Duncannon and Delaware Water Gap, Pennsylvania, where many of the older trees died.

There is some hope that natural forces like the nucleopolyhedrosis virus and the gypsy moth fungus can bring the epidemic under control. One thing is certain, though: just as surely as the chestnut blight cleared the way for oaks to become one of the dominant trees, the gypsy moth is changing the look of our forests once again. It will be interesting to see what the vegetative cover of much of the Appalachian Mountains will be in the coming decades.

Joining the oaks on the drier hillsides are the hickories—bitternut, pignut, shagbark, and mockernut. After the blight, hickory nuts and acorns replaced chestnuts as a major source of nourishment for wildlife.

SHAGBARK HICKORY

LATIN NAME *Carya ovata*

AVERAGE MATURE HEIGHT 70–90 feet

LEAVES hagbark hickory's 8- to 14-inch-long compound leaves have 5 (sometimes 7) leaflets that are 3–7 inches long with fine, sharp-toothed margins. A dark yellowish green above, they are lighter on the bottom and may be smooth or slightly downy.

BARK Similar to that of the shellbark hickory (*Carya laciniosa*), the shagbark hickory's bark is gray with thick scalelike sections that are loose at both ends and lightly attached in the middle.

RANGE IN APPALACHIAN TRAIL STATES Georgia to Maine

MOST LIKELY LOCATIONS Between the summit of Cole Mountain and Forest Service Road 48 in central Virginia; near the Denton Shelter in northern Virginia; on many southern-facing slopes in Connecticut

Also on the dry slopes, pines may become so prevalent as to establish a **pine-oak forest**. Although flowering plants are more efficient at conducting water than coniferous trees, the structure of the waxy needles of the pines permits them to transpire less and retain moisture longer. Yet, with their intolerance of shade, they often yield to the oaks and other trees that have grown larger. Because of this, pine trees will only take over a truly hot and dry ridgeline whose environment is too harsh for others.

The **northern hardwood forest** spreads itself over much of the AT in New England, where the maples, beeches, and birches become masters along many of the ridges, and even into the valleys. Lower elevations and the resulting warmer temperatures preclude this forest type's growth throughout most of the mid-Atlantic states, but from Virginia to North Carolina/Georgia, the northern hardwoods make their reappearance in the cooler climate around 4,500 feet above sea level (the woods around Newfound Gap

Birch grove in Vermont

in the Smokies are a perfect example). Of course, prevailing conditions will cause different trees to predominate in different spots. Yellow birch's ability to grow on top of boulders by germinating in and sending its roots under mosses, which store moisture, enable it to prosper in the dry areas of rockslides. The beeches thrive in rocky areas, while yellow buckeyes have a tendency to take over in moist soils.

The **oak orchard** of the northern hardwood forest is dominated by northern red oak trees whose trunks have been stunted and their branches twisted by harsh weather conditions. The gnarled look of the trees and the absence of understory make these woods resemble fruit orchards. Probably the most easily observed oak orchard along the AT is the summit of Apple Orchard Mountain in central Virginia, which, as you now know, is not covered by apple trees.

Oak trees, whose leaves have a tendency to turn dull shades of yellow, brown, or red in the fall, are still a part of the northern hardwood forest, but it is the increased numbers of birch, beech, and maple trees that give this forest such a vibrant and exhilarating display of colors. The sugar, red, and mountain maples almost burn with intense reds, oranges, and yellows. American beeches are covered in an interesting shade of

---

YELLOW BIRCH *(Silver Birch)*

LATIN NAME *Betula alleghaniensis*

AVERAGE MATURE HEIGHT 70–100 feet

LEAVES Similar to those of the sweet or black birch, the leaves are 3–5 inches long; elliptical or oblong; and pointed at the end with irregular, sharp-pointed teeth. They have 9–11 well-defined veins and are a drab dark green above and a lighter yellowish green below.

BARK The lustrous yellow or silvery-gray bark peels off in thin, paperlike curls. Older trees have bark on the lower trunk that becomes reddish brown with irregular scales.

RANGE IN APPALACHIAN TRAIL STATES Georgia to Maine

MOST LIKELY LOCATIONS Around water sources between Salt Log Gap and Spy Rock Road in central Virginia; Stony Man Mountain in Shenandoah National Park; Mount Greylock in Massachusetts; between Moody Mountain and Black Brook Notch in Maine

yellow, and the leaves of sweet birch, yellow birch, and paper birch reflect the golden rays of an early-morning sun.

It is the absence of chlorophyll that plays the most important role in the look of the woods in the fall. When present, chlorophyll gives leaves their green color and produces simple sugars to nourish trees. Additionally, the chlorophyll masks yellow carotenoid pigments in the leaves. Cooler temperatures and less daylight signal the leaves to quit making the sugars, and as the chlorophyll breaks down, the green fades and the yellows, browns, and oranges emerge. Autumn's reds and purples come from other pigments known as anthocyanins, which develop in the sap of the leaves as a result of a complex interaction between sugars, phosphates, and other chemicals. An early fall of bright sunny days and cool (but not freezing) nights will produce the most brilliant colors.

Much like the northern hardwood forest, the **spruce-fir forest** or **boreal forest** is quite healthy and prevalent—even at lower elevations—in New England, is absent throughout most of the mid-Atlantic, and is found once more on the highest summits and ridgelines of the Southern Appalachians. Spruce, fir, and other evergreens were some of the first seed-bearing plants to evolve into trees, and these woodlands of today, often shrouded in mist or covered by clouds and dripping with moisture, almost have the look and feel of a primeval forest. Just the heady aroma inhaled while hiking through the Great Smokies, traversing the heights of Roan and Unaka Mountains, enjoying the quiet solitude of Whitetop Mountain, summiting Mount Greylock, or crossing the ridgelines in Maine can be enough to transport the modern person back to a time when our ancestors first walked the earth.

Although the spruce-fir forest in the southern climes shares many characteristics and genera of trees with the northern boreal forest, there are subtle differences. Black spruces, balsam firs, and white spruces are the dominant evergreens in New England, but they yield to the red spruces and Fraser firs in the southern mountains. In fact, red spruce is pretty much the only evergreen to thrive in both locations, while Fraser fir is found only on the higher elevations of North Carolina, Tennessee, and Virginia.

With a tourist road leading right to it, Clingmans Dome in the Smokies is probably the most easily accessible of the spruce-fir forests on the AT. Sadly, it is also a place to witness the demise of this forest type. A native of Europe, the balsam woolly adelgid was inadvertently introduced into North America on nursery stock. By the time it was identified in 1908, it had already done extensive damage to balsam firs in New England.

The insect's entire population consists of females that reproduce without mating and are capable of producing more than 200 eggs, and two to three generations mature in one season. The eggs hatch into crawlers less than a millimeter in length. Before this stage of their life ends, the crawlers insert a thread-size mouthpart into the bark of a host tree and begin to feed, causing cellular changes that interfere with the tree's circulation. As a result, respiration and photosynthesis are reduced and the tree weakens and dies.

RED SPRUCE *(Eastern Spruce)*

LATIN NAME *Picea rubens*

AVERAGE MATURE HEIGHT 50–80 feet

LEAVES The stiff, sharp-pointed evergreen needles are 0.5 inch to almost 1 inch long and grow from all sides of the twigs on short stalks. They are a dark yellowish green in color.

BARK The dark reddish-brown to gray bark is broken into irregularly shaped, thin, flaky scales and is often covered with grayish-green lichens.

RANGE IN APPALACHIAN TRAIL STATES Found mostly at higher elevations from Georgia to Virginia/West Virginia and then again in New England

MOST LIKELY LOCATIONS On Clingmans Dome and between Pinnacle Lead and Deer Creek Gap (a virgin stand) in Great Smoky Mountains National Park; Roan Mountain on the North Carolina-Tennessee border; the summit of Whitetop Mountain in southwest Virginia; Stony Man Mountain in Shenandoah National Park; near Old Adams Road and at the junction of the AT and Money Brook Trail near Mount Williams in Massachusetts

(Adult adelgids, which no longer feed upon the tree, are covered in a white "wool" and have a tendency to congregate, forming large patches of wool on the tree trunk.)

The spread of the balsam woolly adelgid, first identified on Fraser firs in the Southern Appalachians in 1956, has been amazingly rapid. No stands of the tree in the south have escaped infestation. More than 95% of mature Fraser firs in Great Smoky Mountains National Park have succumbed, as have more than 85% along the Blue Ridge Parkway.

FRASER FIR *(Balsam;* found in the Southern Appalachians, but this is not *Abies balsamea,* or Balsam Fir)

LATIN NAME *Abies fraseri*

AVERAGE MATURE HEIGHT 30–50 feet

LEAVES The evergreen needles are 0.5–1 inch long; curve upward; and, stalkless, spread at right angles from the hairy twigs. Dark green above, the needles have two narrow white lines on the bottom.

BARK The smooth, grayish-brown bark is thin and often becomes scaly as the tree matures. The bark may be covered with raised blisters filled with a fragrant, sticky resin. These blisters suggested lactating breasts to early settlers, and as a result the Fraser firs were sometimes referred to as she-balsams. Red spruces, which do not have resin blisters, were called "he-balsams."

RANGE IN APPALACHIAN TRAIL STATES North Carolina/Tennessee to Virginia

MOST LIKELY LOCATIONS Clingmans Dome, along the ridge of Mount Mingus, and between Pinnacle Lead and Deer Creek Gap (a virgin stand) in Great Smoky Mountains National Park; on and near the summit of Roan Mountain at the North Carolina–Tennessee border; and the summits of Whitetop Mountain and Mount Rogers in Virginia

This loss has had a great impact on the spruce-fir environment. The trees were superb collectors of moisture from fog and rain, and without that moisture, many flowers, mosses, ferns, and even some animals have begun to disappear. In addition, the fir cones and seeds were a source of food—now lacking—for other animals. Without the shade provided by the trees, dense growths of briars and shrubs have invaded, preventing the development of future Fraser fir seedlings.

However, the Fraser fir may survive extinction. Young firs that escaped the initial infestation have now begun to reach cone-bearing age, and it is possible that succeeding generations will develop a natural resistance to the insect.

Balds

Although technically not a forest type, **balds** occur between 4,000 and 5,000 feet, from Georgia to southwest Virginia but in no other AT states. Open, treeless areas that appear to be naturally occurring and often permit grand 360-degree views, balds are still a mystery to those who have studied them. **Heath balds,** sometimes called slicks by local inhabitants, are composed of an assortment of members of the heath family, such as huckleberry, blueberry, and azalea, with mountain laurel and rhododendron predominating. **Grass balds,** dominated most often by mountain oat grass, have no such shrubs but may include sedges and other low-growing vegetation and grasses. At times, the two types of balds can commingle. When you first see a bald you may be inclined to conclude that it is composed of tundra vegetation and/or is an alpine summit above treeline. Yet there is no treeline this far south, and besides, some balds are not on the highest point of a mountain but occur below summits that are covered in spruce-fir forests. Because they defy the natural order of things, balds and their mysterious origins have been the subject of speculation and debate for many years.

Numerous theories, none of which has gained much prominence over the others, try to explain how balds came to be. One states that balds were caused by fires that completely eliminated the trees, but fires occur in many areas and, in areas other than balds, trees have always reestablished themselves over a period of time. Building on the fire theory, some researchers propose that Native Americans, especially the Cherokee, originally cleared bald areas of trees and intermittently burned them for sacred sites or so that mountain oat grass and berries would flourish, thereby improving conditions for game. Others say the balds are simply areas that were cleared for mountain pastures by early settlers. Yet it has been established that at least some balds were in existence when homesteaders first began to move into the mountains.

Other theories abound. Soil has been suggested as a cause, but there is no one type found to occur in all of the balds. Insect infestation, an overpopulation of browsing animals, or tree destruction from harsh conditions such as drought, ice storms, or heavy winds have all been put forth as reasons for the existence of the balds. Some botanists say there is no one reason—each bald evolved from its own unique set of circumstances.

Finally, a number of noted ecologists say that the hot and dry climatic conditions of several thousand years ago killed the spruces and firs that were near their southern limit. This permitted maples, beeches, and a few other deciduous trees to invade and dominate. The earth then entered a phase of cooler temperatures, killing the broad-leaved trees. Because they need shade to establish themselves, spruces and firs have been unable to repopulate the open areas, permitting grasses and/or heaths to gain the upper hand.

How do balds maintain themselves? Again, theories abound. Some say that tree seeds or saplings are unable to compete with the thick mats of mountain oat grass or to gain a foothold amongst the nearly impenetrable root systems and leaves of the heaths. Another possibility is that conditions usually found at 5,000-foot elevations are just too harsh for trees to reestablish themselves. Some of the latest research seems to indicate that the grazing of animals—deer, elk, bison, and more recently sheep and cattle—have prevented the trees' return.

There must be some truth to this last hypothesis, as some of the balds have begun to shrink since livestock was removed from them. In fact, the U.S. Forest Service and the ATC have cooperated in using artificial methods (fire, bulldozing, timbering) to maintain a few AT balds, such as Siler Bald in North Carolina. The National Park Service is also keeping several balds cleared in Great Smoky Mountains National Park.

The open balds of North Carolina and Tennessee

Yet some spots, like portions of the highlands of the Mount Rogers area, seem to be maintaining themselves as open places. So the mystery of the balds continues.

Bogs

There is another feature of the Appalachian woodlands that is not a forest type but is so significant that it would be an oversight not to discuss it. A spruce-fir forest can bring to mind a woodland that existed when the earth was young, but the eeriness of a bog may make you think you have been transported to another planet. Besides having extraterrestrial-looking flowers that do not survive by the methods of most other plants, these areas are not quite solid, nor are they completely liquid.

There are many different types of bogs and many names for bogs: relict, quaking, glacial, sphagnum, level, flat, raised, domed, slope, geogenous, ombrogenous, ombrotrophic, mineritrophic, transitional, oligotrophic, kettlehole, and others. The differences are subtle, having to do with the original topographic feature, where the bog is situated, how it was created, what plants predominate in it, or how it receives its water and nutrients. In the scientific community there are even discussions and distinctions as to what truly constitutes a bog, as opposed to a fen or a peatland. Yet, in a perfectly acceptable way, the general public, casual observers, and hikers have a tendency to call all of these areas bogs. For most of us then, it is really only necessary to know where bogs are, how they came to be, and what grows in them.

Most bogs found along the AT occur in New England, but bogs can be found, albeit in smaller numbers, as far south as Virginia and North Carolina. From the rim of Garden Mountain in southwest Virginia, the trail overlooks Beartown Wilderness above Burkes Garden, which contains what is thought to be the largest sphagnum bog in Virginia. The Mountain Lake Wilderness in central Virginia serves as a bog-study area for university students. Nearby, it is possible to observe a boggy area in the making just a few feet off the trail. In the 1970s, Big Pond was a large, stagnant, swampy pond with a bit of vegetation growing in and around it. Today, in a process that still continues, much of the surface water has disappeared, having been soaked up by the decayed material of peatlike soil and covered over by vegetation.

Farther north, the trail passes through High Point and Wawayanda State Parks in New Jersey, which contain well over 200 acres of bogs. One of them, Pine Bog, has close to 17 feet of peat accumulation. Near Lost Pond Shelter in Vermont, 15-acre Lost Pond Bog is a model of a high-elevation bog, complete with a quaking border and sphagnum mosses, pitcher plants, and sundews. The small, 1- to 2-acre bogs that fill in depressions in Maine's Mahoosuc Range provide refuge for baked-apple berry, a plant that is rare in the United States outside of Alaska. Along the Barren-Chairback Range of the 100 Mile Wilderness, Fourth Mountain Bog furnishes a chance for up-close examination of carnivorous pitcher plants.

Most of the bogs in the north are the result of glaciers. Some began as embedded ice that melted to leave a lake, some were basins gouged out by moving glaciers, and still others were produced as the glaciers receded and deposited tons of rock and mud that impeded the flow of water. As evidenced by the existence of bogs south of Pennsylvania, not all bogs were started by glaciers. Boulders dropping from the heights may have barricaded a narrow stream valley, or, in much the same way, a beaver dam may have caused a bog to begin to form.

Why do some ponds and lakes develop into bogs while others do not? The answer is that, in some places, over a period of time, there is a net gain in organic matter. In other words, the production of organic material (leaves, grasses, mosses, etc.) occurs faster than the rate of decay. This is where the impeded flow of water comes into play; the organic matter that would normally be carried away by currents begins to accumulate, and as it decays, the oxygen level (which is already low because of the lack of aeration) drops, greatly decreasing the rate of decomposition.

Over a long period of time, the forest around the pond begins to reestablish itself while water-tolerant plants, such as sphagnum moss, grow along the edges. A specialized cell structure permits sphagnum mosses to retain 15–25 times their weight in water, a quality Native Americans exploited by using the dried moss as diapers. The moss has also been used in many parts of the world as a surgical dressing for wounds because, in addition to its absorption capabilities, the acidic nature of its bog origins makes it naturally sterile.

A boggy area in New Jersey

Sphagnum mosses, of which there are scores of species, are the building blocks of most of the bogs found along the AT. Unlike most other plants in the world, they grow from the top and die at the bottom. Through the centuries, layers of this moss become ever-thickening masses that eventually join with the organic deposits, or peat, to close off the open water of the pond, yet they still float upon what has now become subsurface water. Providing an ever drier, partially solid base, the moss permits other, somewhat less water-tolerant plants to begin to grow upon the surface of the bog.

Some of the most interesting of these plants are the carnivorous ones. As school-children we were all fascinated by Venus flytraps, but there are more than 450 species of carnivorous plants worldwide—many of them growing in water-saturated habitats, dry rocky areas, or similarly nutrient-impoverished environments. To compensate for the meager nourishment they obtain from the soil, they have developed the capability of digesting insects and other small animals to obtain essential nitrogen, phosphorus, vitamins, and other trace minerals.

The pitcher plant, found most easily along the AT in the Fourth Mountain Bog along Maine's Barren-Chairback Range, has red-veined vase- or pitcher-shaped leaves that contain a bit of water and enzymes in the bottom. These leaves are perfectly designed to entice and capture. A sweet substance secreted by nectar glands on a leaf's edges attracts the insects, and downward-pointing hairs both entice them to descend farther into the plant and make climbing back out nearly impossible. Inside the leaf are easily dislodged sticky cells that adhere to the prey's feet, further decreasing mobility. Exhausted, the insect slides down to the pool of liquid, where digestive enzymes break down its body so that the plant can absorb it easily through the porous walls of the pitcher.

Believed to have near-tropical origins, sundews have a burst of growth in the heat of midsummer, rising above the surrounding hummocks of sphagnum mosses. Glandular hairs coated with a glistening, sweet, sticky fluid on rosettes of small leaves attract insects, which become entangled in some of the longer outer hairs. In a unique occurrence, the hairs begin a spurt of fast growth, adding cells that enable them to fold over the insect and draw it into more intimate contact with the leaf, where shorter hairs secrete digestive enzymes. If the prey is quite active, the hairs respond quickly and can encircle the victim in less than 20 minutes. If the prey is already dead, the plant seems to recognize that there is no urgent need to ensnare and will take up to several days to complete the process.

Perhaps most intriguing of all carnivorous bog plants, bladderworts have no root systems. They may be free-floating in waters with impeded flow; semiaquatic in peaty areas; or epiphytic, growing on or in wet moss. Usually the plant's flower rises above the submerged and branched stems, on which are attached tiny sacs or bladders. Once believed to be a means of floatation, the bladders are actually traps to obtain nourish-ment. Whenever small aquatic life, such as mosquito larvae, water fleas, isopods, or even small tadpoles and fish, brush against a trigger hair, a tiny trap door snaps open, sucking water and prey into the bladder to be absorbed by the plant with the aid of enzymes and bacteria. When digestion is completed (usually within 15 minutes to 2 hours), cells in the bladder pump out the water, reestablishing a partial vacuum and making the sac ready for the next luckless passerby.

THREATS TO THE APPALACHIAN FOREST

BEFORE ENDING THIS CHAPTER on the Appalachian forest, it is sadly necessary to make mention of threats to the vitality and integrity of this long green tunnel. Besides the chestnut blight, the gypsy moth, and the balsam woolly adelgid already discussed, there are additional natural and human forces attacking the woodlands of the eastern United States.

With their early spring flowers, colorful fruits, and deep red leaves in the fall, dogwoods are some of the most beautiful trees to be found along the AT, but a disease of unknown origin is removing large numbers of them from the landscape. First discovered in the late 1970s in New York, **dogwood anthracnose** has now spread throughout most of the Appalachians.

Breaking down the tree's living tissues, the fungal disease begins in the lower branches and moves upward. The first signs of infection are tan blotches and purple-rimmed spots on leaves. Moving rather swiftly into the twigs, branches, and then the trunk, the disease will kill a tree in a shaded area within two to five years. For some

FLOWERING DOGWOOD

LATIN NAME *Cornus florida*

AVERAGE MATURE HEIGHT 30 feet

LEAVES Growing on short stalks with edges that are more or less wavy, the dogwood's leaves are 3–5 inches long and 2–3 inches wide. They are green above and paler with fine hairs below, and have 6–7 strongly curved veins on each side of the midvein.

BARK Broken into small, square blocks, the rough bark is a dark reddish brown.

RANGE IN APPALACHIAN TRAIL STATES Georgia to Maine

MOST LIKELY LOCATIONS In the Nantahala Mountains of North Carolina and on Bartman Hill in Maryland

reason, trees in sunny areas seem better able to fend off a bout with the disease, yet more than 50% of all dogwoods in eastern Pennsylvania have already died.

As discussed previously, hemlock forests cover a major part of the Appalachians, providing cover and food for wildlife during winter months. Often growing in large stands along stream banks, the trees' shade keeps the temperature of the waters down, even on hot summer days. Without the cooler water, many invertebrates, fish (such as trout), and other cold-water aquatic life would not be able to survive. All of these things, and the trees themselves, are now in jeopardy because of the **hemlock woolly adelgid.** Some botanists predict a virtual elimination of the hemlock species in the not-too-distant future.

Since the 1800s, the **southern pine bark beetle** has been attacking pitch, short-leaf, Virginia, and other pines in the Southern Appalachians. Infestations follow regular cycles of 3–5 years, with irregular ones every 7–10 years. Lately, though, damage to the pines has been more severe, causing foresters to worry and wonder why. Attacking trees weakened by flood, drought, lightning, careless logging, heavy ice and snow, or other conditions, the beetles drill into the bark, constructing chambers and laying eggs, which hatch to feed upon the cambium, the inner living tissue. This opens the way for the invasion of wood-staining fungi that attack and clog the water-conducting capabilities of the cambium, resulting in the tree's death.

The **locust leaf miner** is another beetle that has been around for quite some time but appears to be doing more damage than before. These beetles feed on a number of trees, including apple, cherry, beech, birch, and oak, but they favor black locust. Overwintering in bark crevices, the adult leaf miners feed upon and skeletonize the lower surfaces of newly emerged spring leaves. Soon eggs are deposited from which the larvae emerge to bore into a leaf and feed. By midsummer, this second-generation feeding results in early browning and dropping of leaves, sometimes as soon as late August.

AMERICAN MOUNTAIN ASH

LATIN NAME *Sorbus americana*

AVERAGE MATURE HEIGHT 30 feet

LEAVES The yellow-green, pinnately compound leaves are 6–8 inches long with 11–17 stalklets and sawtoothed leaflets.

BARK The thin bark is light gray and can be either smooth or scaly.

RANGE IN APPALACHIAN TRAIL STATES Georgia to Maine

MOST LIKELY LOCATIONS In the Nantahala Mountains of North Carolina; at the Thunder Ridge Overlook, and between Crabtree Farm Road and the top of The Priest in central Virginia; Stony Man Mountain in Shenandoah National Park; near the crest of Saddleball and the summit of Mount Greylock in Massachusetts; and along Roundtop Mountain in Maine

A healthy tree may be able to withstand an attack, but trees in weakened conditions often die. Because black locusts are pioneer trees—that is, they are some of the first to grow and prepare the way for other trees in fire-damaged, logged, or similarly disturbed areas, the impact of their loss would be felt throughout the forest.

A whole host of other trees are under attack. A **European sawfly** is thought to be responsible for the elevated mortality of the high-altitude mountain ash.

Butternut tree populations are falling victim to the **butternut canker,** while **European beech bark scale** is claiming victims in New England and the Smokies.

The argument could be made that diseases, insects, and pests have assailed the forest for thousands of years. Those who study them, though, tend to say that there is no evidence of a time such as this, when so many different trees appear, all at once, to be in such weakened states (making them more likely to succumb to disease and pestilence). Many point the finger to human factors such as poor logging practices, fragmentation of the forest by development, high ozone levels (which is needed in the stratosphere but is damaging near the earth's surface), and acid rain.

Acid rain is formed when oxides of sulfur (emitted by coal-fired power and industrial plants) and nitrogen (contained in motor vehicle exhaust) are released into the atmosphere, where they become droplets of dilute sulfuric and nitric acids that combine with rain, snow, fog, and dew. Oxides are also released from natural sources such as forest fires, ocean spray, volcanoes, and the decomposition of organic matter, but at much lower rates and concentrations.

Precipitation normally has a pH level of 5.0 to 5.6. (This is based on a scale from 0 to 14, where 0 is most acidic and 7 is neutral.) Studies show that easternmost states have recently been experiencing rainfall with a pH level below 4.5, and the high elevations of western North Carolina, where the die-off of trees is among the most severe, has recorded precipitation with a pH level far below 2.5 (over 1,000 times more acidic than unpolluted precipitation).

The Taj Mahal in India and the statues of Rome have stood for hundreds of years, but within the last several decades their exteriors have begun to deteriorate rapidly, and most experts blame acid precipitation. So, too, does the natural world suffer. Some fish are unable to reproduce, and others die when lakes and streams become acidic. Acid deposition harms trees by removing nutrients from leaves and increasing the soil's acidity, both of which weaken plant systems, making them more susceptible to attacks by insects and disease—sort of like AIDS in humans. Acid rain can also be blamed directly for the death of trees. The red spruce, which shares the same habitat as the Fraser fir, is ample evidence of this. Not under attack by any major diseases or insect infestations, red spruces have been dying at about the same rate as the Fraser firs, and research has shown that acid rain and fog have reduced the trees' root systems by depriving them of mineral foods.

CHAPTER 5
The Grand Floral Parade

The crystal morning's broken with the cooing of a dove,

and you head on up the trail to the highlands up above,

where the colors of the rainbow are the flowers at your feet,

and your heart sings a song with every beat.

~ Walkin' Jim Stoltz

ONE OF THE GREATEST PLEASURES to be found during a visit to the Appalachian Trail is the opportunity to enjoy the grand parade of colors, shapes, sizes, and varieties of wildflowers as their procession of blooms starts in late winter, proceeds into the spring rains, continues throughout the hot summer months, and lingers long into the cooler temperatures of the fall. An amazingly large number of the wildflowers that grow throughout the eastern United States can be observed on even just one short walk along the trail. (Unless otherwise noted, all the flowers in this chapter may be found—at least in small isolated spots—in all the states through which the AT passes.)

Whenever hiking wildflower enthusiasts get together, it seems that one of their favorite topics of discussion is which flower is actually the first to emerge as winter begins to lose its grip on the mountains. There is no one answer, of course. Elevation, latitude, the severity of the winter, and a myriad of other things affect which flower you'll find first. Due to Virginia's overall lower elevation and resulting warmer temperatures, hikers on that portion of the AT may encounter some flowers earlier in the year than hikers amid the mountains of Georgia, North Carolina, or Tennessee. Walkers sauntering along the shoreline of a low-lying lake in central Maine may enjoy the spring flowers sooner than trekkers traversing ridgelines in the White Mountains. No matter where you are, though, there are harbingers of spring that make their appearance year in and year out before any of the other flowers in a particular region.

SKUNK CABBAGE

LATIN NAME *Symplocarpus foetidus*

FLOWER The small flowers of this plant are borne on a rounded spadix sheathed by an enveloping mottled spathe that ranges in color from green to dirty purple.

AVERAGE BLOOM SEASON February to April

LEAVES AND STEMS Appearing after the flower and unfurling from being tightly wrapped, the veined leaves are heart-shaped at the base and resemble cabbage leaves.

RANGE IN APPALACHIAN TRAIL STATES Georgia to Maine

MOST LIKELY LOCATIONS In wet areas on the trail paralleling the Blue Ridge Parkway and in Shenandoah National Park in Virginia

One of the earliest plants to emerge from the ground (and one of the most unique-looking) is skunk cabbage, which grows in moist woods and meadows. To find out how this plant got its name, just rub it a bit and bring your hand up to your nose. Although Native Americans inhaled the aroma as a cure for headaches, once you take a sniff you probably won't want to do so again! As a mechanism to withstand the cold (it sometimes blooms while February snows are still on the ground), skunk cabbage produces its own heat by burning carbohydrates stored in its large root system. Temperatures inside its buds have been found to be as much as 27° higher than the surrounding air.

Also fighting winter's cold temperatures, the tiny white flowers of trailing arbutus can often be found buried beneath a late snowfall at about the same time that dogtooth

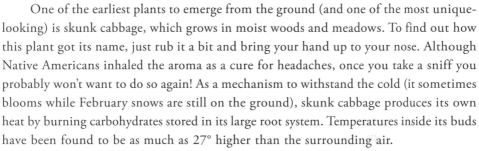

SPRING BEAUTY

LATIN NAME *Claytonia caroliniana*

FLOWER The 0.5-inch, white to pink flowers have distinctive deeper-pink veins coursing along the 5 petals.

AVERAGE BLOOM SEASON March to May

LEAVES AND STEMS 2 leaves grow opposite each other about halfway up a 4- to 12-inch stem.

RANGE IN APPALACHIAN TRAIL STATES Georgia to Maine

MOST LIKELY LOCATIONS Between Unicoi Gap and Dicks Creek Gap in Georgia; on Pearis and Peters Mountains in southwest Virginia; on the slopes of Mount Greylock in Massachusetts; and near Moxie Pond in Maine

TRAILING ARBUTUS

LATIN NAME *Epigaea repens*

FLOWER The white to pink flowers, which grow in little clusters from the ends of the stem or out of the leaf axils, are only about 0.5 inch long, have 5 spreading lobes, and are well known for their strong fragrance.

AVERAGE BLOOM SEASON March to early June

LEAVES AND STEMS This trailing shrub has woody stems covered with fine hairs. The alternate, oblong, leathery leaves remain green throughout the year and are just large enough that you must often move them aside to observe the flowers they are hiding.

RANGE IN APPALACHIAN TRAIL STATES Georgia to Maine

MOST LIKELY LOCATIONS Between Deep Gap and Wallace Gap in North Carolina and in Johns Hollow north of the James River in central Virginia

DOGTOOTH VIOLET *(Trout Lily)*

LATIN NAME *Erythronium americanum*

FLOWER The nodding, 1.5-inch yellow flower has 6 petals and sepals that bend in a graceful, backward curve.

AVERAGE BLOOM SEASON March to May

LEAVES AND STEMS The 4- to 6-inch elliptical leaves are mottled purple-brown and grow near the base of the 6- to 9-inch-high stem.

RANGE IN APPALACHIAN TRAIL STATES Georgia to Maine

MOST LIKELY LOCATIONS Between Deep Gap and Wallace Gap in North Carolina; on a large percentage of hillsides in southwest and central Virginia; in low areas throughout Shenandoah National Park; and on the Wyman and Hall Mountains in Maine

violet—like its western relative the glacier lily—is pushing its way through and above the blanket of snow. True to its name, spring beauty emerges as the weather gets a bit warmer.

Lining the AT with flowers of pinkish white, the spring beauty is genetically quite interesting. We humans all have a stable number of chromosomes: 46. But the number of chromosomes in the spring beauty varies from plant to plant, with more than 50 possible chromosomal combinations.

Making an appearance along with, or soon after, the spring beauty, hepatica's white flowers are found up and down the trail. The blooms were once used by farmers as a sign that planting could safely begin.

Mayapple's fruit ripens in May, but it first pushes its way through the ground in March, when its umbrella-like leaves form huge carpets across the forest floor. In the past this plant was used as a treatment for warts, and even today two substances found

MAYAPPLE

LATIN NAME *Podophyllum peltatum*

FLOWER A single, waxy, nodding white flower grows from the middle of the fork of the 2 leaves. About 1 inch wide, the flower has more than a dozen stamens with yellow anthers that emerge from the center of 6–9 petals.

AVERAGE BLOOM SEASON April to June

LEAVES AND STEMS Rising to a height of about a foot off the ground, the 2 umbrella-like, toothed leaves are divided into 5–7 lobes. Stems with only 1 leaf do not bear flowers.

RANGE IN APPALACHIAN TRAIL STATES Georgia to Maine

MOST LIKELY LOCATIONS Between Neel's Gap and Unicoi Gap in Georgia; on Pearis Mountain in southwest Virginia; and on Thunder Ridge in central Virginia

DWARF IRIS

LATIN NAME *Iris verna*

FLOWER In many ways the dwarf iris resembles its larger domesticated relative. The 3 petals range from deep to pale purple with the 3 sepals being a little larger and of the same color with a yellow-orange spot at their base.

AVERAGE BLOOM SEASON March to May

LEAVES AND STEMS Narrow, pointed, grasslike leaves of 3–12 inches grow on a stem of only 2–5 inches in height.

RANGE IN APPALACHIAN TRAIL STATES Georgia to southern Pennsylvania

MOST LIKELY LOCATIONS Between Springer Mountain and Neel's Gap in Georgia and near the James River and in Bear Wallow Gap in central Virginia

in mayapple are used for medicinal purposes—podophyllin is a cathartic, and peltatin has been used in experiments for the treatment of cancer.

Found at about the same time as mayapple, the dwarf iris was named by the Greeks for their goddess of the rainbow because of its multihued petals and sepals. Iris was the messenger of Juno, and the rainbow was the bridge she used for her frequent errands between the heavens and the earth.

While dwarf iris and other early flowers such as early saxifrage, periwinkle, and star chickweed (Georgia to New Jersey) are contributing to the interest to be found on the floor of the forest, two small trees or shrubs are adding large splashes of color to otherwise still winter-dull hillsides. Serviceberry's drooping clusters of white flowers are accentuated and set off nicely by the deep, rich purple blossoms covering almost every inch of the redbud tree's branches (Georgia to Connecticut).

The pace of the floral procession accelerates when the spring rains of April saturate the soil. Appearing at the same time—or in quick succession—rue anemone, wild ginger, azalea, trillium, Solomon's seal (Georgia to southern New England), false Solomon's seal, Dutchman's-breeches, bloodroot, and fringed phacelia (Georgia to Virginia/West Virginia) turn wooded areas into palettes of color.

Because they emerge at the same time and have a similar appearance, it can be difficult to distinguish Solomon's seal from false Solomon's seal (aka Solomon's plume). It's best done at either the flowering or fruit-bearing time. The little bell-shaped flowers of Solomon's seal hang in pairs from the stem, while the tiny, starred blossoms of false Solomon's seal extend from the end of the stem. Later in the year, the dark blue (almost black) berry of Solomon's seal is easily differentiated from the red berry of false Solomon's seal.

Bloodroot's name comes from the red or orange sap inside its root and stem. Another common name for the plant is red puccoon, derived from the Native American word *pak,* meaning "blood." These earliest inhabitants of North America used the sap as a dye for clothing and baskets. Because the plant must endure the cold temperatures of early spring, the leaves stay curled around the stem to conserve warmth and do not unfurl until pollination occurs.

BLOODROOT

LATIN NAME *Sanguinaria canadensis*

FLOWER The 1- to 2-inch blossom has 8 or more white to pinkish petals around a cluster of many sepals.

AVERAGE BLOOM SEASON March to May

LEAVES AND STEMS A single, 5- to 9-lobed leaf first wraps around the stem, only to open after the flower has bloomed. The leaf persists into late summer.

RANGE IN APPALACHIAN TRAIL STATES Georgia to Maine

MOST LIKELY LOCATIONS Between Springer Mountain and Neel's Gap in Georgia; on the mountains along the North Carolina–Tennessee border; on Tar Jacket Ridge and in Petit's Gap in central Virginia; and throughout Shenandoah National Park

There are some places in the woods where fringed phacelia is so copious that it seems like someone has spread confetti throughout the forest. A close look at the plant reveals tiny but deep fringes (known as fimbrations in botanical terms) around the flower's outer edges.

Also blossoming in response to the nourishment of April showers are blue cohosh, jack-in-the-pulpit, spiderwort, ragwort (Georgia to southern New England), pussytoes, bellwort, buttercup, cinquefoil, meadow rue, and, growing in the moister areas along the trail, marsh marigold.

JACK-IN-THE-PULPIT

LATIN NAME *Arisaema triphyllum*

FLOWER The actual flower is hard to find on this plant. It is at the bottom of the spadix ("Jack"), which is hidden by the flaplike spathe.

AVERAGE BLOOM SEASON April to late June

LEAVES AND STEMS There are usually 2 leaves, divided into 3 or 5 segments, rising from the base of the plant and growing 1–3 feet in height.

RANGE IN APPALACHIAN TRAIL STATES Georgia to Maine

MOST LIKELY LOCATIONS Between Wayah Gap and Nantahala River in North Carolina; Sawtooth Ridge in southwest Virginia; Bald Knob in central Virginia; throughout Shenandoah National Park

Many people think that the green, white, or purple sheath with a hood—the pulpit—that surrounds and covers "Jack" is the plant's flower. Actually, the sheath is just a leaf bract, and you need to lift up the hood and look inside to see the diminutive flowers clustered around Jack's base. When you return in the fall, the pulpit will have fallen away and red berries will have replaced the flowers. After putting the plant's roots through a rather elaborate cooking process, Native Americans pounded them into powder to be used as a type of flour; hence, jack-in-the-pulpit's other common name, Indian turnip. Don't try eating the root, though, as it is poisonous when not prepared using the Native Americans' methods.

GALAX

LATIN NAME *Galax aphylla*

FLOWER Extremely small white flowers cluster on a naked 1- to 2-foot-high stalk

AVERAGE BLOOM SEASON May to July

LEAVES AND STEMS The heart-shaped (almost round), toothed, shiny green (tinged with red in winter) leaves grow close to the ground.

RANGE IN APPALACHIAN TRAIL STATES Georgia to Virginia/West Virginia

MOST LIKELY LOCATIONS Indian Grave Gap in Georgia; in the mountains above the Nantahala River in North Carolina; and along much of the trail paralleling the Blue Ridge Parkway and near Matt Creek in central Virginia

Among those joining the flowery pageant in late April and May are dogwood, bluet, wild geranium, flame azalea (Georgia to southern Pennsylvania), fire pink (Georgia to New Jersey/New York), bowman's root (Georgia to New York), galax (Georgia to Virginia/West Virginia), fly poison (Georgia to New Jersey), phlox (Georgia to southern New England), Indian cucumber root, columbine, bunchberry (Virginia/

DIAPENSIA

LATIN NAME *Diapensia lapponica*

FLOWER The 5 lobes of the white flower, growing on a very short stalk, connect to the 5 stamens.

AVERAGE BLOOM SEASON June to July

LEAVES AND STEMS The leaves and stems of this evergreen plant creep along the ground, creating small tufts.

RANGE IN APPALACHIAN TRAIL STATES New England

MOST LIKELY LOCATIONS Near the summits of Mount Lafayette and Mount Washington in New Hampshire and on Saddleback, The Horn, and Saddleback Jr. in Maine

West Virginia to Maine), diapensia, lily of the valley, whorled pogonia, lady's slipper, gaywings, and sweet cicely.

Despite its name, the dogwood is not named for man's best friend. The tree was once called dagwood because its timber was so strong that it was carved into daggers. Studies of older civilizations show that the dogwood was as highly prized as horns were in the making of such weapons; hence the tree's Latin generic name, *Cornus*. Commonly mistaken for the flower, the pink and white parts are actually leaf bracts encircling the petals of the dogwood's small blossom. Look inside the center of the bracts to see the tiny, greenish flower.

BLUET

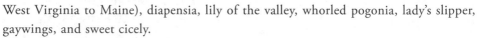

LATIN NAME *Houstonia caerulea*

FLOWER 4 light-blue to almost white petals join together with a slightly yellow center.

AVERAGE BLOOM SEASON April to late June and early July

LEAVES AND STEMS Leaves are opposite and mostly basal on a 2- to 8-inch-tall stem.

RANGE IN APPALACHIAN TRAIL STATES Georgia to Maine

MOST LIKELY LOCATIONS Between Deep Gap and Wallace Gap in North Carolina; on the mountains along the North Carolina–Tennessee border; and along the Long Trail in Vermont

Although northbound AT thru-hikers become intimately acquainted with the tiny bluet as it lines the trail in long mats on the mountains along the North Carolina–Tennessee border, the flower grows well throughout the length of the AT. The species name is Latin for sky blue, an obvious reference to the flower's delicately upturned petals, which seem to reflect the cleanliness and simplicity of an unclouded sky. This may also account for one of its other common names, quaker-ladies.

INDIAN CUCUMBER ROOT

LATIN NAME *Medeola virginiana*

FLOWER Emanating from the top whorl of leaves, the green-yellow nodding flower's sepals and petals bend backwards.

AVERAGE BLOOM SEASON May to June

LEAVES AND STEMS The stem grows from 1 to 3 feet tall and has 2 whorls of leaves, one set about halfway up and the other near the top.

RANGE IN APPALACHIAN TRAIL STATES Georgia to Maine

MOST LIKELY LOCATIONS Between Davenport Gap and Hot Springs in North Carolina; near The Priest in central Virginia; on the slopes of Mount Greylock in Massachusetts; and on Wyman and Hall Mountains in Maine

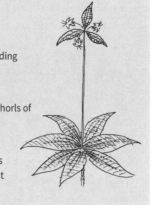

After the pink and purplish petals of the wild geranium drop off, an elongated ovary becomes part of the seedpod, which resembles a bird's head with a long beak rising up from the stem. In fact, hundreds of years ago, inhabitants of the Old World named the plant cranesbill, and even the word *geranium* comes from the Greek *geranos,* which means "crane." Because all parts of the wild geranium contain tannin, it was once used as an astringent, and its leaves were brewed to treat diarrhea and bleeding ulcers.

Indian cucumber root, a member of the lily family, is an intriguing-looking plant that rises on a single stem to a whorl of leaves about halfway up its length and continues on to a second whorl on top. The uppermost leaves can hide the small, dangling, yellow flower. The underground portion of the plant is edible.

COLUMBINE

LATIN NAME *Aquilegia canadensis*

FLOWER Nodding red and yellow blooms are 1–2 inches in size with 5 petals curving upwards as hollow spurs.

AVERAGE BLOOM SEASON April to July

LEAVES AND STEMS The leaves are compound, divided into 3, and grow on a stem 1–2 feet in height.

RANGE IN APPALACHIAN TRAIL STATES Georgia to Maine

MOST LIKELY LOCATIONS Between Nolichucky River, Tennessee, and Damascus, Virginia; and on Bald Knob, Bryant Ridge, Catawba Mountain, and Sinking Creek Mountain in central Virginia

At some time in the distant past, columbine's ornate and unusual flowers reminded people of flocks of hovering birds, and the plant earned the name columba, Latin for "dove." It was also in days gone by that the plant was used to treat numerous illnesses. The juice from a fresh plant was used to treat jaundice and to help reduce the size of a swollen liver. Columbine's leaves and flowers were also believed to be a cure for measles and smallpox. It may not have cured these ills, but since the plant does contain prussic acid, it may have had a narcotic and soothing effect to help ease sufferers' pains.

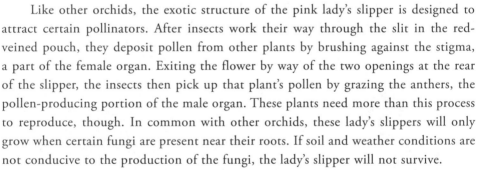

PINK LADY'S SLIPPER *(Moccasin Flower)*

LATIN NAME *Cypripedium acaule*

FLOWER The upper 2 petals are long and slender, and range from yellow-green to purple-brown. It's the other petal, though, that makes this plant so distinctive. It is 1–3 inches long, bulbous in shape, richly pink, and marked with darker pink to red veins, and it folds to a deep cleft in the middle.

AVERAGE BLOOM SEASON Late April to July

LEAVES AND STEMS 2 broad 4- to 8-inch leaves grow from the base of a stem that rises up from 6 to 24 inches in height.

RANGE IN AT STATES Georgia to Maine

MOST LIKELY LOCATIONS Between Davenport Gap and Hot Springs in North Carolina; on Bluff Mountain in central Virginia; close to the Pine Cobble Trail near the Massachusetts–Vermont border; on numerous mountains in Connecticut; in the Carter-Moriah Range of New Hampshire; and north of East B Hill Road in Maine

Like other orchids, the exotic structure of the pink lady's slipper is designed to attract certain pollinators. After insects work their way through the slit in the red-veined pouch, they deposit pollen from other plants by brushing against the stigma, a part of the female organ. Exiting the flower by way of the two openings at the rear of the slipper, the insects then pick up that plant's pollen by grazing the anthers, the pollen-producing portion of the male organ. These plants need more than this process to reproduce, though. In common with other orchids, these lady's slippers will only grow when certain fungi are present near their roots. If soil and weather conditions are not conducive to the production of the fungi, the lady's slipper will not survive.

In the longer daylight hours of late May and June, you'll find rhododendron, mountain laurel, viper's bugloss, sundrops, sundew, pitcher plant, false hellebore, Indian pipe, coreopsis, butter-and-eggs, partridgeberry, and Turk's-cap lily vying for growing space.

If there are two plants that define the beauty, abundance, and panoply of wildflowers found along the AT, especially the southern portion of the trail, they would have to be mountain laurel and rhododendron. Both grow in thickets so dense that they can nearly cover entire mountainsides and, indeed, they do blanket the summits of numerous mountains in Georgia, North Carolina, and Tennessee.

Blooming in late May along with or just after the pink azalea, one of its relatives, Catawba rhododendron's pink to deep purple clusters of flowers are so lush and awe-inspiring that they have attracted people from around the world. Hikers trek well over

Pitcher plant

Catawba rhododendron

2 miles (from the nearest roadway) across the high country of the Mount Rogers area in southwestern Virginia just to be able to enjoy the display of flowers spreading out along the ridgeline in Rhododendron Gap. A few weeks later, on the higher elevations along the North Carolina–Tennessee border, 1,200 acres of Catawba rhododendron bloom in a natural garden on the summit of Roan Mountain. This event is so impressive that it is celebrated by a festival held each year for many decades now.

PITCHER PLANT

LATIN NAME *Sarracenia purpurea*

FLOWER The nodding, round, dark red—almost purple—2-inch flower grows on its own 10- to 20-inch stalk.

AVERAGE BLOOM SEASON May to late July or early August

LEAVES AND STEMS The leaves are what give this plant its name; they really do look like long, slender, 4- to 10-inch pitchers. They're heavily veined with purple streaks, are often half-filled with water, and have bristles on the inside, which help trap insects.

RANGE IN AT STATES New England

MOST LIKELY LOCATIONS In the Fourth Mountain Bog on the Barren-Chairback Range in Maine

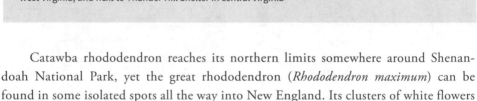

CATAWBA RHODODENDRON

LATIN NAME *Rhododendron catawbiense*

FLOWER Making one of the most colorful displays, the light pink to dark pink to rich purple flowers are about 2 inches across, are bell-shaped, have 5 lobes, and grow in large and ornate clusters.

AVERAGE BLOOM SEASON May to June

LEAVES AND STEMS The distinctive oblong, shiny, leathery, evergreen leaves of 3–5 inches in length grow on shrubs that usually range from 4 to 10 feet in height.

RANGE IN APPALACHIAN TRAIL STATES Georgia to northern Virginia

MOST LIKELY LOCATIONS Along Stover Creek in Georgia; around Muskrat Creek Shelter in North Carolina; on Roan Mountain along the Tennessee–North Carolina border; in Rhododendron Gap in southwest Virginia; and next to Thunder Hill Shelter in central Virginia

Catawba rhododendron reaches its northern limits somewhere around Shenandoah National Park, yet the great rhododendron (*Rhododendron maximum*) can be found in some isolated spots all the way into New England. Its clusters of white flowers appear in time to grow alongside those of the mountain laurel.

If you're hiking in the fall, stop to examine the small capsules on the mountain laurel. Once the plant flowers in June and July, break one open and you'll discover what looks to be brown powder. Each speck is actually a seed of the mountain laurel—so small that it would take thousands of these seeds just to fill a tiny thimble.

Mountain laurel is able to develop into such dense thickets because, in addition to the usual way plants propagate themselves, by cross-pollination of flowers to produce seeds, the mountain laurel reproduces by sending up new shoots from its spreading root system. In addition, branches that happen to touch the ground grow new roots, which then radiate outward and send up shoots of their own.

Illustrating that mountain laurel and rhododendron are not just southern plants, it is possible to find the pink blossoms of rhodora (a relative of the mountain laurel and the rhododendron—all of which belong to the heath family) adding color in the spring to the bogs of the 100 Mile Wilderness of Maine.

From June into September (and sometimes even into October), you should search for and stop to study the unique Indian pipe, which grows in heavily shaded areas. Although recent research suggests that Indian pipe is in a symbiotic relationship with its host, the plant has historically been recognized as being saprophytic, gaining its nourishment from decaying matter through osmosis. Containing no chlorophyll (the substance that gives plants their green color), this herb rises from the soil on translucent, waxy-looking stems as the pinkish-white flower nods back toward the ground, giving the whole plant the appearance of a fancily carved soapstone pipe.

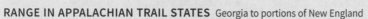

MOUNTAIN LAUREL

LATIN NAME *Kalmia latifolia*

FLOWER Growing in clusters, the nearly 1-inch, cup-shaped flowers vary from pink to white. Radiating from the center, the flower's 10 anthers create a distinctive spoke design.

AVERAGE BLOOM SEASON May to July

LEAVES AND STEMS The shrub usually grows 5–10 feet in height but can, on rare occasions, reach as high as 35 feet. The evergreen leaves are sometimes confused with rhododendron leaves, but are smaller and more slender.

RANGE IN APPALACHIAN TRAIL STATES Georgia to portions of New England

MOST LIKELY LOCATIONS Near Bull Gap in Georgia; on Little Rock Knob on the Tennessee–North Carolina border; throughout Michaux State Forest in Pennsylvania; and near Benedict Pond and on the north slope of Race Mountain in Massachusetts

The partridgeberry is another interesting plant that warrants getting down on hands and knees to observe. Two white flowers, blooming in early summer, fuse together to produce one tiny berry. A close examination of that berry, which changes from green to red during the cooler months, will reveal two scars—one from each flower. The partridgeberry is also an important ground cover; its roots are shallow, but they intertwine to form a compact mat that helps stabilize the soil and keep it from washing away.

Bee balm

Indian pipe

INDIAN PIPE

LATIN NAME *Monotropa uniflora*

FLOWER Usually growing in small clumps, the nodding, nearly translucent flower is most often white but can also be pale shades of pink, yellow, or even blue.

AVERAGE BLOOM SEASON June to September

LEAVES AND STEMS The leaves are nearly unnoticeable and scalelike on a 3- to 10-inch-high stem. Both the leaves and stem are the same color as the flower.

RANGE IN APPALACHIAN TRAIL STATES Georgia to Maine

MOST LIKELY LOCATIONS Near Elk Pond, Rocky, and Catawba Mountains in central Virginia; close to Mount Greylock in Massachusetts; and in the Gulf Hagas area in Maine

PARTRIDGEBERRY

LATIN NAME *Mitchella repens*

FLOWER These small, white to pinkish flowers grow in pairs that are united at their bases on the end of a creeping stem.

AVERAGE BLOOM SEASON May to July

LEAVES AND STEMS The small, 0.5- to 0.75-inch evergreen leaves are smooth, shiny, and opposite on long, trailing stems that grow close to the ground.

RANGE IN APPALACHIAN TRAIL STATES Georgia to Maine

MOST LIKELY LOCATIONS In the James River Face Wilderness in central Virginia; on Mount Greylock in Massachusetts; and in numerous places on the Long Trail in Vermont

Sometimes the AT's protected corridor helps preserve habitat for rare, threatened, or endangered plants, as in the case of the June-blooming Gray's lily. Named for American botanist Asa Gray, this lily is sometimes referred to as the Roan lily, after the mountain on which Dr. Gray first discovered it. In fact, as far as research can determine, Gray's lily is rarely found anywhere else on the AT except Roan Mountain and a few of its neighboring balds. (The Appalachian Trail Conservancy is involved in a continuing study to determine where and what other types of rare, threatened, or endangered plants may happen to be growing within the trail's corridor.)

At other times, a plant that is widespread in the eastern part of the United States is found only in isolated spots along the AT. Climbing fumitory grows on wooded hillsides and rocky slopes from North Carolina all the way north into Ontario, Canada. Yet this plant, which blooms in June and is also called Allegheny vine or mountain fringe, has only been identified at one spot along the entire length of the AT: Fumitory Rocks on the crest of Peters Mountain in Pennsylvania.

By the time the warmer temperatures and breezes of July and August blow across the AT ridgelines, many of the earlier flowers will have disappeared, but growing next to their developing berries and fruits will be black cohosh, oxeye daisy, black-eyed Susan, bergamot (Georgia to southern New England), bee balm (Georgia to New York), touch-me-not, boneset, New York ironweed (Georgia to New York), joe-pye weed, cardinal flower, wintergreen, blazing star (Pennsylvania to New England), nodding ladies' tresses, and gentian.

Bee balm, along with bergamot, is a member of the mint family and has been used as a scent in perfumes and as a flavoring in cooking. Its leaves and early shoots have been added to salads, drinks, and even jellies. Growing in moist woods and along small streams, colonies of bee balm are conspicuous in the forest as their 3-foot-tall stems, which tower above other undergrowth, are topped by tubular flowers of the deepest, richest scarlet to be found on any wildflower. While studying the flower you may notice that the bee balm's stem is different from that of other plants. Run your fingers up and down and you'll find that the stem is not round but square, a characteristic it shares with other members of the mint family.

Another brilliant red flower, the cardinal flower, was once described by naturalist and field-guide author Roger Tory Peterson as America's favorite. Found in the same type of habitat as bee balm—in moist areas and along water runs—the plant is named not for the state bird of Virginia and West Virginia but rather for the color of vestments worn by cardinals of the Roman Catholic Church. In addition to propagating itself by seeds, the cardinal flower can send out little shoots that rise above the ground as a small cluster of leaves. The following year these small shoots develop into mature flowering plants and send out their own shoots. This is why, when you are lucky enough to find one, you'll probably find a whole colony of cardinal flowers.

Because they tend to favor the same environment, jewelweed and stinging nettle are often found growing side by side in large patches lining the pathway. Brushing up against the stinging nettle will give its tiny, stiff hairs an opportunity to scratch your skin and deposit an irritant that will often itch for the rest of the day. One experience of this kind will keep you on the watch for the nettle. Luckily for hikers, the jewelweed's succulent stems contain a juice that helps ease the nettle's sting when rubbed over the itching areas.

For a small burst of refreshing flavor, chew on a leaf of wintergreen, also known as teaberry. It is a short ground cover often found next to the trail growing on creeping stems and erect branches of 2–6 inches with shiny, oval, evergreen leaves and dangling, waxy, egg-shaped flowers. Native Americans used extracts from the plant to lessen the pain of a headache or the discomfort of a fever. They must have known what they were doing because wintergreen contains methyl salicylate—or, as most of us know it, aspirin.

It seems to be a common belief that by the time September and October roll around, the wildflower procession has pretty much come to an end. Yet many of the

JEWELWEED *(Touch-Me-Not)*

LATIN NAME *Impatiens capensis*

FLOWER The almost 1-inch, hanging orange flowers are spurred and spotted with small, reddish-brown dots. The lowest of the 3 sepals curls to the back and makes a sac with a spur.

AVERAGE BLOOM SEASON June to September

LEAVES AND STEMS The plant grows 2–5 feet tall. Its leaves are 2–5 inches long, toothed, and somewhat elliptical in shape.

RANGE IN APPALACHIAN TRAIL STATES Georgia to Maine

MOST LIKELY LOCATIONS Along Thunder Ridge and near Cow Camp Shelter in central Virginia; on Mount Greylock in Massachusetts; and along moist stream areas in Vermont and New Hampshire

summer flowers, such as foxglove, lobelia, angelica, tall meadow rue, marsh pink, monkshood, and grass-of-Parnassus, continue to bloom long after Cub Scouts have left the woods and have begun thinking about Halloween. This is also the time of year when the daisies, asters, and goldenrods are just coming into their lushest period of growth.

Daisies will most often be found in open meadows, along the edges of the forest, or next to old roadways. There are so many species of daisies that it takes a true expert to be able to tell them apart. In fact, according to Peterson, daisies make up the largest family of flowering plants and are possibly the newest family to have evolved and made an appearance on Earth.

Yellow lady's slipper

Viper's bugloss

Wintergreen

Flame azalea

There are more than 100 kinds of asters found in the United States and an equal number of goldenrods. An early American folktale tells of the origin of these two flowers: Two little girls, who were the best of friends, were walking through a field and talking about what they wanted to do when they got older. One, who had long golden hair, said that she would like to do something to brighten people's lives. The other girl, who had deep blue eyes, stated that she just wanted to be able to be close to her best friend. As they walked, they met an old lady and told her of their wishes. The woman gave each of them a magic corn cake, and after eating the treat the children vanished. The next day, however, two new kinds of flowers—goldenrods and asters—appeared growing next to each other in the same field in which the little girls had walked.

Bloodroot

Dutchman's-breeches

Deer in Shenandoah National Park

CHAPTER 6

Furred Creatures Great and Small
(and In Between)

The last word in ignorance is the man who says

of a plant or animal, "What good is it?"

~ Aldo Leopold

Visitors to the Appalachian Trail could potentially dozens of species of mammals while walking in the forest. Some of these animals could weigh nearly as much as a compact car, while some weigh no more than half an ounce. Some live in hollow trees, some inhabit the underground. Several glide gracefully and easily in water, while others zip swiftly through the air.

Although the animals classified as mammals are a widely varied lot, they all have one thing in common: fur. It is the fur that permits warm-bloodedness, which allows them to be active after dark and throughout the year. Unfortunately for the wildlife-watchers among us, many of the mammals along the AT are most active at night, making it more difficult for us to spot them. Then again, this may just be the incentive you need to take a night hike and experience an aspect of the trail many people overlook.

Unless otherwise noted, all of the mammals discussed in this chapter will be found, to some degree, in all the states through which the AT passes.

FAMILY URSIDAE
Bears

BLACK BEARS are the only members of this family to inhabit the eastern United States.

Black Bear *Ursus americanus*

DESCRIPTION In the eastern United States, black bears are almost always black, while in the West they can range from black to cinnamon. Eastern bears are also usually smaller than their western counterparts, while in general, males are larger than females. Size can range from 200 pounds to nearly 600 pounds with a shoulder height of about 40 inches and a length of 4–6 feet.

TRACKS Front paw prints are about 4 inches long and 5 inches wide with five toes. Back paw prints are 7–9 inches long and 5 inches wide; they almost resemble a human footprint, except that the longest toe extends from the middle of the paw. In soft soil it's often possible to identify claw marks in front of the toes.

BLACK BEARS occur in every state along the AT but are probably most abundant in the Great Smoky Mountains, Shenandoah National Park, the state forests of Pennsylvania, and the woods of Maine. Encounters usually end swiftly, with the bear making a quick getaway into the woods and the human standing exhilarated but unharmed. Black bears can become dangerous when they are accompanied by their young, when they are feeding or guarding a kill, or when familiarity with humans has decreased their fear.

Scientifically classified as carnivores, black bears are actually omnivorous, meaning they will consume just about anything. They have been observed eating twigs, leaves, roots, nuts, and berries, and they'll tear the bark off a tree to consume the cambium (the living inner bark of the tree). Everyone knows that bears love honey and honeycomb, but they will also eat the bees and their larvae. Most of the animal protein in their diet comes from grubs, ants, termites, beetles, and other insects, with fish and small mammals, such as mice, chipmunks, and voles, making up the bulk of the small amount of meat they do consume. In fact, animal materials make up less than 10% of their diet.

Contrary to what many people believe, black bears do not hibernate during the winter months. They may sleep away the coldest part of the year, but it is not a deep sleep, and their temperature drops just a few degrees. Consequently, they are easily aroused if disturbed and it is not uncommon for them to be seen roaming around when snow is on the ground.

Besides tracks, a number of other signs can alert an astute observer to the presence of black bears. One of the most obvious is the animal's scat, which is usually cylindrical, somewhat like that of a dog's, and often contains remnants of what the bear has eaten—seeds, leaves of grass, rodent fur and bones, and nutshells. During the time of year that bears are gorging themselves on the abundant variety of berries, the scat will no longer be solid but will resemble a large, black or dark-blue, liquid cow pie. A few other bear signs that may be a little harder to find include logs and stumps turned over or destroyed in the search for grubs and insects, patches of squawroot (a parasitic plant that usually grows on the roots of oak trees) that have been scattered and show signs of being consumed, and branches that have been broken by the bears as they climbed into trees to obtain fruits or nuts.

FAMILY CERVIDAE
Deer and Moose

MALES IN BOTH MEMBERS of this family have antlers. When the antlers begin to grow during the late spring and early summer, they are soft and covered with fine hairs, known as velvet, which contain blood vessels carrying nutrients to help the antlers grow. The velvet drops off near the end of the summer and it is at this time, when the antlers are full grown, that they're used as sexual attractants and, sometimes, as weapons in dominance battles. Antlers still have a purpose to serve when they fall off after the mating season; many creatures of the forest, especially the smaller ones, such as mice, chipmunks, moles, and squirrels, chew on them to obtain much-needed calcium.

Moose *Alces alces*

DESCRIPTION Moose are the largest members of the deer family, with bulls averaging 6–7 feet high at the shoulders and measuring 7–9 feet in length. Massive and covered with dark brown fur, they can weigh from 900 pounds to almost 1,200 pounds. (Females are usually smaller in size and weight.) They have a hump between the shoulders, a big overhanging snout, a large dewlap (fold of skin hanging from the neck) covered by a long tuft of hair, and large gray legs. Palmate antlers can have a spread of as much as 5–6 feet.

TRACKS Moose prints show pointed cloven hoofs usually more than 5 inches in length. In mud, wet snow, or when the moose is running, dewclaw marks may be present.

ONE OF THE MOST THRILLING THINGS to happen to a visitor along the AT is to turn a corner of the trail just in time to catch a bull moose raising its head out of a lake or pond. You might even hear it before you actually see it, as gallons of liquid roll off a massive set of antlers, drip down the muscular neck, and splash loudly back into the water. During the summer, a moose's favorite food is aquatic vegetation, such as water lilies and pondweeds, so you might also see a long strand of foliage hanging from its mouth. Long legs and short necks make it difficult for them to eat or drink in shallow water, which is why you'll sometimes come upon them kneeling down.

A most familiar sight in New England, moose droppings in the fall and winter are pellets that look like piles of coconut-covered brown marshmallows. In summer, droppings are soft and formless, much like a cow pie.

Bulls are usually indifferent but can be quite irritable and dangerous during rutting season, which usually takes place from mid-September to late October. They've been known to attack not only humans but also cars, horses, and even trains. The females (called cows) are very protective, so you should be cautious when they are accompanied by their young.

Once confined to Maine, moose are now regularly seen in New Hampshire and Vermont, with some reports placing them as far south as the Berkshire Hills of Massachusetts and even into Connecticut.

White-Tailed Deer *Odocoileus virginianus*

DESCRIPTION Plentiful throughout the entire route of the AT, white-tailed deer are reddish brown to tan during the warmer months and gray during the winter. Patches of white occur on the nose and throat, around the eyes, on the stomach, inside the ears, and on the back of the tail. They stand about 36–42 inches at the shoulder and are anywhere from 4 feet to almost 7 feet in length. Bucks can weigh up to 300 pounds, while the females usually get no larger than 225 pounds. Antler spread can be as much as 3 feet.

TRACKS Split and pointed, the hoof marks of the white-tailed deer are 2–3 inches long, with the outside toe being just a bit longer than the one on the inside. When a deer walks, the hind feet are placed in almost the exact same spot as the front feet; when leaping, the hind feet often come down in front of the front prints. A close examination of deer prints can tell you what a deer was doing when it made the track. If the points (which face the direction the deer was going) of the two sections of the hoof are nearly touching each other, then the deer was probably just strolling along. When the print shows the two halves splayed, the deer was on the run.

WHITE-TAILED DEER, when frightened, will flee at speeds of up to 35 miles per hour, all the while flashing the white of their tail to alert other deer to the danger. This white flag also helps the young to follow their mothers through the thick forest vegetation. Fawns are born in the spring after a gestation of seven months—one fawn to a doe bred for the first time, then twins, or sometimes triplets, thereafter. White-tailed deer are not as polygamous as other members of the Cervidae family, and it's not uncommon for a male to mate with only one doe throughout his life.

With the extinction of the eastern bison and the disappearance of elk from the Appalachian Mountains, white-tailed deer have become the most populous wild, hoofed animal in the East. With the large number of deer seen along the AT, it may be hard to believe that their population in the Southern Appalachians was nearly decimated near the turn of the 20th century. Some historical accounts say that domestic dogs ran down and killed almost as many as were killed for human consumption. Loss of habitat from farming and timbering only compounded the decline in numbers. To rectify this assault on the natural order of things, herds were imported from the north and released into the mountains by the National Park Service, private clubs, state game agencies, and individual citizens.

With the establishment of national and state parks and game preserves, the enforcement of regulated hunting seasons, and the absence of natural predators (wolves and mountain lions having been extirpated from the Appalachians years before), the deer prospered. The white-tailed deer's increased numbers have been used by some people to argue that hunting regulations should be eased so as to keep deer from browsing on suburban dwellers' backyard gardens. Perhaps a more appropriate way of looking at this problem would be to realize that it is humans who are eating away at the traditional territory of the deer.

Deer are most active in the early evening and early morning but can be seen eating at any time of the day or night. Vegetation that the deer have been eating will have a ragged-edge appearance. Because they lack upper incisors, deer more or less rip forage off a plant instead of biting it off. Also, if you look closely at the lower vegetation they've been feeding on, such as jewelweed or stinging nettle, you'll see that the tops of the plants have been nipped off at an almost uniform height. Deer stop feeding at the point it becomes uncomfortable for them to bend any farther. This point is known as the browse line, and in years of scarce food, the browse line may be lower than normal, as the deer continue to eat downward to obtain any nourishment they can.

FAMILY CANIDAE
Wolves, Foxes, and Coyotes

RELATED TO DOMESTIC DOGS, all North American members of this family have doglike characteristics, such as long, narrow muzzles, erect ears, bushy tails, and slim legs. They rely heavily on a keen sense of smell when on the prowl, not only to smell the prey itself, but also to detect scent posts marked by the secretions of other animals.

Gray Fox   *Urocyon cinereoargenteus*

DESCRIPTION The gray fox's body is covered mostly with a frosted gray fur, while the sides of the neck, legs, and stomach, as well as the backs of the ears, are a reddish rust color. The inner ears, neck, and belly are white. Standing approximately 15 inches high at the shoulder, a gray fox's length averages 24 inches (the tail is an additional 14 inches), and its weight is about 10 pounds.

TRACKS The front print is about 1.5 inches long, and the hind print is just a bit smaller and narrower. Both show four toes and claws in front of the heel pad.

BECAUSE FOXES ARE PRIMARILY NOCTURNAL and highly secretive, sighting one is a rare occasion. If you do happen to see one on the AT, it will most likely be a gray fox. They populate heavier forests, wooded areas, and rocky mountain ridges, as opposed to the red fox's more open-meadow and cultivated-area habitats.

Omnivorous, gray foxes dine on fruits, nuts, grasses, berries, insects, birds, and small mammals, such as rabbits (which are a large part of their diet). They are the only foxes in the country that can climb trees and will do so when threatened. Because of this ability, they are often found foraging in leaning trees or those that are thickly branched.

The gray fox, which was once native only to the Deep South but is now found elsewhere in America, often makes its home in natural cavities, such as those found among boulder fields or in caves or hollow trees. Occasionally it will dig into the ground for a den, which may or may not be marked by a mound. Like many other animals, gray foxes cache food; their hidden reserves will appear as small mounds of heaped dirt and/or vegetation.

Red Fox   *Vulpes vulpes*

DESCRIPTION The red fox's body is just slightly larger than the gray fox's, and its legs and muzzle are a bit longer. Usually its fur is yellowish red on top of the body, white on the underside, and varying degrees of black on the feet, legs, and back of the ears. They have numerous phases of color variations that can include being almost totally black, being black with a frosting of white (the silver fox), or having dark bands across the back and shoulders. The tip of the tail remains white in all phases.

TRACKS The red fox has larger paws than the gray fox, and its hind prints will be about 0.5 inch shorter than its front prints. Because their paws are more heavily furred than the gray fox's, the red fox's tracks are not as sharp and the toes are often blurred, but they do sometimes show imprints of the fur.

FOND OF OPEN MEADOWS, cultivated fields, and brushy areas, red foxes will usually occupy an underground den when their litter of pups is small and needs to be cared for. So as to have a commanding view of their surroundings, most of the time they prefer to sleep on raised areas—on rock piles, above a stream bank, or on a hilly slope. Even in winter, adult foxes sleep outside their dens, curled up with their tails over their noses and feet, oftentimes becoming covered by falling snow.

Red foxes are well known for their cunning in escaping hunting dogs, hunters, and other predators, but their cleverness is also used in other ways. Naturalists have documented cases of red foxes carrying strips of bark in their mouths, entering and then immersing themselves in a creek, leaving just their nostrils and the bark above the water. After submerging themselves briefly, the red foxes would come out of the water, drop the bark, and scurry away. Upon examination, the human observers found the pieces of bark to be covered with fleas.

Coyote *Canis latrins*

DESCRIPTION About the size of a medium dog, coyotes stand approximately 25 inches high at the shoulder and have a body length of close to 3 feet, the tail being an additional 14 inches or so. Its long fur is mostly gray with black tips on many of the hairs. The bushy tail has a black tip.

TRACKS As with other members of the dog family, the coyote's front foot is larger than the hind foot. Each print shows all five of the pads (four toes and the heel) along with marks from the four claws. It may be hard to distinguish from that of the gray fox, but it will be larger.

A LARGER RELATIVE of the fox, coyotes are probably newcomers to the Appalachian Mountains. Although there have been reports of coyote-like animals in the eastern United States since the first colonists arrived, most experts conclude that the sightings were of gray wolves (which were quickly extirpated from the East.) Coyotes were first confirmed in New York sometime in the 1920s and have now been found to have spread to every state along the AT. The theory is that they migrated from the West, moving northward and then eastward through southern Canada and dropping back down into the United States past the Great Lakes. Since tagged coyotes have been found to travel up to 400 miles, the theory could certainly be true.

Because Eastern coyotes are larger than their Western counterparts—averaging 35–40 pounds as opposed to 20–25 pounds in the West—biologists thought they might be a new species or subspecies. In fact, recent research has shown them to have a mix of wolf genes, possibly from having crossbred on the migration through Canada. However, there seems to be no consensus in the scientific community, so coyotes along the AT are still given the same Latin name (which translates to "barking dog") as those in the West. Its common name comes from the Nahuatl Indians of Mexico, who called the animal *coyotl*.

Coyotes are true scavengers, eating just about anything that comes their way—fruits, berries, and other vegetative matter, as well as frogs, snakes, and insects. However, the main part of their diet consists of rabbits, squirrels, groundhogs, and other small mammals. They are so efficient at controlling the rodent population that they are certainly more beneficial than detrimental. When bringing down larger animals, such as a deer, two or three coyotes may work together, running in relays to tire the prey. Studies seem to suggest, though, that most of the eastern coyote's deer meat comes from roadkill rather than from their own hunting prowess.

Red Wolf *Canis rufus*

DESCRIPTION *Note: When the first version of this book was published, there was a very real chance of seeing a red wolf along the AT as it wound its way through Great Smoky Mountains National Park. At that time a program that had been established to reintroduce the red wolf into the park looked like it was going to be a success. Sadly, that proved not to be the case, as some of the wolves were killed when they wandered outside the park, and any pups that were born were not able to survive. The program was discontinued near the turn of the 21st century. Today, the only place red wolves exist in the wild in the eastern United States is near the Atlantic coast of North Carolina. This updated entry has been left in the book in the hopes that, one day, it may again become relevant to the lands along the Appalachian Trail.*

In some ways the red wolf resembles the coyote, but it usually is larger and longer-legged. Those that had been released in the Smokies had been attaining a weight of 50–60 pounds and stood about 15 inches high at the shoulder. Lengths are in the 3-foot range, and tails measure an average of 15 inches. Their closely cropped fur is reddish and interspersed with black hairs. There are varying phases, from reddish gray to a yellowish color to nearly black.

TRACKS Individual prints show all five paw pads and marks from the four claws; inner toes are larger than outer ones. Front and hind prints are about 4.5 inches long—nearly 2 inches larger than those of the coyote.

RED WOLVES ONCE ROAMED THE EAST from southern Pennsylvania to Florida but had been eradicated from the area by the end of the 19th century. Eventually confined to a swampy region along the Louisiana–Texas border, their numbers had dwindled to less than 100 by the 1970s. In fact, a 1980 field guide stated that "it may be doomed to extinction." The goal of the reintroduction program in Great Smoky Mountains National Park had been to eventually have 50–75 of these outstanding creatures roaming the park and the surrounding federal lands of the Pisgah, Cherokee, and Nantahala National Forests.

Red wolves, like their gray wolf cousins, are social animals that have a family group, but they hunt alone, not in packs. In the forests of the Smokies, their diet consisted of birds, raccoons, rabbits, deer, mice, and other small mammals. These wolves were extremely shy and posed virtually no threat to hikers.

FAMILY DIDELPHIDAE
Opossums

Opossum *Didelphis virginiana*

DESCRIPTION The opossum is a curious-looking animal with short legs, a long head that comes to a point, black ears not covered by fur, and a long, thin, naked tail that is black for about a third of its length, then becomes white. Approximately the size of a house cat, it ranges from 15 to 20 inches in length (the tail is another 10–20 inches long) and it weighs, on average, about 10 pounds. The fur is grayish in color, with longer white hairs covering black-tipped fur underneath.

TRACKS The track of the 2-inch-wide hind paw shows a first toe that has no claw (which is opposable and can be used for grasping). The three middle toes are close together, with a fifth pointing outward. The front paw is a bit smaller, with the five toes spreading outward like the fingers on an open human hand.

NORTH AMERICA'S ONLY MARSUPIAL (meaning it carries its young in a pouch), the opossum at one time was considered to be a distinctly Southern animal. Yet, it has now spread to the point that it is found in every state along the AT. Opossums do sometimes pay a price for living in a colder climate. Ears and tails, which are not covered by fur, are subject to frostbite, and it is not uncommon to see an opossum in New England with portions of these body parts blackened or even missing.

When ready to give birth, the female licks her fur from the vaginal opening to her pouch, giving the young an obvious pathway to climb up and begin nursing. Born after a gestation period of only 12–13 days, the young weigh less than 0.1 ounce each, measuring about one-half to two-thirds the size of a honeybee—an entire litter of up to 14 or 15 could easily fit into a tablespoon. Unfortunately, the mother only has 13 nipples, so one or two perish almost immediately.

Opossums are omnivorous, and with 50 teeth (the most of any North American mammal) they can eat just about anything. A large part of their diet consists of carrion, but they also eat fruits, vegetables, nuts, eggs, insects, snakes, frogs and toads, mice, and food scraps scavenged from campsites or even stolen directly from hikers' unguarded packs. Primarily nocturnal, they are almost exclusively seen by AT travelers on night hikes. Their clawed feet and prehensile tail (capable of grasping or wrapping around) make them excellent, if somewhat clumsy, climbers.

FAMILY
ERETHIZONTIDAE
Porcupines

PORCUPINES ARE THE ONLY MEMBERS of this family to occur in the United States. They inhabit the AT from West Virginia to Maine, but they, and evidence of their existence, are most often seen in New England.

Porcupine *Erethizon dorsatum*

DESCRIPTION Porcupines have a stocky, hunched body with a small head, a short tail, and short legs and ears. Larger than most people imagine, they normally weigh 15–25 pounds, but weights of up to 40 pounds have been recorded. Head and body measure about 20 inches, with the tail adding another 7–9 inches. Most of the body, especially the rump and tail, is thickly covered with black to brown quills. (Porcupines in western America tend to have yellowish quills.)

TRACKS Prints of the porcupine are quite distinctive. Both the front and hind paws leave a pebbled impression (especially in soft soil and snow), a result of heavily calloused feet. The oval-shaped paw prints may have impressions of the five toes but almost always show the long claw marks ahead of the main print. The hindprint of more than 3 inches (with claw marks) is often found ahead of the 2-inch foreprint. Tracks are sometimes blurred when the porcupine's stomach rubs the ground or its tail swishes across the trail as it moves along at a waddling gait.

MANY AN UNWARY HIKER has learned firsthand of the porcupine's nearly insatiable search for salt. Sweat-soaked boots, packs and straps, and clothing are all fair game to the porcupine, and it is not uncommon for novice campers to wake up in the morning to find these items gnawed upon or chewed into unusable rubbish. The remedy is to be sure to hang absolutely everything out of a porcupine's reach. (People sleeping in trail shelters have even reported that they've been awakened by a porcupine walking across their chest to gain height as it makes a grab for hanging food.)

Hikers' sweaty bodies leave salt on shelter floors, privy seat covers, and picnic tables; some of these structures have been nearly destroyed by porcupines. Trail maintainers—especially those in Vermont, where the problem seems to be most pronounced—have taken to covering these items with tin or sheet metal. Yet there are many shelters and privies where porcupines have even gnawed on the metal.

Normally strict vegetarians, porcupines enjoy feasting on leaves, twigs, berries, grasses, and plants. In winter, when green vegetation is absent, porcupines subsist almost entirely by chewing through the outer bark of numerous trees, including spruce, hemlock, pine, and some deciduous trees, to feed on the cambium, which is the inner living bark of a tree. Unfortunately, they may feed upon one tree for long periods of time, girdling the tree (chewing the bark off completely around the trunk) and causing its death.

Protected by 32,000 quills, a porcupine has few natural predators, but woe unto those who decide to attack. When threatened, the porcupine raises its quills, lowers its head, and strikes with its tail. Contrary to a belief that continues to this day, porcupines are not able to shoot their quills. The quills are, however, loosely attached to a sheet of muscle below the animal's skin, enabling them to come off easily and to quickly embed in the skin or fur of the attacker.

The hollow quill's tip is barbed with overlapping scales, and, once embedded, body heat from the porcupine's victim causes the small barbs to expand, making the quill that much harder to get out. Muscular movement also pulls the quill deeper and deeper into the tissue; sometimes it will move completely through an animal's body, piercing an internal organ along the way. This is why you must remove the quills as quickly as possible if your dog is attacked. A veterinarian will be able to do this with the least pain to your pet, but if you're unable to get to a doctor, cut the end off the hollow quill, which releases air pressure, collapsing the quill a bit and making it somewhat easier to remove.

FAMILY PROCYONIDAE
Raccoons

MEMBERS OF THIS FAMILY are a disparate group that includes the olingos of South America, the lesser pandas found in Asia, and the coatis and ringtails (which some biologists consider members of a subfamily) of the American Southwest. The only member of this family found along the AT is the raccoon.

Raccoon *Procyon lotor*

DESCRIPTION About the size of a small dog, a raccoon measures 18–28 inches long and can weigh 12–45 pounds. Its bushy, 8- to 15-inch tail has four to six alternating black and brown rings. It is most easily recognized by the black mask outlined in white across the eyes. The dense fur is grayish in color with black-tipped overlying hairs.

TRACKS Most often found next to streams and ponds, the raccoon's tracks are quite easy to identify. Hind prints about 4 inches long resemble human feet with especially lengthy toes. Front and hind paws have five toes. Claw marks are almost always distinct; if absent, the prints could be confused with those of the opossum.

MORE THAN LIKELY, the raccoon's common name comes from the Algonquian Indians of Virginia, who refer to the animal as the arahkun. Their Latin species name, *lotor,* meaning "washer," originated from the belief that raccoons washed their food before eating. It is true that if they are around a stream or pond they will dip the food in the water before taking a bite. However, raccoons living in dry regions consume most of their food without doing this and suffer no ill effects. There is still some disagreement among zoologists as to why the animals perform such a ritual. Some speculate that it is simply done to make food easier to swallow. Others say that the water makes the paws more sensitive and better able to feel and pick out the bits of food that should be rejected.

Because raccoons can adapt to just about any kind of habitat, they are one of the most widespread mammals along the AT, living near fields, in the forests, next to housing developments, and throughout the mountains. Their scat is cylindrical like that of a dog, and like that of the opossum or skunk, it is often found on logs, stones, and large tree limbs. Break the scat open with a stick and you'll find evidence of what the raccoon has recently eaten—maybe seeds, nuts, corn or other garden crops, insect wings, fur, and bits of bone.

These are true omnivores; their diet seems to consist of almost anything and everything that is edible. They have been observed consuming insects and their larvae, squirrels, rats, mice, voles, other small mammals, berries, fruits, nuts, eggs, and small birds. They have even been known to frequent muskrat houses to prey on the young and to raid campsites where food or dirty dishes have been left out.

Aquatic creatures, such as frogs, crayfish, salamanders, fish, and mollusks, appear to be their favorite food. In fact, it is along streams or beside ponds that prints and other evidence of raccoon activity are most often found. Their nimble fingers are quite adept at popping open freshwater mussels, and the discarded shells, as well as those of clams, crayfish, and turtles, are strong signs that some raccoon has been feasting upon these delicacies.

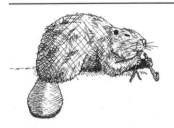

FAMILY CASTORIDAE
Beavers

THE ONLY LIVING GENUS in this family, the beaver, is found nowhere else but North America.

Beaver *Castor canadensis*

DESCRIPTION North America's largest rodent and the second-largest in the world after South America's capybara, beavers average 28 inches in length with a horizontally flattened, naked, scaly tail that can be considerably more than a foot long. Usually weighing somewhere between 40 and 60 pounds, some individuals have reached weights of more than 100 pounds. The fur is a rich, dark brown.

TRACKS Beaver tracks may be hard to find because their long, broad tail often drags on the ground, obscuring the prints. However, when seen, the tracks are quite distinctive because the hind foot is webbed, leaving a 5-inch-wide, fanlike track in the mud. The front tracks, about half as long as the rear ones, usually show only three or four of the foot's five toes.

BEAVERS ARE ONE OF THE MOST family- and colony-oriented animals to be found along the AT. A colony, which may be composed of up to 12 individuals, will usually consist of a male and female (which biologists believe mate for life), a number of 2-year-old young, and the members of the previous year's litter. Having only one litter a year, beavers mate during the winter. After a gestation period of about four months, two to six young arrive during April, May, or June. Born with their eyes open and fully furred, the kits may be swimming around, even submerged, with the mother by the end of the first day. (While underwater, all beavers have clear membranes that slip over and protect the eyes, valves that close off nostrils and ears, and bits of skin that cover the mouth but leave incisors exposed so that branches and food can still be carried.) Parents spend great amounts of time educating their young, swimming and diving with them, leading them to food, showing them the intricacies of getting in and out of lodges, and alerting them to danger.

Watching beavers build a dam or home is to really understand the phrase "busy as a beaver." Two adult beavers can bring a 3-inch sapling down in about three minutes. When working on a dam, they will fell a tree (often 2–3 feet in diameter), trim off the branches in convenient sizes, and carry the logs with their teeth to the dam. Dam construction is adapted to local conditions: to lessen pressure from a fast-moving creek, the dam will be bowed upstream, and in times of high water, the beaver will open up temporary spillways. Working together, two beavers can construct a 12-foot-long, 2-foot-high dam in only two nights of labor.

Observers have witnessed an amazing display of cooperation among young, unskilled beavers clumsily trying to build dams or lodges: When it becomes obvious that things are not going correctly, the young beavers will stop working, disappear, and then return with older beavers, who repair and rebuild as necessary while the original workers help and learn.

Although it seems that beaver activity is most prevalent along the AT near the lakes, ponds, and streams of New England, the animals inhabit all of the states along the trail.

FAMILY FELIDAE
Cats

THE WILDCATS found along the AT all share similar traits: short faces with eyes that face forward to provide binocular vision and depth perception; relatively small, rounded ears; muscular legs; and retractile claws.

Bobcat *Felis rufus*

DESCRIPTION Bobcats average 33 inches in length, stand about 2 feet high at the shoulders, and normally weigh between 20 and 35 pounds, but some have reached as much as 60 pounds. Their golden-brown fur is short and dense with black streaks and spots; their winter coat is grayer. A short, stubby tail is tipped in black, the ears are slightly tufted, and the chest and stomach are covered in white fur.

TRACKS Bobcat tracks are about 2 inches in diameter (front and hind) and are almost rounded. No claw marks are made, but all four toes and the heel pad from each paw are usually visible. Heel pads are concave in front, giving them a scalloped look, and lobed in the rear; this will distinguish bobcat tracks from those of canines, which are lobed only in the rear and have no scalloping in the front.

PRIMARILY CREPUSCULAR, highly secretive, and shy, bobcats are rarely seen by AT hikers. They usually spend daylight hours in hollow trees, under rocks, or hidden by heavy brush. Other than scat, tracks, or scratch marks, bobcats leave little evidence of their existence. The scratch marks are evidence of perfunctory efforts to cover the scat, which is marked off in short segments by constrictions and almost always contains the hair of rabbits or small rodents.

The bobcat receives its name from its short, stubby tail. About 400 years ago in the northern part of England, the word *bob* meant a "bunch," as in a bob of flowers. Hair that had been gathered in a bunch, which made it appear shorter, was called bobbed hair. Eventually, *bob* came to mean anything that was cut short, such as the tail of a horse or a wildcat.

Lynx *Felis lynx*

DESCRIPTION Similar to the bobcat in size, shape, and general looks, a lynx's fur is longer and the black marks less distinct. The tail is bushier than that of the bobcat; the legs are longer; and the long, black ear tufts are much more pronounced.

TRACKS Because the lynx has heavily furred paws, its tracks are larger and rounder than those of the bobcat but are similar in appearance.

A BIT LARGER and grayer than the bobcat, the lynx consumes birds, small rodents and mammals, and occasionally a deer. However, its chief source of protein is the snowshoe hare. Because of this, the lynx has a population cycle that parallels that of the hare's, peaking about every 9–10 years. Of all of the AT states, the lynx is found only in the northern portions of Maine, New Hampshire, Vermont, and New York.

Mountain Lion *Felis concolor*

DESCRIPTION *Note: Mountain lions have been officially gone from the Appalachian Mountains for more than a century, yet people continue to report sightings. Although many of the cases turn out to be false (deer, bobcats, and even dogs can be mistaken for lions), other reports are harder to dismiss. Park rangers with some wildlife training have reported for several decades seeing animals that fit the description of mountain lions. Other people contend that there is still no concrete or reliable evidence of their existence (such as identifiable scat or carcasses). So the debate rages on. If you do think you see a mountain lion along the AT, try to catch a glimpse of its tail—which would be longer than that of any other animal found in the Eastern forests.*

Mountain lions stand an average of 28 inches high at the shoulder, measure 6–7 feet in length, and have long tails that could be anywhere from 21 to 35 inches long. While they are usually close to 150 pounds, they can weigh as much as 250 pounds. Most of the fur is tawny to grayish in color; the tip of the tail is dark brown to black. This same color is found on the backs of the small, rounded ears and on the sides of the nose.

TRACKS Because a mountain lion's track is not much larger than that of a lynx, it is hard to distinguish between the two. Checking the straddle (the width of a set of tracks) and the stride (the distance between sets of tracks) may be helpful. A lynx's straddle is usually less than 7 inches, and its stride is about 15 inches. The mountain lion has an average straddle of 9 inches; its stride ranges from 12 to 28 inches.

IN UNDISTURBED WILDERNESS REGIONS, mountain lions may be astir during the day in search of mice, rabbits, birds, and insects. However, they seem to prefer deer, and their absence from an area has been linked to white-tailed deer overpopulation.

FAMILY SUIDAE
Swine

THE ONLY MEMBER of this family along the AT is the wild boar, which is not native to North America. Imported from Europe near the turn of the 20th century, boars were originally placed in hunting preserves to provide sport. A number escaped, and their descendants now inhabit the mountains of Tennessee, North Carolina, Georgia, and maybe a few neighboring states.

Wild Boar *Sus scrofa*

DESCRIPTION Resembling domestic pigs with coarse hair and grizzled, gray-tipped guard hairs, wild boars stand 3 feet high at the shoulder, can be as much as 6 feet in length, and weigh an average of 200 pounds. Unlike domestic pigs, their long tail (about 10 inches) is straight, not curled, and they have 3- to 5-inch tusks that curve upward.

TRACKS Wild boars have cloven hoofs like deer, but the two halves are spread farther apart and the tracks will show markings of dewclaws.

WILD TURKEYS and bears dig up the ground in search of food, but wild boars, which are most active at dusk and dawn, will leave large patches of earth looking as if they had been churned over by a rototiller. Their rooting reduces the number of wildflowers; destroys the eggs and shelters of ground-nesting birds; and, because they are foreign to the mountains' ecosystem, threatens native species. It is estimated there are currently several hundred wild boars in Great Smoky Mountains National Park. In an effort to reduce the damage they do, the boars are trapped and moved to private hunting preserves. However, because they are such prolific breeders and have few natural predators, trapping seems not to be reducing their numbers, but just keeping them in check.

Wild boars have been known to attack ferociously when cornered, injured, or traveling with their young. Do not approach or intimidate them in any way.

FAMILY MUSTELIDAE
Otters, Skunks, Minks, Weasels, and Allies

MOST MEMBERS of this family are rather small, with long, slender bodies; short legs; thick coats of soft fur; and anal scent glands.

River Otter *Lutra canadensis*

DESCRIPTION A river otter's dark brown fur will look almost black when wet. Weighing about 20 pounds, they average 28 inches in length and have an 11- to 19-inch tail that is thick at the base and tapers to a point. At night their eyes reflect light as a pale amber.

TRACKS Although river otters have webbed feet, the webbing often does not show, except in very soft mud. The five toes are quite spread out, with each showing a bit of the claw. The inner toe of a hind track sometimes sticks out to one side. Tail drag marks are occasionally seen between the paw prints.

EXCELLENT SWIMMERS, river otters have valves in their ears and nostrils that close underwater. At home on land as well, they often build dens with underwater entrances by digging tunnels into the bank of a stream. Very playful, river otters have been seen bodysurfing on the rapids of a stream, sliding on the mud of a river bank into the water, and coasting on snowfields. To coast, they make running starts, jump onto the snow, tuck forelegs along their sides, trail hind legs behind in a very streamlined fashion, and go sledding off downhill.

Social animals, river otters are quite vocal. The sounds they make include growls, snorts, grunts, quick chirps, and shrill yells. Whistles apparently are a means of communication between otters that have been separated by a large distance; mates appear to chuckle softly together as a sign of affection.

Striped Skunk *Mephitis mephitis*

DESCRIPTION About the size of a house cat, the striped skunk weighs around 10 pounds, has a body length averaging 15 inches, and has a long, bushy tail approximately 10 inches long. Its basic color is black, with two wide stripes of white on the back that meet to form a cap of white on the shoulders and head. The tail sometimes has a white tip. It should be noted that coloration varies widely, and striped skunks can range from being nearly all white to mostly black.

TRACKS Both front and hind prints show five toes (middle toes are the foremost) and usually claw marks. The hind print can be almost 2 inches long, is wider at the front, and shows much of the heel pad; other than the toe arrangement, it can resemble a tiny human footprint.

A LESS-ADMIRED MEMBER of the Mustelidae family, a skunk is usually quite peaceable by nature and will even go through a warning ritual before releasing its spray. It will first stamp its feet, raise its tail, and then do a type of handstand on its forepaws. When these warnings fail, it bends its body into a U (so that head and rear are facing the enemy), lifts its tail, and squeezes two scent glands near the anus, shooting a stream of oily, sulfurous spray accurately into the attacker's eyes.

Striped skunks are nocturnal (some biologists classify the animal as crepuscular, or active during twilight) omnivores that will consume just about anything, including bits of food left on dirty dishes around a campsite. The striped skunk is found in every state along the AT; a relative that possesses the same type of scent glands, the Eastern spotted skunk (*Spilogale putorious*), inhabits the mountains south of central Pennsylvania.

The word *skunk* is from the Algonquian Indian word *seganku* or *segahgo*. In fact, it is believed that *Chicago* means "skunk place" in the local Indian dialect. The skunk's scientific name, *Mephistis*, was a Roman term for a poisonous gas seeping out of the earth.

Mink *Mustela vison*

DESCRIPTION The mink possesses glistening, luxurious, soft fur that is most often a deep, rich brown but can be almost black. White spots occur along the chin and throat. Its long, slender body averages 21 inches in length, weighs between 2 and 3 pounds, and has a moderately bushy tail of approximately 7 inches.

TRACKS The mink's hind feet come down directly behind its front ones, so tracks have a double-print pattern. Heel pads and all five toes (and occasionally marks from semi-retractile claws) show on each print. Toes are arranged almost in a semicircle around the heel pad.

MINKS SHARE NUMEROUS TRAITS with other individuals of their family tree. Like skunks, they have anal glands that secrete a fetid discharge that many people find more offensive than that of the skunks, although minks do not spray it. Ferocious hunters, minks, like weasels, kill by biting their prey's neck. Their diet includes fish, frogs, snakes, crayfish, birds, turtles, and rabbits. The preferred food appears to be muskrats; evidence of that animal is found in mink scat more often than the remains of any other living thing. Minks are opportunists when it comes to making their homes. Often they will make their home in a beaver pond, taking advantage of the work the beavers have done. They also take over the den of muskrats after killing and eating them.

Long-Tailed Weasel *Mustela frenata*

DESCRIPTION Weasels' long, slender, lithe bodies have long necks; short, rounded ears; black-tipped, bushy tails; and brown fur that is paler on the stomach and underside. During winter months in the northern latitudes, the fur changes to a pure white. Although the males are often twice as large as the females, weasels average 9 inches in length, have tails about 5 inches long, and weigh approximately 8 ounces.

TRACKS Like the mink, a weasel's tracks may have a double-print pattern, but there are many variations. Often the hind print is inside or near the front print; other times they are side by side, and sometimes one is slightly ahead of the other. Each print is about an inch long and usually shows only four of the five toes and the crescent-shaped heel pad.

WEASELS DESERVE THEIR REPUTATION as skilled and ferocious hunters. They have been known to attack prey several times their size, climb 20 feet up into a tree after a squirrel or chipmunk, and slip through the narrowest of openings in pursuit of prey. Rarely are they unsuccessful in the hunt. Yet there seems to be disagreement among naturalists as to the true nature of the weasel. Some biologists claim that, driven by bloodlust, weasels will go on killing sprees, dispensing death merely for pleasure. Others, who have observed the weasels over a period of time, maintain that all of their victims are either eaten immediately or cached for consumption later. Although they will eat just about any other animal, weasels subsist chiefly on mice, rats, and other small rodents.

Long-tailed weasels are found in every AT state; a relative, the least weasel (*Mustela nivalis),* which shares many of the same characteristics, has a slightly more limited range. Like other members of the family, weasels have anal glands that produce a strong odor.

Fisher *Martes pennanti*

DESCRIPTION Fishers are large, fox-size members of the weasel family, weighing an average of 10 pounds (males are larger than females) and measuring about 23 inches in length, with a bushy tail adding another 14 or so inches. The very dark brown fur has white-tipped hairs that give an elegant frosted sheen.

TRACKS The fisher's tracks are similar to those of the mink but are larger (2 inches wide) and will most often show claw marks. When walking, a fisher has a stride of about 8 inches; when it's running, the prints will be paired and show a leap of nearly 3 feet.

AT ONE TIME, fishers in the East were found only in the northernmost portions of New York and New England. Yet they have been expanding their range, having been seen as far south as West Virginia and Virginia. Still, the best chance of seeing one while on the AT would be along the trail in Maine.

Fishers are good swimmers, but despite their name, they spend very little time in water, and their diet consists of almost no aquatic life. Skilled hunters, they are large and strong enough to kill a small deer. They seem to have a particular appetite for porcupines. Their assault on the quilled creatures is ingenious and effective. Using a frontal attack, the fisher quickly bites the porcupine's nose and eyes, retreating before its victim can respond. The fisher continues to do this until the porcupine weakens from injury and blood loss. The prey is then flipped over, its stomach (where there are no quills) is split open, and the feasting begins.

Marten *Martes americana*

DESCRIPTION Similar in appearance to the weasel, martens, which are smaller than fishers, weigh 2 pounds on average and are about 15 inches in length with a bushy tail of 7 inches. With a pointed snout and a foxlike face, martens have short legs and rounded ears. Their soft fur varies from dark brown to blond, while the breast and throat are pale orange-buff.

TRACKS The marten's tracks are similar to, but larger than, those of the mink, and smaller than a fisher's. In winter the marten's feet are so heavily covered in fur that the toe pads often do not show.

WITH A RANGE more limited than that of the fisher, martens are most often glimpsed on the AT in Maine and possibly a bit of New Hampshire. Living in evergreen forests of fir, spruce, and hemlock, martens spend much of their time in trees, where the female builds a nest of leaves in a cavity to give birth to two to five young in the spring. Quite inquisitive, martens have been known to wander into campsites for no apparent reason other than to find out what is going on.

FAMILY LEPORIDAE
Rabbits and Hares

THE MEMBERS OF THIS FAMILY have long ears, long hind legs, soft fur, short cottony tails, and bulging eyes that enable them to watch for danger over a wide area. Fossils of rabbits have been found dating back to 60 million years ago. The main difference between rabbits and hares is that hares are born fully furred and open-eyed, while rabbits are hairless and blind at birth.

Eastern Cottontail *Sylvilagus floridanus*

DESCRIPTION A fairly large rabbit, it has ears well over 2 inches long, a head and body approximately 15 inches long, and a fluffy tail about 2 inches long. The soft fur is grayish brown on top with the underparts usually white. The nape of the neck is characteristically rust-colored; the tail is brown above and white below.

TRACKS When the cottontail is moving, the hind prints, which are oblong and 3–4 inches long, will show in front of the 1-inch-wide, nearly round front prints. Each print may show traces of four toes.

EASTERN COTTONTAILS are the most common rabbits in the United States, so more than likely it will be this rabbit you'll see on the AT. Cottontails certainly do "breed like rabbits": Each female is able to produce several litters of three to nine young each year. Within hours of giving birth, the female is able to mate and conceive again. In addition, a female born in early spring is ready to mate by late summer. One male and one female, together with offspring, could produce 350,000 rabbits in just five years! Yet, being preyed upon by nearly every omnivore and carnivore of the forest or sky, rabbits live quite precarious lives, and most do not make it much past their first birthday.

A relative, the New England cottontail (*Sylvilagus transitionalis),* is almost the same size as the eastern cottontail, but is redder in color and has a black patch between the ears. Although its range has included all AT states, its numbers have been declining recently, and it is now rarely seen along the trail.

Snowshoe Hare *Lepus americanus*

DESCRIPTION The snowshoe hare is one of the smallest hares found in North America, weighing less than 4 pounds and measuring only 17 inches in length. Its ears, at 3 inches, are longer than those of the eastern cottontail rabbit. During the summer, the snowshoe hare's fur is a dark gray-brown, and the chin, throat, belly, and underside of the tail are white. The upper portion of the tail is black. In winter the entire body becomes white, except for the nearly black tips on the ears.

TRACKS Very narrow at the heel, the hind print of this hare shows the toes to spread out widely, leaving a "snowshoe" print on the surface of snow.

SOME FIELD GUIDES say that snowshoe hares are found only north of the mid-Atlantic states, some insist they reach their southern limit in West Virginia, and others state that the hare is found in the mountains of Georgia. Although there have been field reports of sightings that far south, most thru-hikers who sight snowshoe hares on the AT report seeing them only in New England.

A soft, fluffy coat that changes color with the seasons gives this animal its other common name, the varying hare. The process by which the fur changes color is known as a photoperiodic phenomenon, meaning change is governed by the amount of sunlight in a day. When the days grow shorter in the fall, the hares begin to change color, with the white appearing in patches, which helps to camouflage the animals in early, light snowfalls that don't cover the ground. By the time the ground is fully blanketed in white, the hare will also be completely white. As days become longer in the spring, the coloration reverses, once again in patches so that the hare blends in with its surroundings—spots of melting snow interspersed with the brown of twigs and undergrowth.

A relative of the snowshoe hare, the European or cape hare (*Lepus capensis*) was introduced into the United States in the 1890s and is now the largest hare in North America. Along the trail, cape hares occur in eastern Pennsylvania, New Jersey, New York, and portions of New England. However, because they prefer open fields to heavy forest, they are rarely seen by AT hikers.

FAMILY SCIURIDAE
Squirrels, Chipmunks, and Groundhogs

A WIDE VARIETY of individuals are included in this family. Prairie dogs and marmots (found west of the Mississippi River), woodchucks, ground squirrels, chipmunks, and tree squirrels are all members. Looks, habits, body styles, and diets are quite diverse.

Woodchuck (Groundhog) *Marmota monax*
DESCRIPTION Woodchucks have large, stocky bodies with small, rounded ears and short legs. They range in size from 14 to 22 inches in length, weigh up to 12 pounds, and have a bushy tail that can be 4–8 inches long. Their grizzled brown fur has light frosting, and the cheeks have a hint of white.

TRACKS Woodchuck tracks are similar to, but larger than, those of other rodents. The complete heel pad usually shows, and claw marks can be seen in front of all toes.

WOODCHUCKS WERE ONCE called whistle pigs by people living in the mountains of Virginia and West Virginia. The name is certainly appropriate because, once frightened, woodchucks will let out a loud, piercing whistle followed by a series of softer ones as they run for shelter. Some observers claim that woodchucks also have a more elaborate and longer-lasting whistle that could almost be described as a song.

Unlike many other animals, woodchucks dig their own burrows, which can be more than 4 feet deep and more than 25 feet long. In fact, many other mammals, such as raccoons, foxes, skunks, opossums, and rabbits, will expropriate space for their own home in woodchuck tunnels. True hibernators, woodchucks spend the winter months underground on a mat of grass, curled into a tight ball. Their heart rate drops to only four beats per minute, they take only one breath every six minutes, and their body temperature decreases from 97°F to less than 40°F.

Eastern Gray Squirrel *Sciurus carolinensis*

DESCRIPTION The upper part of the eastern gray squirrel's body is grayish in color, but the head, the shoulders, a portion of the lower back, and the feet have a light brown wash. The fluffy, flattened tail is darker at the base and is frosted with silver hairs. Averaging 9 inches in length (with the tail being an additional 8 inches), eastern gray squirrels weigh about 20 ounces.

TRACKS The hind paws leave a triangular print more than 2 inches long, while the front prints are nearly round and 1 inch in length. A fleeing squirrel's paired hind prints will appear slightly ahead of paired front prints, leaving tracks that look like exclamation points.

EASTERN GRAY SQUIRRELS can be seen almost anywhere along the AT, jumping from tree limb to tree limb and scurrying across the ground. Diurnal, they are especially active in the early morning and late afternoon throughout the year. In winter they usually live in hollow trees, while their summer homes are leafy nests balanced in the upper branches. In late summer and early fall, they are actively eating and gathering the nuts of hickory, beech, walnut, and oak trees, which they drop to the ground to retrieve and store for winter. At times hikers must be wary, for several squirrels dropping nuts along the same portion of trail can make for quite an aerial bombardment.

A larger and darker (almost black) relative, the fox squirrel (*Sciurus niger*) favors oak-hickory forests and ranges from Georgia to southern Pennsylvania.

Red Squirrel *Tamiasciurus hudsonicus*

DESCRIPTION Smaller than the eastern gray squirrel, the red squirrel is about 8 inches long, weighs approximately 7 ounces, and has a tail close to 5 inches in length. Its fur is grayish red on top, while the underside is almost white. In summer the color tends to be almost a greenish yellow with a black line dividing the upper portions from a white underside.

TRACKS Because red squirrels are so light and because of the way they walk, tracks rarely have toe prints, but when they do, the tracks will show four toes on the front prints and five toes on the hind prints (which are about 1.5 inches long). Red squirrels tend to keep their forepaws parallel when running.

Because they prefer coniferous forests of spruce, pine, and hemlock, red squirrel populations are greater in the northern AT states, but they might be seen as far south as Georgia. Very territorial, they are quick to show their anger at any intruder by stamping their feet, jerking their tail, chattering, and releasing a series of loud chucks, barks, squeaks, spits, and growls. Although protective of its own territory, the red squirrel is not above raiding from others to obtain a bird's eggs or a hiker's snack foods.

Northern Flying Squirrel *Glaucomys sabrinus*

DESCRIPTION This small squirrel has a fold of skin that stretches along each side from its front paws to its ankles on the rear paws; it has a furry, wide, flattened tail, and large, black, shiny eyes. The soft, dense fur is a deep brown above and white below. Weighing no more than 5–6 ounces, northern flying squirrels are about 10 inches long, and their tails are another 4–7 inches in length.

TRACKS The northern flying squirrel's tracks are so similar to those of the red squirrel that even experts have a hard time distinguishing between the two; usually the feet of the flying squirrel are smaller.

Although not really a flyer, the northern flying squirrel can glide more than 80 feet through the air. It climbs high up onto a tree trunk and leaps into the air, spreading its arms and legs to stretch out its skin fold, which acts like a kite or glider wing. During the flight it can twist its tail or the lateral membranes to steer or change its angle of descent. Just before landing, it jerks its tail and lifts the front part of its body, effectively braking itself in flight. Upon landing almost silently on all four feet, it quickly runs to the other side of the tree to avoid predators that may have seen its glide.

The omnivorous northern flying squirrel is found in all AT states but, because it's nocturnal, is rarely seen. A smaller and a bit grayer relative, the southern flying squirrel (*Glaucomys volans),* shares the same gliding abilities and many of the same traits and habits; its range is almost the same as the northern flying squirrel's, being found everywhere along the trail but the northern part of Maine.

Eastern Chipmunk *Tamias striatus*

DESCRIPTION One of the smaller members of the squirrel family, chipmunks weigh less than 5 ounces, are about 6 inches long, and have flattened tails of about 4 inches.

The upper portion of the body is grayish to reddish brown, with a black-and-white stripe running along the back that ends at the rump; the underside is white. There are also buff stripes around the eyes.

TRACKS The front print is round and shows four toes and claws. The triangular-shaped hind paw has five toes and claws, is almost 2 inches in length, and prints ahead of the smaller forepaws.

MORE THAN A DOZEN SPECIES of chipmunks inhabit North America, but the eastern chipmunk is the only one found along the AT. Their cheeping calls and their scampering antics accompany hikers along many miles of the trail. Omnivorous, chipmunks eat snails, insects, small birds, and even mice and snakes. In summer, their faces are often stained by blackberry and raspberry juice, while fall sees them running toward burrows to cache the nuts they're transporting inside bulging cheek pouches.

An aggressive digger, a chipmunk's home is a long, winding tunnel that could extend for more than 30 feet. Several chambers open out from the main tunnel to serve as bedrooms, bathrooms, and food storage. Inside the sleeping quarters is a nest of leaves and grasses with an emergency supply of food underneath.

FAMILY CRICETIDAE
New World Rats and Mice

WITH MORE THAN 60 SPECIES, this is the largest family of native mammals found in North America. Just by virtue of their number, these animals have a wide range of sizes, from the 3- to 4-pound muskrat to the 0.25-ounce northern pygmy mouse. One species or another inhabits nearly every type of habitat available. In addition to those species detailed below, which are probably the most common found along the trail, the following do have ranges in AT states but may be seen less often: the southern red-backed vole (*Clethyrionomys gapperi*), North Carolina to Maine; the southern bog lemming (*Synaptomys cooperi*), North Carolina to Maine; the white-footed mouse (*Peromyscus leucopus*), Georgia to mid-Maine; the golden mouse (*Ochrotomys nuttalli*), Georgia to southern Virginia; and the eastern harvest mouse (*Reithrodontomys humilis*), Georgia to southern Pennsylvania.

Muskrat *Ondatra zibethicus*
DESCRIPTION Muskrats are thick-bodied, short-eared rodents whose long, scaly tails of about 10 inches are essentially naked and vertically flattened. The dense underfur on their average 12-inch, 3-pound bodies is gray but overlaid with long, coarse, brown guard hairs.

TRACKS Both of the muskrat's front and hind paws have five toes, but the inner toe of the forepaw is so small that it often does not show in prints. The 2- to 4-inch hind print can be ahead of, behind, or sometimes overlapping the shorter and narrower front print. Occasionally the mark of a dragging tail is also visible.

FOUND NOT IN THE HIGHER ELEVATIONS but along streams, lakes, and ponds, muskrats occur in every state along the AT. Occupying much the same environment as beavers, muskrat homes also resemble those of their neighbors, except they are usually smaller and constructed chiefly of aquatic vegetation instead of a mixture of tree parts. Along streams or deeper lakes, muskrats will become bank dwellers, digging tunnels that begin above or below water level and go to within several inches of the ground surface, where the sleeping quarters are. Usually an additional tunnel is dug as an escape route, since predators, such as great horned owls, raccoons, and mink, will pursue muskrats right into their homes.

Active primarily at night, muskrats are excellent swimmers that can stay underwater for extended periods of time, propelled by their slightly webbed hind feet and guided by their tails. A mouth that closes behind protruding incisors permits them to chew underwater.

Their diet consists chiefly of aquatic plants, such as cattails, water lilies, pondweeds, and arrowheads, although vegetation growing on land is also included. Like beavers, muskrats are also fond of freshwater mussels, clams, small fish, snails, frogs, and crayfish. Muskrat meat, sometimes known as marsh rabbit, kept food on the tables of many of the early settlers and was still quite a common dish in some parts of the country until the mid-1900s, when its popularity began to fade. Even today, in this age of synthetic materials, muskrat fur is sometimes still used as trim on garments.

Eastern Wood Rat *Neotoma floridana*

DESCRIPTION Looking unlike most people's expectation of what a rat is and more like an overgrown mouse, the eastern wood rat has a round face and a body with light-brown fur above and grayish-white fur below. The bushy, flattened, 7-inch tail is also bicolored. The largest rats along the AT, eastern wood rats measure about 9 inches long and weigh 7–16 ounces.

TRACKS The wood rat's tracks are hard to distinguish from those of other rodents because, like other rodents, the wood rat has five toes on triangular hind paws and four toes on the forepaws.

AT ONE TIME wood rats were found abundantly from Georgia to Connecticut, but by the 1980s their numbers had become alarmingly small north of central Pennsylvania. Mystified scientists studying the problem put forth several theories. One theory was that the arrival of gypsy moths so defoliated oak trees that acorns became scarce, causing large-scale wood rat starvation. Another stated that the modern world's destruction of habitat was to blame. Still a third theory pointed out that a major predator, raccoons, increased in number at the same time wood rats' numbers were decreasing. Eventually it was confirmed that raccoons were to blame, sort of. The eggs of a parasitic round-worm are found in raccoons' feces and, since wood rats will feed on seeds found in the scat, the eggs are ingested. Hatching inside the wood rats, the larvae eventually work their way into the rats' brains, causing death. As an example of how all things in nature are interrelated, once raccoon populations began to dwindle as a result of rabies and canine distemper epidemics, the wood rat's numbers began to rise.

Since their tracks are hard to distinguish from those of other rodents, the best way to discover whether wood rats are in the area is to search for their bulky nests—piles of sticks and debris in a bush or cave, or a large pile of sticks almost 4 feet high against a tree. Since these are the pack rats of legend, their nests may also contain all manner of debris, such as a hiker's missing spoon or a buckle chewed off a backpack.

Meadow Vole *Microtus pennsylvanicus*

DESCRIPTION This rather stocky vole has short, rounded ears; small eyes; and a tail less than 2 inches in length. The upper part of its body varies from a dark brownish gray in winter to a yellowish brown in summer. The underside is gray and sometimes a little buff. The head and body measure an average of 5 inches and the weight is somewhere near 2 ounces.

TRACKS The meadow vole has a variety of print patterns. Sometimes the front prints and hind prints overlap, almost obliterating each other. Other times the 0.5-inch hind print is ahead of the slightly smaller front print. Tracks have the familiar rodent pattern of four toe and claw marks showing on the forepaw and five toe and claw marks on the hind paw.

MEADOW VOLES ARE ACTIVE throughout the year, living exclusively on vegetation such as grasses, sedges, clover, flowers, bark, and leaves. Voracious eaters, they consume nearly their weight in food each day. These voles are often referred to as field mice and make their homes in surface tunnels of grass and underground burrows. When frightened, they, like rabbits, stamp their hind feet. They are prolific breeders—a captive female was recorded to have produced 17 litters of three to nine young in less than one year.

Woodland Vole (Pine Mouse) *Microtus pinetorum*

DESCRIPTION A small, chunky animal with rather small ears, the woodland vole has short, soft fur that is a shiny rust color on top and light gray on the underside. About 4 inches long with a brown tail 1 inch in length, it weighs about 1 ounce.

TRACKS Biologists say there is no practical difference between woodland vole tracks and those of the meadow vole.

Found everywhere along the AT, woodland voles live much of their lives in underground burrows several inches below the surface that they dig with their forefeet and teeth. In winter they can become quite communal and huddle together for warmth. Despite its common name, pine mouse, these voles are found more often in deciduous woods than in pine forests.

Deer Mouse *Peromyscus maniculatus*

DESCRIPTION The upper portion of a deer mouse's body ranges in color from a gray buff to a deep red-brown; the underside is white. The approximately 4-inch tail is also distinctly bicolored and covered by short hairs. The body measures 2–4 inches and weighs an average of just less than 1 ounce.

TRACKS Like many other mice, the tracks of deer mice show the front prints behind and between the hind prints. Sometimes the tail drags—when it does, the hind print and front print may be blurred into one large print.

Deer mice most often nest in hollow logs but may have additional small burrows nearby as refuges from predators. One of the mouse species customarily found at trail shelters, their diet includes fruits, berries, insects, and certain fungi but chiefly consists of seeds and nuts. Many of these foods are cached in hollow logs and other areas protected from the weather.

FAMILY MURIDAE
Old World Rats and Mice

This is the largest of all mammal families, but only three species, which were accidentally introduced into the New World, inhabit North America. All three species have long tails and large ears. These are the rodents that do the most harm to humans by damaging or destroying tons of crops each year and carrying such fatal diseases as typhus, spotted fever, and bubonic plague. It is believed that the organisms carried by these rats have killed more people in the last 1,000 years than have died in all of the wars throughout history.

Norway Rat (Brown Rat, Water Rat, and Sewer Rat) *Rattus norvegicus*

DESCRIPTION The most notable features of the Norway rat are large, naked ears, small eyes, and a scaly, almost hairless tail that can be almost as long as the rest of the body. Weighing anywhere from 7 to 16 ounces, it averages 9 inches in length. The coarse fur is brown to gray on the back and light gray on the underside.

TRACKS The hind print of the Norway rat shows five long toes with claw marks and can be 2 inches long. The front print is less than half that length and shows four long toes and claw marks. The toes on the outside of each print point almost sideways instead of ahead.

THE NORWAY RAT is believed to have arrived in North America on ships carrying Hessian troops hired by Great Britain to battle American colonists during the Revolutionary War. These rats have since spread to every corner of the United States. Nocturnal and omnivorous, they eat all manner of vegetables, grains, fruits, eggs, meats, leather, paper, cloth, carrion, and garbage. When not living inside the structures people have built (especially places where grain and other foods are stored), these rats usually nest in 2-inch-diameter burrows underground.

Another member of this family, the black rat (*Rattus rattus),* might be seen along the AT, but it usually makes its home in seaport areas along the coasts of North America.

House Mouse *Mus musculus*

DESCRIPTION The small house mouse weighs less than 1 ounce, measures about 3.5 inches, and has a scaly tail almost as long as its body. The fairly short fur is grayish brown on top, with a paler, buff underside. The rather large ears are covered in fur.

TRACKS The tracks of the house mouse are very similar to and hard to distinguish from those of the deer mouse (see page 127).

THE HOUSE MOUSE is the one that you will most likely find in shelters and the one that will probably get into your pack and food sack. They can climb straight up vertical walls and gnaw through floors, walls, and baseboards. Chewing and shredding just about anything, they have made nests overnight in the pockets of a backpack or inside a boot.

Originally from Asia, house mice spread across Europe and arrived in America on ships sailed across the Atlantic Ocean by Spanish, French, and English explorers and colonists. They are prolific breeders; it is estimated that a single pair with offspring could produce well over 3 million house mice in less than three years, but disease and natural predators keep their numbers in check. There is an additional natural control: if their population becomes too dense in a given area, many of the females become infertile.

FAMILY ZAPODIDAE
Jumping Mice

FOUR SPECIES OF THIS FAMILY occur in North America. Two are found exclusively west of the Mississippi, one occurs from southern Georgia and Alabama northwest to Alaska, and the last one (profiled here) inhabits the mountains from Alabama to eastern Canada. All are champion sleepers that hibernate six to eight months of the year.

Woodland Jumping Mouse *Napaeosapus insignis*

DESCRIPTION The small woodland jumping mouse is close to 4 inches long and averages no more than 1 ounce. At 5–6 inches, its white-tipped, nearly hairless tail is longer than its body. As mice go, this is a rather good-looking one with bright yellowish-orange sides, a brownish back, and a white underside.

TRACKS The woodland jumping mouse spends almost all of its active time in grassy and bushy areas, thereby rarely leaving any tracks to find in dirt or mud. However, when you do find one, the hind print will be rather large (for an animal this size) as much of its large back jumping leg will also print.

INHABITING THE MOIST, cool environment of heavy coniferous and hardwood forests, the woodland jumping mouse lives up to its name, being able to make grand leaps averaging 6–8 feet. Scientists believe it plays an important role in woodlands by consuming large amounts of an underground fungus, *Endogone*. The mouse's digestive juices are thought to be essential for the germination of the fungus's spores, which are dispersed throughout the forest via the animal's scat.

FAMILY TALPIDAE
Moles

MOLES LIVE ALMOST THEIR ENTIRE LIVES underground, rarely coming to the surface. They have streamlined bodies; the pelvis is narrow, allowing them to easily change direction in their burrows, and the velvety-soft fur is grainless, enabling them to effortlessly move forward or backward. Because they spend so much of their time underground, you are unlikely to ever see mole tracks, but you will see evidence of their tunnels in the little ridges of broken dirt that cross the trail.

Eastern Mole *Scalopus aquaticus*

DESCRIPTION The eastern mole's front feet are wider than they are long, the palms are turned outward, and the slightly webbed toes have strong claws. The tight, velvety fur has a silvery sheen and tends to be slate-colored in the northern part of the eastern mole's range and tan to brown in the more southern states. The snout is naked, flexible, and relatively long. Eastern moles measure an average of 5.5 inches, their mean weight is 4 ounces, and their nearly naked tail is about 1.25 inches long.

ALONG THE AT, the eastern mole ranges from Georgia to Massachusetts and is found mostly in open areas such as fields and meadows, but it also inhabits spots that are lightly wooded. Although the largest part of their diet is earthworms, these moles can be a boon to farmers since they also feed on the larvae of many pests, such as rose chafers, Asiatic garden beetles, and Japanese beetles. An excellent burrower, an eastern mole can dig a new tunnel more than 14 feet in length in just one hour.

Hairy-Tailed Mole *Parascalops breweri*

DESCRIPTION The hairy-tailed mole measures 4.5–5.5 inches long and can weigh almost 2.5 ounces. Its tail of about 1 inch is covered with hair. The body fur is a dark slate color with a bit of a sheen to it; the underside is paler.

THE HAIRY-TAILED MOLE has a voracious appetite, eating up to three times its own weight every day. They stay underground during the day, coming to the surface to feed at night. Because these moles are active year-round, they have a tendency to dig tunnels quite a distance below the surface that are better insulated from the cold. In fact, the tunnels are so well constructed that many generations may use them. Preferring well-drained soils in open fields, brushy areas, and sometimes woodlands, hairy-tailed moles inhabit AT states from Georgia to Maine.

Star-Nosed Mole *Condylura cristata*

DESCRIPTION The star-nosed mole is the one whose photograph you were fascinated with as a child. The 22 fingerlike, fleshy projections, called tentacles, surrounding its nose give it an alien-world look. The large front feet are as long as they are wide. The dark-brown to black body measures 4–5 inches in length, weighs 1–2.75 ounces, and has a hairy tail close to 3 inches long.

WHEN THE GROUND IS FROZEN during the winter, making it hard to search for food, the star-nosed mole becomes an excellent swimmer, moving its tail and feet to drive itself forward in search of fish and other aquatic life. Since its tentacles are continually moving when foraging on land, biologists believe they are helpful in negotiating burrows and in locating food. Once the star-nosed mole begins to eat, it tucks the tentacles together, out of the way. These are social animals, and more than a dozen have been found occupying the same acre.

FAMILY SORICIDAE
Shrews

IT IS BELIEVED that shrews (and moles) are related to mammals that existed at the same time as dinosaurs.

Usually living alone, shrews are very territorial and will battle just about any animal they perceive as a threat, even their own kind. They are outrageously active and nervous and have such a high metabolism that they must eat at least every three hours and consume up to twice their weight daily. Subsisting chiefly on insects and other small mammals, a poison in their saliva can paralyze their prey. A shrew's tracks are so little that they most often look like nothing more than indistinct dots, and burrows are so small as to be easily and wrongly identified as earthworm tunnels.

In addition to those species described below, it is possible that the following may be found on the AT: the smoky shrew (*Sorex fumeus*); the northern water shrew (*Sorex palutris*), North Carolina to Maine; the long-tailed or rock shrew (*Sorex dispar*), North Carolina/Tennessee to Maine; the pygmy shrew (*Microsex hoyi*), North Carolina to Maine, but absent from Maryland to southern New England; and the least shrew (*Cryptotis parva*), Georgia to New York.

Short-Tailed Shrew *Blarina brevicauda*

DESCRIPTION The short-tailed shrew is the largest shrew inhabiting North America. It measures 3-4 inches in length, has a short tail 1 inch long, weighs almost a full ounce, possesses no external ears, and has eyes so small they are scarcely evident. The fur is a solid color of grayish lead throughout the body.

SHORT-TAILED SHREWS spend much of their time digging subterranean tunnels through which they wander in search of underground fungi, worms, insects, snails, centipedes, beetles, and other invertebrates. Occasionally they will consume mice and smaller shrews. Ferocious, a short-tailed shrew attacks by biting its quarry's face and neck, paralyzing the victim with a poison in its saliva, and then sometimes eating the helpless victim alive after it is dragged back to the shrew's nest. The venom is not fatal to humans, but a bite will hurt for quite a few days.

Males release a musky secretion from glands on their hips and stomach to mark their burrows so other males, who may be searching for mates, will not enter. Meetings of two adults, male or female, can erupt into savage fights over territory and mates. Yet mates have been known to stay together almost permanently. Short-tailed shrews are some of the most common mammals found in North America.

Masked Shrew (Cinereous Shrew) *Sorex cinereus*

DESCRIPTION One of the smallest mammals in the United States, the masked shrew weighs, at the most, 0.3 ounce, measures about 2 inches in length, and has a tail that may be 1–2 inches long. The fine fur is brown above and silvery gray on the underside. The tail is also bicolored.

LIKE THE SHORT-TAILED SHREW, the masked shrew is one of the more widely distributed mammals inhabiting North America. Yet, being chiefly nocturnal, it is rarely observed. It feeds primarily on spiders, larvae, slugs, and snails, and its nest is often a pile of grass, leaves, and other bits of vegetation located under a log, inside an old hollow tree stub, or hidden by dense foliage.

FAMILY VESPERTILIONIDAE
Evening Bats

SOME BATS, being the only mammals that fly, migrate during the spring and fall, but several members of this family hibernate in place during the winter months. All have a simple, unmodified nose, upward-projecting earlobes that contain a tragus (a piece of skin that helps enhance hearing), and a tail that barely extends beyond the complete interfemoral membrane (a thin piece of skin stretched between the two hind legs). The species found in this family live almost exclusively on insects; the fear that bats will fly into your hair is based on the fact that they often fly close to animals, including humans, in search of insects that swarm about warm-blooded animals.

The three species described below are probably the most common along the trail, but the following are also known to occur in AT states: the Rafinesque's or eastern big-eared bat (*Plecotus rafinesquii*), Georgia to North Carolina/Tennessee; the Townsend's or western big-eared bat (*Plecotus townsendii*), Virginia and West Virginia in isolated colonies; the evening bat (*Nyctideius humeralis*), Georgia to southern Pennsylvania but only occasionally found in the Appalachian Mountains; the hoary bat (*Lasiurus cinereus*); the big brown bat (*Eptesicus fuscus*); the eastern pipistrelle (*Pipistrellus subflavus*); the small-footed myotis (*Myotis leibii*); the Indiana or social myotis (*Myotis sodalis*), Georgia to New England but absent from much of New Hampshire and Maine; and the Keen's myotis (*Myotis keenii*). A species from a different family, Molossidae, the Brazilian or Mexican free-tailed bat (*Tadarida brasiliensis*), occurs in very isolated cases in the Southern Appalachian Mountains.

Silver-Haired Bat *Lasionycteris novtivagans*

DESCRIPTION The silver-haired bat can be distinguished from all other North American bats by the color of its fur—brownish black with silvery tips that make it appear frosted. The head and body are 2–3 inches long, the tail is approximately 1.5 inches long, the wingspread is almost a foot, and the weight is less than 0.5 ounce. The interfemoral membrane has fur on its upper side. The small ears are naked and rounded.

THE SILVER-HAIRED BAT is more migratory than many of its relatives and is often found in many parts of its range only during the fall and spring migration. With a relatively slow flight, it hunts around streams and ponds in the early evening for various insects, preferring flies and moths. The silver-haired bat is not a cave bat but is found resting during the warmer months in hollow trees and even bird's nests. In winter it hibernates in buildings, rock crevices, and trees.

Little Brown Myotis *Myotis lucifugus*

DESCRIPTION The little brown myotis has a wingspread of 10 inches and a body that weighs less than 0.5 ounce. It measures, with tail, approximately 3.5 inches in length. The short fur on the back is a rich brown with glossy tips, the underside is lighter, and the throat is sometimes almost white.

DURING THE DAY the little brown myotis, one of the most prevalent bats in America, roosts in barns, houses, caves, and other sheltered spots away from light. Very migratory, it may fly several hundred miles south to hibernate for the winter. It mates in the fall, but sperm is stored in the female's uterus, and fertilization does not take place until the following spring. One young is born in June or July and nurses constantly, except when the mother is searching for food. Mother bats gather together in nursery colonies in caves, where the concentration of bodies raises the temperature to protect the newborns. When upset, the mother flies away with the youngster attached to a teat and carried crossways with its rear legs gathered beneath an armpit.

Red Bat *Lasiurus borealis*

DESCRIPTION Male red bats are bright red with a bit of white frosting on the tips of the fur hairs on the breast and back. Females are noticeably duller, having more of a brownish look, but the frosting is more pronounced. The red bat weighs less than half an ounce, has a wingspread of 12 inches, a tail about 2 inches in length, and a body 2.5 inches long. The upper part of the interfemoral membrane is furred.

THE ACTIONS OF RED BATS during the winter seem to vary from individual to individual and from place to place. Many red bats migrate to the southern part of the United States, with some continuing to Bermuda. Others do not travel at all but hibernate throughout the colder months, and certain individuals have been observed emerging to forage on warm days. In summer, they hang upside down in thick vegetation that provides relief from the sun but is open beneath to permit them to fall headlong into flight. Red bats often hunt in pairs, flying over the same route again and again in search of moths, flies, leafhoppers, and beetles.

CHAPTER 7
Serenaders on the Wing

You ask me: Why do I live on this green mountain?

This is another sky, no likeness to that human world below.

~ Li Po

Appalachian Trail visitors can hike for many miles or go for days on end without seeing or hearing any mammals, but just about any excursion on the trail is guaranteed to be rewarded with the glimpse of a pair of multihued wings zipping through the forest greenery or the sound of a melodious song drifting about on the wind, providing a soundtrack for the day's outing.

Birds evolved from reptiles, and most of the scientific community now accepts the idea that their ancestors were those largest of reptiles, the dinosaurs. The scaly skin still on their legs shows their relationship to their progenitors. Over time, various kinds of birds developed, gained dominion, and then disappeared. It was once thought that birds, as a group, were at their zenith about half a million years ago, during the Pleistocene epoch. However, a study (not necessarily accepted by everyone) that was led by the American Museum of Natural History in the 2010s suggests that there could be as many as 20,000 bird species in the world today, the majority of which are passerine, or perching birds.

As birds moved away from their reptilian forefathers, their most significant step was the evolution of feathers from modified scales. Not only did feathers give the birds' bodies shape and balance and protect them from heat and cold (permitting them to become warm-blooded animals), but the feathers also gave the birds the ability to fly. Most birds have three main kinds of feathers: Contour feathers—the ones that give a bird its color—cover most of the body, and the manner in which they grow gives birds their streamlined shape. Small interlocking hooks on these flight feathers give added strength to wings. Filoplumes (hairlike feathers) and down (soft, fluffy feathers) grow beneath the contour feathers and provide insulation. In warm weather, they are pressed flat and close to the body, cutting down on air spaces and allowing body heat to escape. In cooler temperatures, they are fluffed out to add air spaces, thereby retaining body heat.

Despite their toughness, feathers do wear out, so at least once a year birds molt, replacing their feathers with a new set. Often, this molting results in feathers of a different color, preparing the bird to breed or to better camouflage itself within changing seasonal surroundings. (Unless otherwise noted, the descriptions of particular birds in this chapter pertain to the adult male of the species in their spring and summer, or breeding, plumage; females and immature chicks tend to be duller in color.)

The development of feathers alone did not permit flight. Body changes had to be made, and as a result, heavy sets of teeth were replaced by beaks; bones became hollow and lighter; vertebrae, pelvic, and shoulder girdles became fused into lighter yet stronger body cases; and muscles developed to give power to the forelimbs—which evolved into wings.

Flight requires a high expenditure of calories, and as a result, birds' diets include foods with concentrated sources of energy, such as insects, nectar, seeds, and fruits. To aid and speed digestion, their metabolic rate allows food to be transformed into energy as quickly as possible. Their body temperature is higher than that of mammals, ranging from 104° to 110° Fahrenheit, and their hearts—larger in proportion to body size than any other vertebrates'—circulate blood at an astounding rate.

Because smaller birds have a larger surface area in relation to the volume of their bodies—which means greater heat loss—they have greater energy demands and even higher metabolic rates. As an example, the tiny ruby-throated hummingbird (*Archilochus colubris*), loses so much heat that its diet is primarily nectar—almost pure sugar.

In their constant quest for nourishment, birds have learned to migrate to the places where food sources are the most abundant during a particular time of year, and the Appalachian Mountains provide an ideal, continuous, 2,000-mile-long course for them to follow from Alabama to Canada. Possibly using prominent peaks and other landmarks to guide them, they travel north from the Southern states and as far as South America during the spring, making use of the heated air that swells northward from the Gulf of Mexico, pushed forward by strong tailwinds. If the warm air encounters a cold front, which decreases the winds, the birds simply land and spend time feeding, waiting for the next blast northward. This is probably the best time of year to observe large numbers of birds, as numerous species are often found in relatively small areas (and the males are in their resplendent breeding plumage).

The annual cycle usually begins in the Southern mountains during the latter half of March, when such species as the American robin (*Turdus migratorius*), the solitary vireo (*Vireo solitarius*), and the black-and-white warbler (*Mniotilta varia*) wander back into the mountains from their winter homes in the Piedmont and Coastal Plain. Also at this time, year-round residents like northern cardinals (*Cardinalis cardinalis*), Carolina chickadees (*Parus carolinensis*), and song sparrows (*Melospiza melodia*) become more active.

The majority of spring migrants are seen from early April to late May, as birds that have spent the summer in the Southern states or the tropics arrive to either nest or pass through on their way north. Because of the scarcity of food and foliage at higher elevations this time of year, they most often gravitate to the valleys and lower ridgelines.

Nesting activity lasts from mid-May into early July, and this may be when birds are the easiest to see as they stay close to "home," ready to defend their territory. Although some species are strongly associated with one habitat, many shift their use patterns throughout the year. This high mobility makes it hard to generalize about a particular species' habitat use, but most bird field guides usually focus on this time of year—and the places that birds build their nests—when describing a species as favoring, or being found in, a certain habitat or vegetation zone. With that in mind, it is possible to discuss which habitats certain birds are likely to be encountered in along the AT.

RUFFED GROUSE

LATIN NAME *Bonasa umbellus*

DESCRIPTION About 17 inches in length, ruffed grouse have fanlike tails, which on males have an unbroken outer band of black. The ring on females' tails is broken by a small, brown gap. Crest feathers and those around the neck (the ruff) become raised when the birds are courting or alarmed.

VOICE The female coos and makes clucking notes, while both sexes emit a sharp "kwit, kwit" note when alarmed.

RANGE IN APPALACHIAN TRAIL STATES Georgia to Maine

Grouse are common throughout the length of the AT, inhabiting deciduous, mixed, and coniferous forests. The ruffed grouse (*Bonasa umbellus*) is the bird that makes a hiker think a tractor is starting up in the distant woods or that the hiker is having a heart attack. In order to attract a mate, the male grouse drums its wings against its body, and the resulting low, muffled sound seems to resonate within a hiker's chest. They've also caused hearts to skip a beat when several suddenly come flying out of the underbrush, flapping noisily just a few feet in front of startled faces. During the spring, a female grouse may burst out of the brush and go running down the trail as if she has a broken wing. The act is designed to lead a potential predator away from a nest or nearby chicks. If the display fails, she turns around and, hissing loudly, charges the intruder. A smaller relative that uses these same tactics, the spruce grouse (*Denragapus canadensis*), does not have a crest of feathers on its head like the ruffed grouse. In New

England—about the only place it is found along the AT—the spruce grouse is often referred to as a partridge.

The Canada jay (*Perisoreus canadensis*) lives year-round in the evergreens of the higher elevations and on the open ridgelines of New Hampshire and Maine. AT hikers often encounter these birds when they swoop down to gobble up trail mix accidentally dropped on the ground. Locals call them camp robbers because these jays are brave enough to boldly hop into camp and make off with bits of food from a hungry hiker's plate—as the hiker is eating!

BLACK-CAPPED CHICKADEE

LATIN NAME *Parus atricapillus*

DESCRIPTION This 5.5-inch chickadee has buff sides, white cheeks, and a black cap and bib. Wingspan may be up to 8.5 inches.

VOICE The call is a whistled "chick-a-dee-dee-dee-dee." The song is a whistled "fee-bee," with the first note higher than the second.

RANGE IN APPALACHIAN TRAIL STATES From the mountains of North Carolina/Tennessee to Maine

Also inhabiting the higher elevations of the New England coniferous forests is the boreal chickadee (*Parus hudsonicus*), whose brown feathers on the top of its head can help distinguish it from the black-capped chickadee (*Parus atricapillus*). A consumer of seeds, berries, and insects, the black-capped is found in just about every environment along the AT.

Most often seen in the coniferous forests of New England (but, interestingly, also residents of Shenandoah National Park), ravens (*Corvus corax*) can best be distinguished from the wider-ranging crows (*Corvus brachyrhynchos*) by their calls and the shapes of their tails. The usually larger raven has a wedge-shaped tail and a low, hoarse type of "gronk." A crow's tail is square or slightly rounded, and its call is a long, descending "caw."

Usually nesting close to streams or other bodies of water, the winter wren (*Troglodytes troglodytes*) is most often seen on the coniferous forest floor foraging for insects and spiders, while the olive-sided flycatcher (*Contopus borealis*) spends much of its time perched on the upper branches of dead trees waiting for passing insects.

Ground feeders, white-throated sparrows (*Zonotrichia albicollis*) are vertical migrators, spending winters in the valleys and lower elevations and rising into the mountains to nest and raise their young during the warmer months. A relative, the dark-eyed junco (*Junco hyemalis*), follows the same feeding and migration patterns.

The quite tame, and tiny, northern saw-whet owl (*Aegolius acadicus*), which roosts in dense evergreens in the winter, has a song consisting of softened, whistled notes—about two per second—that may go on for long, almost endless periods of time. Long-eared owls (*Asio otus*) sometimes form communal winter roosts of more than 50 birds in dense coniferous forests. In addition to emitting a low, moaning "whooooo," they have a large vocal repertoire that includes twittering and catlike whines.

GREAT HORNED OWL

LATIN NAME *Bubo virginianus*

DESCRIPTION More than 20 inches in length with a wingspan of 55 inches, great horned owls have yellow eyes, widely spaced ear tufts, a white throat collar, and horizontal bars across the stomach.

VOICE Low, resonant "hoos" in a series of 3–8

RANGE IN APPALACHIAN TRAIL STATES Georgia to Maine

Barred owls (*Strix varia*) are some of the most vocal of owls that also have an abundant vocabulary. A pair will often alternate calling back and forth, sometimes during the day. Hikers who are just preparing to bed down for the night have sometimes been frightened into sleeplessness by one of their other cries—a bloodcurdling scream. One of the largest of owls, the great horned owl (*Bubo virginianus*), and one of the smallest, the eastern screech owl (*Otus asio*), are, due to their ability to adapt to suburban areas, probably the two owls that most people are familiar with. All owls cough up the pellets of undigested fur, feathers, and bones that you may have broken apart as a student in biology class.

TURKEY VULTURE

LATIN NAME *Cathartes aura*

DESCRIPTION When soaring, the dark brown feathers of the nearly 30-inch-long turkey vulture show silver on the trailing half of the wings.

VOICE Grunts and hisses at nesting site and often when competing for food

RANGE IN APPALACHIAN TRAIL STATES The year-round range is from Georgia to Pennsylvania/New Jersey; the summer range reaches to Maine.

The most frequently seen soaring bird along the AT is the turkey vulture (*Cathartes aura*) whose 6-foot wingspan gives it a majestic look and a V-angled silhouette when seen circling on thermals above cliff facings and over long ridgelines. The lack of feathers

YELLOW-BELLIED SAPSUCKER

LATIN NAME *Sphyrapicus varius*

DESCRIPTION With a black-and-white-streaked face and a red patch on the forehead, this 8- to 9-inch woodpecker also has a long, white wing patch and a yellowish belly. Males have a red throat patch, while females have a white one.

VOICE A "cherr" that spirals downward in pitch

RANGE IN APPALACHIAN TRAIL STATES Tends to winter in the Southern states, is almost a year-round resident in the mid-Atlantic states, and is usually only found north of New York during the summer months

on their red heads enables them to more easily extract themselves from inside the body cavities of the carrion they feed upon. Ranging mostly from Georgia to the southern portion of Pennsylvania, but expanding their range a little farther northward, black vultures (*Coragyps atratus*) have short black tails and must flap and glide a bit more than the turkey vulture to maintain a soaring flight.

When walking through a mature deciduous forest, you may notice holes of varying sizes drilled into the bark of the trees. Woodpeckers have special air pockets in their heads to soften and absorb the shock of hammering these tree trunks. Yellow-bellied sapsuckers (*Sphyrapicus varius*) drill rows of small, circular holes; sap rises into the cavities; and, true to their name, these woodpeckers feed by sucking the liquid out with long, bristly tongues. Often ants and other insects are attracted by the trees' sweet juices and the sapsucker can obtain both dinner and dessert from just one hole.

Pileated woodpeckers (*Drycopus pileatus*) inhabit the same environment as yellow-bellied sapsuckers, but the holes they make are large, deep, and almost rectangular. Be sure to listen for the demented call of a pileated woodpecker when in the deep woods. If you don't know what it sounds like, just think of Woody Woodpecker; he and his laugh were patterned after the acorn woodpecker's call, which sounds somewhat like the pileated's call. If, as many ornithologists believe, the ivory-billed woodpecker (*Campephilus principalis*) truly has become extinct, then the nearly 20-inch pileated has inherited the status of being North America's largest woodpecker.

Because they share many of the same identifying marks—white back, white underparts, white-spotted black wings, and black-and-white-streaked heads—the downy woodpecker (*Picoides pubescens*) is hard to distinguish from the larger hairy woodpecker (*Picoides villosus*). Besides overall body size, the best way to tell them apart is that the downy's bill is about half the size of its head, while the hairy's bill is almost as long as its head. Like all the woodpeckers mentioned, the northern flicker (*Colaptes auratus*) can be found along the entire AT during at least some portion of the year.

RED-EYED VIREO

LATIN NAME *Vireo olivaceus*

DESCRIPTION About 6 inches long with a wingspan of about 10 inches, the red-eyed vireo has an olive-colored back, a gray cap, and a noticeable white eyebrow stripe bordered with black. You usually have to be at close range to be able to identify the bright red eyes.

VOICE Whistled phrases separated by pauses are repeated over and over again—as many as 40 times a minute. This has been described as a monotonous tweedling.

RANGE IN APPALACHIAN TRAIL STATES Residents of North America for only part of the year, red-eyed vireos are found from Georgia to Maine during the warmer months

Bore holes in the ground may be the mark of an American woodcock (*Scolopax minor*). Its 3-inch beak has a flexible tip and upper mandible whose forward half can be bent upward. Using this tip like a pair of fingers, the woodcock nimbly pulls out of the ground the earthworms that make up the bulk of its diet; it has been observed consuming its weight in worms within a 24-hour period.

Inhabiting the AT forests during the summer months, eastern wood pewees (*Contopus virens*) and great crested flycatchers (*Myiarchus crinitus*) often provide the melody hikers wake up to in the morning. The flutelike songs of the veery (*Catharus fuscescens*) and the wood thrush (*Hylocichla mustelina*) and the "Teacher! Teacher! Teacher!" cry of the ovenbird (*Seiurus aurocapillus*) sometimes furnish background music for an entire day.

The song of what may be the eastern deciduous forest's most common nesting bird, the red-eyed vireo (*Vireo olivaceus*), is also sung throughout the sunlit hours. Often joining in this symphony is the "Drink-Your-Tea!" of the rufous-sided towhee (*Pipilo erythrophthalmus*) and the down-slurred whistle "Here! Here! Here! Here!" of a tufted titmouse (*Parus bicolor*). In the higher elevations of New England, the upward-lilting song of the Swainson's thrush (*Catharus ustulatus*) might be added.

During rest breaks, AT hikers have been entertained by the antics of the small brown creeper (*Certhia americana*), which feeds by spirally creeping up one tree and then dropping to the base of another and starting up again.

One of the largest birds inhabiting the eastern forests throughout the year, wild turkeys (*Meleagris gallopavo*) need great expanses of undeveloped, timbered country to survive, and the extensive wooded areas of the AT support a large population of this bird, which seems to prefer walking over flying. Chances are good that during the summer you will see a family flock making use of the pathway in front of you; the sexes tend to separate during the colder times of the year. Ranging from 2.5 to 4 feet in size, turkeys are almost always hunting for food. Scratchings along the edge of the trail may

WILD TURKEY

LATIN NAME *Meleagris gallopavo*

DESCRIPTION The naked head is bluish in color with red wattles (more pronounced in the males) down the throat. The body is covered by iridescent brownish-olive feathers, and the male possesses a beard of hairlike feathers hanging from the breast.

VOICE Gobbles similarly to domestic turkeys. Females cluck to keep brood together.

RANGE IN APPALACHIAN TRAIL STATES Georgia to southern New England

mark where they have been digging for beetles and other insects; searches for their favorite nuts, such as acorns, leave large areas of the forest floor cleared of decaying leaves and other small deadfall. Like deer, a portion of the turkey's diet includes poison ivy.

In a midsummer forest of deep greens, dark browns, and rocky grays, the flaming-red body and dark black wings of a male scarlet tanager (*Piranga olivacea*) stand out and make him hard to misidentify. He is often accompanied by the female, whose slightly smaller body is yellowish below and greenish above, with grayish-brown wings. Recognized by a distinctive red bib, the rose-breasted grosbeak (*Pheucticus ludovicianus*) is found throughout the northern states but extends its population as far south as Georgia by remaining at the elevations provided by the Appalachian Mountains.

The term *woodlands* is sometimes applied by birders to places that are in the transition phase between fields and dense forests. Such spots are usually areas that were once heavily forested and are now recovering from the effects of fire, flooding, ice storms, logging, farming, or some other human disturbance. More undergrowth and bushy plants will be found here than in the deep woods, and this undergrowth, when coupled with thickets found along the woodland's edge, provides habitat for a wide variety of birds.

The least flycatcher (*Empidonax minimus*) and the yellow warbler (*Dendroica petechia*) both spend their days searching for insects and nesting in the crotches of small trees in the woodlands environment. Other warblers, such as the chestnut-sided

A tufted titmouse perches on a tree branch.

HOUSE SPARROW

LATIN NAME *Passer domesticus*

DESCRIPTION During the summer, the male house sparrow has a rich chestnut-colored back and nape, white cheeks, and a prominent black rib. After molting in the fall, gray feather tips tend to obscure these features. Females have buff eyebrows and lack the black bib.

VOICE The song is a series of repeated musical chirps.

RANGE IN APPALACHIAN TRAIL STATES Georgia to Maine

warbler (*Dendroica pensylvanica*), the mourning warbler (*Oporornis philadelphia*), and the common yellowthroat (*Geothlypis trichas*), share the same nesting and feeding habits. In addition to insects, the indigo bunting (*Passerina cyanea*) consumes seeds, berries, and grains. This sparrow-size bird is such a deep blue that, in all but the brightest of lights, it may look black. An indigo bunting's eggs may also make you question whether your eyes can tell one color from another, for in varying lights, they will look green, blue, and white.

With a catlike mewing call, gray catbirds (*Dumetella carolinensis*) deftly slip through the tangled vines or branches of low shrubs as they leave their well-hidden nests. During the winter, the tiny American tree sparrow (*Spizella arborea*) inhabits open woodlands along the AT, but as its Latin species name suggests, spends the summer in the subarctic lands of northern Canada and Alaska.

At about the time hikers camping next to a field (such as Rice Field Shelter in southwest Virginia or Campbell Shelter in central Virginia) are trying to fall asleep, they may be serenaded by a nocturnal whip-poor-will (*Caprimulgus vociferus*), which will whistle out its name for hours on end. From Georgia to Connecticut, the song could be mixed with that of a quail, the bobwhite (*Colinus virginianus*), which also repeats its name over and over for long periods of time.

Throughout the length of the AT, you might notice small handcrafted birdhouses placed along the edges of open meadows and small boggy areas. Due to the loss of nesting cavities as well as competition from European starlings (*Sturnus vulgaris*) and house sparrows (*Passer domesticus*), eastern bluebird (*Sialia sialis*) populations steadily declined during the middle of the 20th century. In 1978, after the formation of the North American Bluebird Society, bird enthusiasts began to place nesting boxes in the bluebird's natural habitats, and as a result, the populations have begun to recover. The male of most bird species is almost always the more colorfully plumed, but the upper parts of the female bluebird can be as deeply blue as those of her male counterpart.

Native Americans were the first to put hollow gourds on poles for purple martins (*Progne subis*) to nest in. Martins have historically lived in trees, in caves, and among

EASTERN KINGBIRD

LATIN NAME *Tyrannus tyrannus*

DESCRIPTION About 8 inches long, this bird appears black on its upper part and white on its lower. A white tip across the width of its tail is a discernible identifying mark.

VOICE A rapid series of high notes of "zeer zeer zeer" or "dzee dzee dzee." It also repeats the sequence "kit-kit-kitter."

RANGE IN APPALACHIAN TRAIL STATES Spending winter in South America, eastern kingbirds inhabit the AT from Georgia to Maine during the warmer months.

rocks, but today many people have constructed elaborate condos for these birds, which prefer to live in large colonies. Their short, wide beaks enable them to scoop up grasshoppers, moths, butterflies, and other insects while on the wing. In the fall, purple martins gather by the thousands and move south to the Amazon Valley of Brazil.

Lacking the aid of human benefactors, killdeer (*Charadrius vociferus*) nest in small depressions on bare ground or in grassy pastures. Although it is a plover—a bird usually associated with shores and beaches—the killdeer is more often found in open farm country or along the edges of meadow ponds. Like the grouse, it performs the broken-wing act (see page 136).

Songbirds populate agricultural fields and open meadows in great numbers. The vesper sparrow (*Poocetes gramineus*), field sparrow (*Spizella pusilla*), and chipping sparrow (*Spizella passerina*) all feed on the insects and weed seeds found in such places.

A bluebird rests on a barbed wire fence.

Often seen sitting on a fence post with its head and beak raised upward in song is the brown and yellow eastern meadowlark (*Sturnella magna*). Hoarsely singing out its name, the phoebe (*Sayornis phoebe*) is one of the first to arrive in the spring from its winter home on the Gulf Coast and is one of the last to leave in the fall. This extended period of inhabitation along the AT makes its song a familiar one to thru-hikers throughout their entire trek.

A robin-size flycatcher, the eastern kingbird (*Tyrannus tyrannus*) sits on low limbs and darts out after flying insects. Very territorial, they chase larger birds out of their area, making a variety of maneuvers and aggressive attacks, such as diving onto

COMMON LOON

LATIN NAME *Gavia immer*

DESCRIPTION 32 inches long with a wingspan of close to 60 inches, the common loon has a checkered black-and-white back with a dark green head during the summer and is dark brown and white during the winter.

VOICE Silent during the winter, this loon's call during the summer has been likened to a yodeling, forlorn cry or deranged laugh. They sometimes bark out a "cwuck" while in flight.

RANGE IN APPALACHIAN TRAIL STATES Although occasionally seen in Vermont and New Hampshire, the common loon is most often sighted in Maine.

invaders' backs. Afterward, they perform an unusual tumbling flight, seemingly acting upon triumphant emotions.

Preferring the cattails of marshy areas, red-winged blackbirds (*Agelaius phoeniceus*) will sometimes nest in the tall weeds along bog edges or other watery areas. They are the only all-black bird with bright red and yellow shoulder patches, so identification is quite easy. Summering in the spruce bogs and wet woodlands of New England and wintering in woods and fields south of Massachusetts, the rusty blackbird (*Euphagus carolinus*) is a dull black all over and has pale yellow eyes. Several warblers, especially palm warblers (*Denroica palmarum*) and northern waterthrushes (*Seiurus noveboracensis*), and a wren, the marsh wren (*Cistothorus palustris*), also visit the northern bogs and marshy areas during the warmer months.

Spending most of their summers in the open waters of the lakes, ponds, and streams of New England, common loons (*Gavia immer*) venture ashore only during the breeding and nesting season. Inside their nests of vegetable debris, most often constructed on sandy spits jutting out into the water, the female lays two dull-green eggs that hatch after an incubation period of about 29 days. Loons dive and swim underwater so swiftly that they can easily outswim fish, which comprise the bulk of their diet. They also dive to escape danger, and they are capable of staying submerged for up to three minutes. When hikers are camped in pondside shelters or campsites, such as Little Rock Pond in Vermont, Ethan Pond in New Hampshire, and Sabbath Day Pond and Moxie Bald Lean-To in Maine, the maniacal, laughing calls of loons may make them feel as if they are within the confines of some primitive forest or jungle.

All of the loon's several calls have an eerie sound, but each serves a different purpose. The long, drawn-out wail is used to keep a pair in contact, the yodel-like call is used to mark territory, and the tremolo expresses alarm and danger.

Not just in New England but throughout the AT, other birds found on or near water, especially during the summer months, are mallard ducks (*Anas platyrhynchos*), American black ducks (*Anas rubripes*), and blue-winged teals (*Anas discors*)—all of which prefer shallow water where they feed on bottom vegetation. Most often seen on larger bodies of water during the winter are common mergansers (*Mergus merganser*) and common goldeneyes (*Bucephala clangula*).

The great blue heron (*Ardea herodias*), the eastern United States' largest and most widespread heron, frequents marshes, swamps, and river and lake edges but has even been seen wading in Whitetop Laurel and Beaverdam Creeks within the town limits of Damascus, Virginia. Standing motionless in the water, it waits for its dinner of a fish, snake, mouse, frog, or small bird to come close enough to be quickly grabbed and consumed. With a wingspan of nearly 70 inches, the flight of a great blue is truly something to behold. This large bird of approximately 50 inches in height makes its summer home as far north as Ontario, Canada, but usually migrates back to coastal waters south of Massachusetts for the winter. The green-backed heron (*Butorides striatus*), a much smaller relative, inhabits a wider range but is seen less often on the AT than the great blue.

The fall migration begins in September as songbirds take advantage of cold fronts moving in from the north to ride the winds southward. As on their northward journey, they land if the winds die down, feeding and waiting for the next front to move through. For many bird enthusiasts this migration seems somewhat less spectacular than the one in the spring. The birds' singing is diminished, travel appears to be at more of an unhurried pace, and the colorful plumage of the breeding season has been replaced by duller winter feathers.

For hawk-watchers, though, fall is the most exciting time of the year. Having arrived somewhat inconspicuously in the spring, hawks take advantage of seasonal atmospheric conditions to travel southward by the thousands in autumn. Heated air from rays of the sun striking cliffs and rock outcroppings couples with warm air rising from the lowlands to create forceful drafts, or thermals, that the hawks use to soar upward. In addition, by gliding near the crest of the ridges, they are able to take advantage of the northwesterly winds striking the Appalachians, where air currents are forced across the mountain crests, providing more uplift.

BALD EAGLE

LATIN NAME *Haliaeetus leucocephalus*

DESCRIPTION About 40 inches in length, the mature bald eagle has a white head, a white tail, and a very dark body. Immature birds have a large amount of white under their wings and on their breasts.

VOICE Repeated harsh and piercing screams while in flight; a series of chirps at the nesting site

RANGE IN APPALACHIAN TRAIL STATES It is possible, but rare, to see a bald eagle just about anywhere from Georgia to Maine.

An osprey carries nesting material.

Many places along the AT provide front-row seats from which to watch this seasonal phenomenon. Some of the premier sites include Peters Mountain and Rockfish Gap in central Virginia, Stony Man Mountain and Mary's Rock in Shenandoah National Park, Washington Monument State Park in Maryland, and Sunrise Mountain in New Jersey. A blue-blazed pathway on Blue Mountain near Eckville, Pennsylvania, leads from the AT to the Hawk Mountain Sanctuary. Established in 1934 as the first refuge developed to protect migrating birds of prey, the sanctuary now hosts hundreds of visitors who gather each fall to witness the thousands of birds winging by.

Sometimes as early as mid-August, ospreys (*Pandion haliaetus*), American kestrels (*Falco sparverius*), and a few bald eagles (*Haliaeetus leucocephalus*) may begin the procession southward. The migration begins in earnest in mid-September, when temperatures are still quite mild, as the broad-winged hawks (*Buteo platypterus*) take to the skies. Peak daily sightings of several thousand are not uncommon, and on record days more than 10,000 have been reported. One of the most rewarding aerial attractions along the AT is the opportunity to witness a kettle—a flock of broad-wings riding a thermal, the hundreds of birds rising as one giant spiral in the sky. Broad-wings may end up taking journeys of more than 4,000 miles, migrating from the woodlands of Maine to forests in Peru.

In the early weeks of October, peregrine falcons (*Falco peregrinus*) join the movement, on their way to Mexico and Central America. Up until the mid-1950s, peregrines could be seen rocketing about the skies above the AT at speeds in excess of 100 miles per hour. Yet, like the osprey, bald eagle, and other raptors, they fell to the cumulative effects of DDT. The insecticide caused some hatchlings to be born deformed, but more often it weakened the shells of the birds' eggs to the point that the eggs simply could not hold together long enough for the chicks to be born. Now that DDT has been banned in the United States, breeding peregrine falcons in captivity and then releasing them into the wild has proven somewhat successful, thanks to the combined efforts of scientists, concerned citizens, governmental agencies, and the Appalachian Trail Conservancy and its volunteers.

Release sites along the AT have included Big Bald in North Carolina, Cold Mountain in central Virginia, Hawksbill Mountain in Shenandoah National Park, and Holts Ledge in New Hampshire. In recent years, peregrine falcon pairs have been seen near Bear Mountain Bridge in New York, on Deer Leap Mountain close to the AT in

RED-TAILED HAWK

LATIN NAME *Buteo jamaicensis*

DESCRIPTION Averaging 23 inches in length, mature red-tailed hawks have yellow feet, mottled brown-and-white wings and backs, and a rounded tail whose upper surface is noticeably red (but hard to make out when soaring).

VOICE A piercing, downward-sliding scream

RANGE IN APPALACHIAN TRAIL STATES From Georgia to southern New England throughout the year; found in northern New England during the summer months

Vermont, and at Holts Ledge in New Hampshire. Nesting falcons are very vulnerable to human disturbance, and there have been instances when portions of the AT have been temporarily detoured to protect them. If you happen to be hiking along a stretch of the AT that you've been wanting to do for a long time and you come across a sign rerouting you, don't be disappointed; as you take the alternate route, be content in knowing you are helping the world's fastest creatures slowly make a comeback.

As the cooler nights and shorter days of October cause color changes in the leaves, one of the smallest hawks, the sharp-shinned hawk (*Accipiter striatus*), becomes the dominant migrant. Joining the procession at this time are the larger but less numerous Cooper's hawks (*Accipiter cooperii*), which feed upon common medium-size birds such as jays, starlings, and mourning doves.

Making use of the cold winds of November, red-tailed hawks (*Buteo jamaicensis*) zip by the now-leafless trees, not as large flocks but usually as solitary birds winging their way southward. Compared to the others, their journey may be short, sometimes only taking them from the rolling farmlands of the Berkshire Hills of Massachusetts to open spaces close to the AT in Maryland. Making their way to a warmer climate at about the same time are red-shouldered hawks (*Buteo lineatus*) and northern harriers (*Circus cyaneus*).

Soaring over an Appalachian Trail that could be covered by December snows, northern goshawks (*Accipiter gentilis*), which may have spent the summer in northern Canada, and golden eagles (*Aquila chrysaetos*), possibly hatched in the spring in the tundra around Canada's Hudson Bay, bring the migratory season to a close.

The annual cycle will begin anew when phoebes, winter wrens, black-and-white warblers, and solitary vireos begin to wing their way northward along the mountains in mid-March.

CHAPTER 8

Of Moist Skin and Scales

In the woods too, a man casts off his years, as the snake

its slough, and at what period soever of life, is always a child.

In the woods, is perpetual youth.

~ Ralph Waldo Emerson

MILLIONS OF YEARS AGO, certain creatures crawled out of the ancient oceans and began to spread across the land. Even though they were able to breathe in the open air and move about on the ground, evolution left these amphibians poorly adapted for terrestrial life. Their moist skin, which aided in respiration and helped prevent dehydration, kept them confined to damp or watery environments. In addition, their jellylike eggs could not survive in air, so they had to return to water or to sheltered, moist cavities to breed.

The amphibians gave rise to reptiles, animals completely adapted to life on land. The dry, scaly skin of reptiles enables them to venture far from water and, unlike amphibians (which can breathe through their moist skin), they use only their lungs for respiration. Reptiles were further able to divorce themselves from the aquatic environment because their eggs, like those of birds, are tough-shelled to prevent desiccation.

AMPHIBIANS

THE WORD *AMPHIBIAN*, derived from Greek words meaning "living a double life," is applied to animals that typically begin life in water and later move out onto land. Amphibians living along the AT include the members of two major orders, the salamanders and the frogs and toads.

Salamanders

The abundant precipitation that falls upon the AT provides the perfect environment for salamanders. Because they range from being aquatic to completely terrestrial, you may see salamanders not only in small streams or in the trailside springs from which you obtain your drinking water but also scurrying from one hiding place to another under forest litter and rocks.

All salamanders look like lizards, but they have moist skin and lack the scales, claws, and external ear openings that characterize the reptiles. Close to 40 species may be found along the trail. The largest family, the lungless salamanders, are believed to have originated in the Southern Appalachians. What is most fascinating to biologists is that lungless salamanders appear to still be evolving. For example, research has shown that a Jordan's salamander (*Plethodon jordani*), also called an Appalachian woodland salamander, found on one ridgeline can be different from those found a few peaks away. They range from Georgia to southern Virginia, but because their need for certain habitats traps them in isolated populations, biologists theorize that those in one place may evolve into an entirely different species from those in another.

Even different species are so similar that not only is identification difficult, but it is also hard to dismiss the notion that they evolved from a common ancestor. The Shenandoah salamander (*Plethodon shenandoah*), found only on the talus slopes of Stony Man and Hawksbill Mountains and The Pinnacles in Shenandoah National Park, is so similar to the red-backed salamander (*Plethodon cinereus*) that it can be distinguished only by its darker, nearly black belly. The territorial red-backed salamander, ranging from North Carolina to Maine, keeps the Shenandoah salamander from colonizing the moist forest floor around its rocky habitat. The Shenandoah survives only because it is able to exist in dry conditions unsuitable for the red-backed salamander.

Another member of the lungless family, the four-toed salamander (*Hemidactylium scutatum*), lives under forest litter and rocks near boggy areas and is found in disjunct populations from Georgia to New England. Its reddish tail is constricted at the base so that it breaks off easily to provide an escape from predators.

Spending a great portion of their lives in water, newts, a family of the salamander order, may wander miles away from their home stream, but they almost always return to breed. Researchers say that the nervous systems in some newts can map the terrain

Red-spotted newt (in red eft stage)

they cross and the mapped information can be recalled when it is time to return. The red-spotted newts (*Notophthalmus viridescens viridescens*) have an additional mechanism at their disposal: they can detect the earth's magnetic field and are able to use it as a directional reference.

Newts are most often seen along the trail in their immature stage, when they are referred to as efts. Efts are born on land, but once they reach adulthood, they spend most of their lives in water. The most common is the red eft, an immature red-spotted newt, which ranges from Georgia to Maine. Feeding on insects, worms, amphibian eggs, larvae, and small crustaceans, they are bright red or orange and have a distinctive series of black-edged red-orange spots on their backs.

Frogs and Toads

Although as tadpoles they have well-developed tails that are their exclusive means of movement, frogs and toads can be distinguished from other amphibians by the absence of a tail in the adult stage. Scientists speculate that tails disappear as frogs and toads mature because tails would get in the way of their large hind legs, which are designed for leaping and hopping. Frogs may be differentiated from toads by their generally longer legs, smoother skin, and greater swimming abilities. Toads are usually plumper than frogs and they hop more than leap. In addition, the toads' conspicuous warts secrete chemicals that are poisonous to predators.

Having spent the winter in old logs and stumps and under leaf litter, wood frogs (*Rana sylvatica*), found from Georgia to Maine, are among the first to emerge in the spring. They average about 2 inches in size, can range from pink to tan to dark brown, and have prominent ridges of skin running down the body from behind each eye. As the sound floats upon the surface of a pond, the series of short, raspy, low-pitched clacking calls that a single male emits during breeding season is quite weak, but a group calling together as a chorus can sound like ducks quacking in the distance. The only North American frogs found above the Arctic Circle, wood frogs can be frenzied breeders. After depositing fertilized eggs in sometimes massive communal clusters, they retreat into the forest, often wandering far from water.

Tiny spring peepers (*Hyla crucifer*) are the next to add their voices to the spring symphony with their chorus of high-pitched, birdlike "peeps," becoming almost deafening when heard at close range. Although they have been heard into late October, peepers are most vocal in early spring, as AT hikers who camp in April and May next to the pond about 4 miles north of Hot Springs, North Carolina, can attest. Later in the summer, spring peepers will be found 50–60 feet up in the trees.

Mountain chorus frogs (*Pseudacris brachyphona*) resemble spring peepers but have smaller toe pads and a white line on the upper lip. After breeding in shallow ponds, ditches, and small pools along stream edges, they prefer hilly woodlands from Georgia to the southern portion of Pennsylvania.

Nocturnal pickerel frogs (*Rana palustris*) live in a variety of aquatic environments close to bogs, slow-moving water, and damp areas with low, dense vegetation. Their slender bodies are smooth-skinned and tan, their bellies and the undersurfaces of the hind legs are bright yellow to orange, and there is a light stripe across the jaw. The mating call of the male pickerel has been likened to the low, rolling snore of a very tired human being.

The largest frog inhabiting the United States, the cannibalistic bullfrog (*Rana catesbeiana),* may attain a length of up to 8 inches and can be found along the entire AT. With powerful hind legs, it has been seen jumping 8–9 feet in one leap. Heard throughout the summer, its familiar, low, deep call of "jug-o-rum" carries for more than a quarter mile and has greeted many hikers as they approached Punch Bowl Shelter in central Virginia.

About half the size of the bullfrog, green frogs (*Rana clamitans*) may also be seen up and down the trail. Their call is a low, explosive, twangylike "c'tung," but they often let out a high-pitched "squeenk" when startled and jumping for safety.

Common throughout the more northern trail states, northern leopard frogs (*Rana pipiens*) can inhabit freshwater sites with abundant vegetation, as well as brackish marshes and even damp fields. The male's harsh call—a low, grating snore of about 3 seconds—is followed by several short, guttural grunts. These are more than likely the species of frog you dissected in high school biology class.

Cope's gray tree frog (*Hyla chrysoscelis*) and the common gray tree frog (*Hyla versicolor*) are identical in appearance and share the same range from Georgia to Maine. Both live high in the trees and descend only at night, either to mate or to just join in a chorus of loud, clattering trills. Their breeding habits have been likened to a marathon, with the actual mating act lasting up to four hours. Another tree frog, the northern cricket frog (*Acris crepitans*), ranges from Georgia to New York but is somewhat of a rare sight along the trail. Its call is reminiscent of the sound of two small pebbles clicking together.

The plump-looking American toad (*Bufo americanus*) is the toad you are most likely to encounter from Georgia to Maine. Brown to olive in color, it has various patterns of lighter, yellowish skin and warts of different sizes on its back, sides, and legs. Behind each one of its eyes is a raised, smooth, brown lump—the parotoid gland—that secretes a sticky white poison used as a defense. In addition to inflaming the mouth and throat of a predator, the toxin causes nausea, irregular heartbeats, and occasionally death. Often burrowing into soft soil, American toads inhabit a variety of environments, from heavy forests to open meadows to backyards in the inner city.

The color of Woodhouse's toad (*Bufo woodhousei*), ranging from Georgia to New Hampshire, varies widely, but there is always a light, cream-colored stripe down the center of the back. This toad sometimes hybridizes with American toads, making some individuals hard to identify.

Because eastern spadefoot toads (*Scaphiopus holbrooki*), ranging from Georgia to New Hampshire, are burrowing animals that only emerge after dark and breed only after heavy rains, they are rarely seen by AT hikers. Their olive-colored, stocky bodies are covered in relatively smooth skin; their warts are not as easily discerned as those on the American toads. A chorus of eastern spadefoots can sound almost like the cacophony of a flock of crows.

Pickerel frog

REPTILES

REPTILES EVOLVED FROM ANCIENT AMPHIBIANS about 300 million years ago and reached their zenith during the Mesozoic era, when they became the dominant vertebrates inhabiting the land, sea, and air. From that point they declined, and of the ones living today, two orders inhabit the Appalachian Trail environment—the turtles and the lizards and snakes.

Turtles

Turtles are the most ancient of all living reptiles and have changed little since their origins about 200 million years ago. Yet their unique makeup does not appear closely related to other reptiles, and their true origin continues to baffle those who study them.

Because of its wide range of habitats, from moist forestlands to wet meadows and floodplains, the eastern box turtle (*Terrepene carolina*) is probably the most seen turtle along the AT. It was given its name because it is the only turtle able to box itself in completely, being able to tightly close its plastron (lower shell) against its high-domed, yellow-to-orange mottled carapace (upper shell).

The painted turtle (*Chrysemys picta*) is the most numerous turtle in North America. The distinctive red markings on the sides of its shell and the red and yellow stripes on its tail, legs, and head make identification easy. Found up and down the trail in quiet waters with muddy bottoms and plentiful vegetation, they are often seen basking on logs floating in the water along the AT as it follows the C&O Canal Towpath in Maryland.

Endowed with powerful jaws, the snapping turtle (*Chelydra serpentina*) can grow up to 18 inches in length and weigh more than 40 pounds. Its saw-toothed tail may be as long as its tan to dark brown carapace, which is serrated toward the rear. Under water, snapping turtles usually do not bite, but on land they can become mean and aggressive, with even hatchlings snapping wildly at objects perceived as intruders.

The bog turtle (*Clemmys muhlenbergi*) was once thought to be an endangered species, but research has shown it is just so secretive that it is rarely seen. One of the smallest turtles in the world, it quickly burrows into mud or debris when disturbed and spends the winter buried deep in the muck of underground waterways.

Yellow dots on the head and shell of the spotted turtle (*Clemmys guttata*), ranging sporadically from Virginia to Maine, make it easy to identify. Like the painted turtle, it has been seen along the C&O Canal Towpath in Maryland. Spotted turtles are amazingly intelligent; scientific studies have shown they have an ability to correctly negotiate mazes.

Usually found along the AT from northern Virginia to Maine, wood turtles (*Clemmys insculpta*) are easily recognized by their bright, orange-red skin and a carapace that looks like it has a series of deeply grooved, irregular pyramids on top of it. Prefer-ring moist woods, they move into open land to feed, and retreat to ponds, swamps, and slow-moving waters in dry seasons. Once collected for food, wood turtles are suffering from habitat loss and are a protected species in a number of states.

Endowed with a musky odor as a warning to predators, stinkpot, or eastern musk, turtles (*Sternotherus odoratus*) have two light stripes on their heads and are scarce in their range along the AT from Georgia to New Hampshire. Highly aquatic, they bask in shallow water or on floating vegetation with just the center of their carapace—which is often covered with algae and moss—showing to the sun.

Lizards and Snakes

Lizards have rough, scaly skin. Like snakes, they shed, or molt, their skin as they grow. Because they are cold-blooded, lizards need to lie in the sun to warm themselves, and even though many of them can swim, they don't spend all their time in the water.

In the same family as the iguanas of the American Southwest, abundant eastern fence lizards (*Sceloporus undulatus*) inhabit the more sun-exposed places along the AT. Rarely are they seen in dense woods or higher elevations. Males in search of mates are very territorial and defend against competitors by bobbing their heads up and down and standing high to display the bright, black-bordered blue patches of their bellies. Many subspecies of this lizard are scattered throughout the United States.

Of the lizards found along the trail, members of the skink family are seen most often. Five-lined skinks (*Eumeces fasciatus*) range from Georgia to southern New England and are probably the most abundant lizards on the AT. The immature have five well-defined lines along their back and bright blue tails. With age these characteristics fade and become less obvious. These skinks live belowground but are often seen basking on logs or the lower portions of tree trunks, or wandering the forest floor in search of insects, worms, spiders, other lizards, and even mice. The five-lined skink's tail will detach when grasped, allowing it to escape and grow another. As an additional defense, their bite is powerful enough to draw blood.

The broad-headed skink (*Eumeces laticeps*) is the largest Appalachian Trail skink, growing up to 12 inches in length. The five broad, light stripes found on the young fade as males mature, but females usually retain at least a remnant of this pattern. Found from Georgia to about the Maryland–Pennsylvania border, they inhabit moist woodlands at the mid- to lower elevations, preferring warmer temperatures than the five-lined skink.

Inhabiting about the same range, though found only in modest, localized popu-lations, ground skinks (*Scincella lateralis*) are the smallest lizards along the AT. Their brown bodies have black stripes along the sides, and they rarely grow to be more than 5 inches long.

Although snakes seem to hold a special fascination for people, they are among some of the most misunderstood animals in the world. They are not slimy, but rather possess a dry, scaly skin. A snake's long, forked tongue is harmless; it is used to collect odorous particles to be brought into the mouth and into contact with smell-sensitive organs, supplementing sensations received through the nostrils. Snakes may be, and have been, encountered just about anywhere along the trail, but among the spots you are most likely to encounter them are Blackrock in Shenandoah National Park; Buzzard Rocks in northern Virginia; and Balanced Rock, about 0.5 mile north of Dan's Pulpit, in Pennsylvania.

All snakes can swim, but contrary to what many people appear to believe, water moccasins (*Agkistrodon piscivorus*), also called cottonmouths, do not occur along the Appalachian Trail. These venomous snakes populate only the coastal areas and the Piedmont of North Carolina and Virginia. Though found in Georgia and Tennessee, they do not inhabit the higher elevations through which the AT passes in these states.

The two venomous snakes that do inhabit trail lands are the copperhead (*Agkistrodon contortrix*) and the timber rattlesnake (*Crotalus horridus*). Both can be differentiated from other snakes by their thicker bodies, thin necks, triangular heads, and vertical pupils—although if you can make out the pupils, you are probably too close. They also have a heat-sensitive pit, which aids in locating warm-blooded prey, on each side of their heads between the eye and nostril.

Although there are variations, the copperhead's tan body has darker-colored, hourglass-shaped markings unique to its species. Basking during day in the spring and fall, and having a tendency to become nocturnal in warm summer temperatures, they can be well camouflaged by leaf litter on the forest floor.

Timber rattlesnakes have large, heavy bodies, typically with dark blotches in the front that become fused to form crossbands in the back. Color can range widely from yellow to pinkish gray to black, but the tail is almost always black. In some populations, the identifying features fade and body color gets darker as the snake matures, making them look almost like black racer snakes. Of course, no matter what color, rattlesnakes will usually rattle when threatened.

Please refrain from slaying these, or any snakes, along the trail. Not only do they have as much right, if not more, than you to be in the woods, they provide a valuable service by keeping rodents and other pests in check. Due to indiscriminate killing, both of the venomous snakes are becoming rarer sights. Although bites do occur, very few are reported on the trail, and few deaths have been attributed to either snake. However, since all snakebites do contain certain bacteria, medical attention should be sought as quickly as possible if you are bitten.

The nonvenomous eastern hognose snake (*Heterodon platyrhinos*), whose defense mechanisms can be almost comical at times, is one of the snakes you are most likely to see on the trail between Georgia and Vermont. When first threatened, the hognose may shake its tail in the leaves, mimicking the sound of a rattlesnake. Upon further provocation, it will puff up (thus its other common name, puff adder), hiss, and flatten its neck like a cobra. If all else fails, the hognose will simply roll over and play dead. However, it will give this charade away because, if turned onto its stomach, it promptly flips over onto its back again.

Very common along the AT, the black racer snake (*Coluber constrictor*) is uniformly black with a bit of white on the chin. Growing to be more than 6 feet long, it is often encountered stretched out to its full length across the trail. Although it can move at great speeds, it sometimes refuses to give way, remaining steadfast on a favorite sunning spot and vibrating its tail in dead vegetation to imitate the sound of a rattlesnake.

The common garter snake (*Thamnophis sirtalis*) is the most widely distributed snake in North America. Because coloration varies, identification can be difficult. Individuals can be various shades of red, brown, blue, or green, with prominent back and side stripes. Yet the stripes may be absent and a spotted pattern can be present. Almost always associated with damp environments, they do frequent some of the higher peaks along the trail. In addition to biting when threatened, they release an offensive-smelling, musky liquid. Also with stripes, the eastern ribbon snake (*Thamnophis sauritus*) has been confused with common garter snakes, but this semiaquatic snake is almost always encountered in damp meadows or near pond and stream edges in lower elevations.

Copperhead (left) and rattlesnake

The widely distributed brown snake (*Storeria dekayi*) also expels a musk when feeling endangered. Growing to only about 18 inches, they can be gray, brown, or reddish brown, and have two rows of small dark spots on both sides of a pale stripe on their backs. They have been found huddling together in great numbers during hibernation.

Often mistaken for copperheads because of their tan or copper skin, northern water snakes (*Nerodia sipedon*) do not have hourglass markings, but do have dark crossbands on the neck area (which sometimes go to midbody) with dark blotches and alternating lateral bars on the remainder of their bodies. Active both day and night, they frequently climb onto low, overhanging limbs. Sadly, they are killed by people who mistake them for water moccasins as they bask on logs in the water. They are not venomous, but an anticoagulant in their saliva will cause bite wounds to bleed profusely.

Also mistaken for copperheads because of their tan color and darker blotches down the length of their bodies, eastern milk snakes (*Lampropeltis triangulum*) received their common name from the once-held belief that they were capable of milking cows. They tend to favor woodlands along the length of the trail, but have been observed slithering through the balds of North Carolina, Tennessee, and Virginia.

Ringneck snakes (*Diadophis punctatus*), which discharge a musk when frightened, are readily distinguished by their bright yellow or orange collars, and yellow, orange, or red undersides. Identifying red-bellied snakes (*Storeria occipitomaculata*) is harder because individuals may be brown, gray, or black and can have one wide stripe or four faint narrow stripes or five stripes down the back. Three orange to yellowish spots on the nape of the neck sometimes fuse into a single band.

CHAPTER 9
Some Suggested Hikes

It is better to wear out one's shoes than one's sheets.

~ Genoese proverb

IT IS ALL WELL AND GOOD to read this and other books about the Appalachian Trail, but to really appreciate it you need to be out there hiking on it. So go take a hike!

The following listing of hikes is not so much a "best of" but rather a "get acquainted with" the AT. Some hikes were selected for their grand vistas, others for ease of access, and still others for their waterfalls or the beauty of their forests. To give you an option, almost all of them make use of connecting routes. You can either do a round-trip journey or elect to do a longer circuit hike.

On a *round-trip* hike, you go to your destination on the AT and return by the same route. On a *circuit* hike, you take a circular route to return to your starting point, rewalking very little, if any, of the same ground. A *one-way* hike is just that—you walk in one direction, ending the trip at a different point from where you started. A one-way hike necessitates a car shuttle.

Because use of the Appalachian Trail has increased and because its resources need increased protection, you should practice leave-no-trace hiking and camping techniques. Endorsed by almost every organization connected with the outdoors, the Leave No Trace Seven Principles have been developed to protect a fragile natural world from increased usage. *Leave No Trace Seven Principles © 1999 by the Leave No Trace Center for Outdoor Ethics: lnt.org*

1. **PLAN AHEAD AND PREPARE**
   - Know the regulations and special concerns for the area you'll visit.
   - Prepare for extreme weather, hazards, and emergencies.
   - Schedule your trip to avoid times of high use.

- Visit in small groups. Split larger parties into groups of four to six.
- Repackage food to minimize waste.
- Use a map and compass to eliminate the use of marking paint, rock cairns, or flagging.

2. **TRAVEL AND CAMP ON DURABLE SURFACES**
   - Durable surfaces include established trails and campsites, rock, gravel, dry grasses, or snow.
   - Protect riparian areas by camping at least 200 feet from lakes and streams.
   - Good campsites are found, not made. Altering a site is not necessary.

   IN POPULAR AREAS:
   - Concentrate use on existing trails and campsites.
   - Walk single file in the middle of the trail, even when it's wet or muddy.
   - Keep campsites small. Focus activity in areas where vegetation is absent.

   IN PRISTINE AREAS:
   - Disperse use to prevent the creation of campsites and trails.
   - Avoid places where impacts are just beginning.

3. **DISPOSE OF WASTE PROPERLY**
   - Pack it in, pack it out. Inspect your campsite and rest areas for trash or spilled foods. Pack out all trash, leftover food, and litter.
   - Deposit solid human waste in catholes dug 6–8 inches deep at least 200 feet from water, camp, and trails. Cover and disguise the cathole when finished.
   - Pack out toilet paper and hygiene products.
   - To wash yourself or your dishes, carry water 200 feet away from streams or lakes, and use small amounts of biodegradable soap. Scatter strained dishwater.

4. **LEAVE WHAT YOU FIND**
   - Preserve the past: examine, but do not touch, cultural or historic structures and artifacts.
   - Leave rocks, plants, and other natural objects as you find them.
   - Avoid introducing or transporting non-native species.
   - Do not build structures or furniture or dig trenches.

5. **MINIMIZE CAMPFIRE IMPACTS**
   - Campfires can cause lasting impacts in the backcountry. Use a lightweight stove for cooking and enjoy a candle lantern for light.
   - Where fires are permitted, use established fire rings, fire pans, or mound fires.
   - Keep fires small. Only use sticks from the ground that can be broken by hand.

- Burn all wood and coals to ash, put out campfires completely, and then scatter the cool ashes.

6. **RESPECT WILDLIFE**
    - Observe wildlife from a distance. Do not follow or approach them.
    - Never feed animals. Feeding wildlife damages their health, alters natural behaviors, and exposes them to predators and other dangers.
    - Protect wildlife and your food by storing rations and trash securely.
    - Control pets at all times, or leave them at home.
    - Avoid wildlife during sensitive times: mating, nesting, raising young, or winter.

7. **BE CONSIDERATE OF OTHER VISITORS**
    - Respect other visitors and protect the quality of their experience.
    - Be courteous. Yield to other trail users.
    - Step to the downhill side of the trail when encountering pack stock.
    - Take breaks and camp away from trails and other visitors.
    - Let nature's sounds prevail. Avoid loud voices and noises.

For further information, *The Green Guide to Low-Impact Hiking and Camping* by Laura and Guy Waterman is an excellent resource, providing details on not only the "how" of no-trace principles but also the "why."

If you want to spend some energetic but rewarding days filled with the camaraderie of the trail, contact one of the maintaining clubs (see Appendix E, page 179) and join them on a work hike to build, rebuild, or maintain a section of the AT.

GEORGIA

Blood Mountain

DISTANCE & CONFIGURATION 6.8-mile circuit

DIFFICULTY Moderately strenuous

HIGHLIGHTS The view from the summit of Blood Mountain is one of the best in all of the North Georgia mountains.

TRAILHEAD DIRECTIONS From Dahlonega, take US 19 north 19.5 miles to the Byron Reece Memorial, where you will park. (From Blairsville, take US 19 south about 13.5 miles to the memorial.) The AT crosses US 19 0.5 mile south of the parking area, in Neels Gap, where the Walasi-Yi Center offers a hikers' hostel, groceries and snacks, and a backpacking shop with an extensive selection of outdoors equipment and books. Parking is limited.

TRAILHEAD GPS COORDINATES N34° 44.556' W83° 55.268'

BEGIN THE HIKE by ascending the blue-blazed trail from the memorial parking lot for 1.0 mile to intersect the AT. Make a right turn, but almost immediately bear left onto blue-blazed Freeman Trail. Following this pathway around the southern slope of Blood Mountain, you'll again come to the AT, this time in Bird Gap, 2.8 miles into the hike.

Bear right and ascend gradually along the AT, crossing two streams in quick succession before coming into a gap at 3.5 miles; keep following the white blazes as you continue to ascend. The highest point of the AT in Georgia, the summit of Blood Mountain (4,461'), is reached at 4.4 miles. Be sure to climb onto the rocks next to the stone shelter (built by the Civilian Conservation Corps in the 1930s) to obtain an Olympian view southward, all the way to the AT's southern terminus on Springer Mountain.

Beginning your descent, you'll pass other rock outcroppings providing vistas to the southwest and the northeast. Just about the time it feels as if your knees are ready to buckle under you from negotiating the steepness of the pathway, the route returns you to the Byron Reece Memorial Trail at 5.8 miles. Bear left and follow the blue blazes back to your car at 6.8 miles.

NORTH CAROLINA

Standing Indian Mountain

DISTANCE & CONFIGURATION 5.0-mile round-trip, or 10.5-mile circuit using Lower Ridge and Kimsey Creek Trails

DIFFICULTY Strenuous

HIGHLIGHTS Dramatic views from Standing Indian; the delightful environment of a mountain stream if you do the circuit hike

TRAILHEAD DIRECTIONS Follow US 64 west 15.6 miles from Franklin and turn left onto Forest Service Road 71, which becomes dirt; follow it 6.0 miles to the AT parking area in Deep Gap.

TRAILHEAD GPS COORDINATES N35° 02.564' W83° 33.300'

FOLLOW THE AT north to ascend from the parking area in Deep Gap and enter the Southern Nantahala Wilderness Area. Just after crossing a small stream at 0.8 mile, take the short, blue-blazed pathway to the right to check out the Standing Indian Shelter.

Return to the AT and continue to ascend along an old woods road, reaching blue-blazed Lower Ridge Trail at 2.4 miles. Bear right to attain Standing Indian's summit, which, at 5,498 feet, is the highest point on the AT south of the Smokies. From this height, the view of the Tallulah River Gorge can be quite breathtaking, as is the vista of ridge upon ridge of North Georgia mountains. If you happen to be here in June, the

Atop Standing Indian Mountain

area around the summit bursts forth with hundreds of purple Catawba rhododendron blossoms. Great rhododendron's paler petals appear in July.

Returning to the trail junction, those doing the round-trip hike will simply retrace their steps along the AT. If you are doing the circuit hike, continue on the blue-blazed Lower Ridge Trail, which tends downhill, rather steeply in places. Just after crossing the Nantahala River on an automobile bridge, this pathway ends in the U.S. Forest Service's Standing Indian Campground at 6.8 miles.

From there, follow blue-blazed Kimsey Creek Trail, which at 7.1 miles veers away from the river and at 7.7 miles begins following Kimsey Creek to its headwaters near Deep Gap, where the hike comes to an end at 10.5 miles.

NORTH CAROLINA/TENNESSEE

Charlies Bunion

DISTANCE & CONFIGURATION 7.8-mile round-trip, or 12.7-mile circuit using the Dry Sluice Gap, Grassy Branch, and Sweat Heifer Creek Trails

DIFFICULTY Moderately strenuous for the round-trip, strenuous for the circuit

HIGHLIGHTS Northern hardwood forest and excellent vistas from Charlies Bunion; Kephart Prong and views of Oconaluftee Valley on the circuit hike

TRAILHEAD DIRECTIONS The parking area at Newfound Gap in Great Smoky Mountains National Park is on US 441, 16 miles south of Gatlinburg, Tennessee, or 20 miles north of Cherokee, North Carolina.

TRAILHEAD GPS COORDINATES N35° 36.675' W83° 25.521'

WALK NORTHWARD ON THE AT from the parking area, ascending through a mixture of spruce-fir and northern hardwood forests. In 1.7 miles, the Sweat Heifer Creek Trail (one of the pathways you'll be using if you do the circuit hike) comes in from the right; keep left, and soon afterward you will reach a good view to the south of Clingmans Dome, the AT's highest point. Descend to the junction, at 2.7 miles, with the Boulevard Trail, which bears left to reach Mount LeConte Lodge (in 5.3 miles).

Continue right on the AT, passing by Icewater Spring Shelter at 3.0 miles, the site of the first composting privy in the park. In another 0.8 mile you reach Charlies Bunion, where it is time to take a break and enjoy the expansive view. To the east is the route of the AT along the Sawteeth Range, to the northeast is Greenbrier Pinnacle, while almost due north and directly below are the deep gorges of the Porters Creek drainage system. Continuing with the sweeping vista, Mount LeConte rises to the northwest, with Mount Kephart and the Jump-Off capping the western horizon.

From here, if you are doing the round-trip hike, simply retrace your steps to your vehicle. If you are doing the circuit hike, descend northward on the AT to the junction with the Dry Sluice Gap Trail at 4.2 miles. Bear right onto this pathway, and with very little change in elevation, come to the Grassy Branch Trail at 5.7 miles. Following that route to the right, you'll descend into the isolated valley of Kephart Prong to arrive at Kephart Shelter, 8.0 miles into your journey.

Ignoring the descending Kephart Prong Trail, ascend (strenuously in some places) via the Sweat Heifer Creek Trail, which follows an old railroad grade in places through fire cherry and a northern hardwood forest, providing views into the Oconaluftee Valley. Park historians believe the trail's name is derived from the custom of herding livestock over the mountain on a wagon road in the 1930s. When you arrive back at the AT at 11.7 miles, bear left and gradually descend to Newfound Gap at 12.7 miles.

SOUTHWESTERN VIRGINIA

Grayson Highlands and Mount Rogers National Recreation Area

DISTANCE & CONFIGURATION 11.6-mile circuit

DIFFICULTY Moderate

HIGHLIGHTS Wild ponies and miles of open meadows somewhat reminiscent of the Continental Divide in Montana and Wyoming

TRAILHEAD DIRECTIONS The entrance to Grayson Highlands State Park is off US 58, about halfway between Damascus and Independence, Virginia. Once inside the park, follow its main road to the Massie Gap parking area.

TRAILHEAD GPS COORDINATES N36° 38.007' W81° 30.505'

FROM THE PARKING AREA, take the blue-blazed Rhododendron Trail (which is basically a National Park Service dirt road) through open meadows to meet the AT in 0.5 mile. Bearing left to follow white blazes, you'll soon leave the state park, enter national forestlands, and come to the junction with the Wilburn Ridge Trail, which goes right to the highest points of Wilburn Ridge. (You can use this pathway as an alternate route if you wish; it rejoins the AT in 1.4 miles.)

High, open meadows, 360-degree views, mountain air blowing across your face—hiking doesn't get much better than this. Be sure to soak in your surroundings as you enjoy the vistas spread out before you. Above you and to the west are the spruce- and fir-covered summits of Mount Rogers and Whitetop Mountain. Behind are the rolling grasslands you traversed to reach here and the summits of Haw Orchard and Stone Mountains, while far to the south are the mountain peaks of North Carolina, with Grandfather and Sugar Mountains rising prominently.

At 2.6 miles, leave the white blazes to follow blue blazes (a former route of the AT) through Rhododendron Gap and across the crest of Pine Mountain. Rejoin the AT at 4.7 miles, and turn right to follow the white blazes into a wooded area. Emerging into open country again, cross the fences of "The Scales" (a onetime cattle weighing area) at 6.1 miles, and ascend through fields to the meadowlands atop Stone Mountain.

Pass a spring to the left of the trail at 7.6 miles, and continue following white blazes to merge with an old railroad grade at 8.3 miles. Crossing the East Fork of Big Wilson Creek, Little Wilson Creek, and Quebec Branch (at 9.8 miles), you'll begin a long ascent back to Wilburn Ridge. Having returned to the Rhododendron Trail, turn left, following blue blazes to complete the journey at 11.6 miles.

CENTRAL VIRGINIA

Apple Orchard Falls

DISTANCE & CONFIGURATION 2.4-mile round-trip to the falls or 7.9-mile circuit using the Apple Orchard Falls and Cornelius Creek Trails

DIFFICULTY Strenuous

HIGHLIGHTS 150-foot Apple Orchard Falls; a walk along two mountain streams, old woods roads, and a railroad grade on the circuit hike

TRAILHEAD DIRECTIONS The hike begins at the Sunset Field Overlook, milepost 78.7 on the Blue Ridge Parkway (7.0 miles north of the Peaks of Otter Lodge, north of Bedford, Virginia).

TRAILHEAD GPS COORDINATES N37° 30.466' W79° 31.448'

BEGIN A GRADUAL DESCENT on the Apple Orchard Falls Trail from the overlook parking area, crossing the AT in 0.2 mile and an old roadway at 0.8 mile. Entering a hemlock forest, the pathway descends steeply through rhododendron, crosses the creek, and arrives at the falls at 1.2 miles. The falls drop about 150 feet over a stone facing, and the water takes many paths down the rocks, so be sure to walk around to gain different perspectives. If you are doing the round-trip hike, retrace your steps from here back to your car. If you are completing the circuit hike, continue to descend on the trail, but be aware of unsure footing.

The grade becomes a bit gentler at 1.8 miles as good campsites begin to appear. The Apple Orchard Falls Trail comes to an end at 3.6 miles when it meets Forest Service Road 59. Turn left and ascend Cornelius Creek Trail. By the time you have passed numerous rippling cascades, inviting wading pools, towering hemlocks, and old logging roads and railroad grades and have crossed over Backbone Ridge, you will have gained more than 1,700 feet in elevation. You will intersect the AT at 6.6 miles.

Turn left, following white blazes over the shoulder of Rich Mountain before descending to intersect the Apple Orchard Falls Trail at 7.7 miles. A right turn onto that blue-blazed pathway will return you to the overlook at 7.9 miles.

SHENANDOAH NATIONAL PARK

Lewis Spring Falls and Blackrock

DISTANCE & CONFIGURATION 3.3-mile circuit using the Lewis Spring Falls Trail

DIFFICULTY Moderate

HIGHLIGHTS The easily reached Lewis Spring Falls, a grand view from Blackrock, and the opportunity to savor a meal while enjoying the scenery from the picture windows of Big Meadows Lodge. (No camping is permitted anywhere along this hike due to its proximity to the lodge.)

TRAILHEAD DIRECTIONS The entrance to Big Meadows Lodge is near milepost 51 of the Skyline Drive, between the Swift Run Gap Entrance Station on US 33 and the

Thornton Gap Entrance Station on US 121. After turning onto the road to the lodge, follow signs to the amphitheater parking area.

TRAILHEAD GPS COORDINATES N38° 31.841' W78° 26.369'

FIND THE PATHWAY between the amphitheater parking area and the lodge. Follow it downhill 0.1 mile to the junction with the AT, which you will cross over to continue along blue-blazed Lewis Spring Falls Trail as it gradually drops through the forest. Turn right at 1.2 miles, and steeply descend along the side pathway to enjoy the cascades near their base.

Return to the main pathway and turn right. Make a right onto another short side route at 1.7 miles to enjoy the view overlooking the head of the falls. Upon rejoining the main pathway, you'll huff and puff a bit up the steep slope to come onto the Lewis Spring service road and intersect the AT at 2.3 miles. Bear left to follow white blazes.

Ascend steadily along the western side of a ridgeline to intersect (at 2.7 miles) a pathway leading to the right 0.1 mile to Blackrock Viewpoint. While it is almost always worthwhile to take these short side routes, you'll be just as well rewarded if you continue along the AT for several more yards for basically the same extraordinary view westward. On clear days your eyes can gaze out across the width of the Shenandoah Valley, up and over Massanutten Mountain, and all the way to the distant Great North and Allegheny Mountains along the Virginia–West Virginia border.

Proceeding along the AT, skirt the cliffs of Blackrock, and return to the initial intersection of this hike with the Lewis Spring Falls Trail, where you'll bear right to the parking area at 3.3 miles. Here you may want to take a few additional steps to enjoy some country cooking at the lodge's restaurant.

WEST VIRGINIA

Harpers Ferry

DISTANCE & CONFIGURATION 1.3-mile circuit

DIFFICULTY Easy

HIGHLIGHTS The AT passes through West Virginia for only about 3.0 miles, one of which passes through Harpers Ferry National Park, providing a chance to walk through a bit of history.

TRAILHEAD DIRECTIONS Park your car at the Harpers Ferry National Park Visitor Center (171 Shoreline Drive), off US 340 south of Harpers Ferry, and take the free shuttle bus into the historic town.

TRAILHEAD GPS COORDINATES N39° 19.299' W77° 44.598'

ATC headquarters at Harpers Ferry

FROM THE BUS PARKING LOT, walk back toward US 340, look for a post with a white blaze marking the trail, and ascend the AT steeply along the face of a cliff. Be careful to avoid copious growths of poison ivy. The blue-blazed pathway at 0.2 mile leads left to the headquarters of the Appalachian Trail Conservancy, definitely worth a visit. Continuing on the AT, pass by other side routes, arriving at Jefferson Rock at 0.7 mile.

Upon viewing the confluence of the Shenandoah and Potomac Rivers from this rock formation in 1783, Thomas Jefferson described the scene as "stupendous" and "worth a voyage across the Atlantic."

Folklore states that the flat stone is not the actual rock Jefferson stood upon. Angered by Jefferson's 1800 campaign promise to cut defense spending, a company of soldiers is said to have pushed the rock bearing his name over the cliff. Historians generally agree that Jefferson visited this rock formation, but which rock he sat upon and whether that rock was pushed down the hill are not known.

Entering the heart of the city, made a component of the national park system in 1944, the trail is now obviously a tourist route, complete with handrails and pavement. Pass by the ruins of Saint John's Episcopal Church (built in 1852); Saint Peter's Catholic Church (constructed in 1833); and the oldest structure in town, the Robert Harper House, which was erected between 1775 and 1782.

Descend the stone steps hand-cut from the hillside near the beginning of the 1800s, and turn right onto High Street; then turn left onto Shenandoah Street.

Pulpit, overlooking a major bend of the Lehigh River, at 1.5 miles. Return to North Trail and bear right, enjoying the traverse of the main crest of the mountain. During late June and into July, your forward progress may be impeded by the urge to gather handfuls of abundant blueberries.

Intersect the AT at 3.9 miles, turn left, and begin a gradual descent back to the Outerbridge Shelter, at 5.6 miles. The area around the shelter is evidence of nature's healing power. In the 1970s and early 1980s, there was almost no vegetation here, having succumbed to the effects of the industrial factories in the gap. Today, however, plant life is so lush that views are quite limited.

Continuing to descend, return to the parking area at 6.3 miles.

NEW JERSEY

Kittatinny Mountain

DISTANCE & CONFIGURATION 6.5-mile circuit using the Iris Trail

DIFFICULTY Moderate

HIGHLIGHTS A walk through hickories, scrub oaks, hemlocks, and pitch pines, skirting the shore of Lake Rutherford for a time; several views of lakes and ponds and the Pocono Mountains. (Please note that fires are permitted only at designated campsites in New Jersey.)

TRAILHEAD DIRECTIONS Parking is available adjacent to the High Point State Park headquarters, which is on NJ 23, less than 5 miles south of I-84's Exit 1 (Port Jervis, NY).

TRAILHEAD GPS COORDINATES N41° 18.322' W74° 40.208'

Lake Rutherford

THE AT AND THE YELLOW-BLAZED MASHIPACONG TRAIL share the same pathway entering the woods at the south end of the parking lot. In 0.2 mile, Mashipacong Trail heads right; you want to bear left onto red-blazed Iris Trail (identified by a white post to the left of the AT).

After a very gradual rise, the pathway gently descends to permit you to walk above the western shoreline of Lake Rutherford, the water supply for the town of Sussex. Passing by the blue-blazed pathway to the Rutherford Shelter, you'll ascend to rejoin the AT about 3.0 miles after beginning the hike.

Turn right to ascend a short distance more before descending to cross a stream. Ascend slightly again, finally reaching Dutch Shoe Rock (where a blue-blazed pathway descends right 0.4 mile to Rutherford Shelter). After enjoying the view northeast over Lake Rutherford from various perspectives, you will cross over to the other side of the ridge for a chance to survey the Pocono Mountains in Pennsylvania at 5.1 miles from the start.

After descending to cross the valley floor, ascend to a spot, at 5.5 miles, overlooking Sawmill Pond to the west, soon passing by Blue Dot Trail (which descends to the pond). From here the AT tends downward, arriving at the parking lot at 6.5 miles.

NEW YORK

Fitzgerald Falls

DISTANCE & CONFIGURATION 0.6-mile round-trip

DIFFICULTY Easy

HIGHLIGHTS What could be better? A great waterfall is reached with very little effort. (Please note that fires are permitted only at designated campsites in New York.)

TRAILHEAD DIRECTIONS The trail crossing is on Lakes Road, 4.2 miles north of the intersection of Lakes Road and NY 17A in Greenwood Lake.

TRAILHEAD GPS COORDINATES N41° 16.411' W74° 15.2516'

LEAVE THE PAVED ROAD to descend to and cross over Trout Brook on a wooden footbridge. In springtime or after heavy rains (the best time to visit the falls), you will be happy to find that the Appalachian Trail has been rerouted off of its original path, which had necessitated additional brook crossings and a traverse of often flooded ground. (Avoid the blue-blazed pathway that goes off to the left.) Framed by hemlock trees, picturesque Fitzgerald Falls, dropping 25 feet down a narrow fissure in the rock facing, is reached at 0.3 mile. Retrace your steps to return to your vehicle.

CONNECTICUT

Housatonic River

DISTANCE & CONFIGURATION 4.8-mile one-way

DIFFICULTY Easy

HIGHLIGHTS One of the longest river walks on the AT, this hike has almost no change in elevation and parallels the Housatonic River the entire way. (Camping is permitted in Connecticut only in designated sites and shelters; fires are prohibited everywhere.)

TRAILHEAD DIRECTIONS Drop one car off at the southern end of the hike by taking CT 341 west from Kent, crossing the Housatonic River, and turning right onto Skiff Mountain Road, about 0.3 mile west of US 7. In 1.0 mile, bear right onto River Road and go a little more than 1.5 miles to the AT parking area for St. John's Ledges. Drive your other car back to Kent and turn north onto US 7; continue 9.0 miles to Cornwall Bridge. Take CT 4 back across the Housatonic River to turn onto River Road; follow it 1.5 miles to the parking area at the site of Swift's Bridge, destroyed by floods in 1936.

TRAILHEAD GPS COORDINATES N41° 45.497' W73° 27.018' (end);
N41° 49.380' W73° 23.208' (start)

FROM THE PARKING AREA at Swift's Bridge, take the AT south down an embankment to follow an old dirt road below cultivated fields. With almost no change in elevation, you are free to enjoy the light of the sun playing off the waters of the slow-moving river, listen to the sounds of bird life, watch the scampering of chipmunks, or let your mind wander to far-off places.

Camping is permitted next to Stony Brook, which you will cross at 2.0 miles, and at the shelter near Stewart Hollow Brook at 2.4 miles.

At 3.9 miles, you will reach the site of the North Kent Bridge, which was destroyed in 1936. Prior to that time, the AT had crossed the river here to continue southward via Kent Falls and Mohawk Mountain. Although the road is passable by car at this point, continue to enjoy your walk, cross over Mount Brook, and return to your waiting vehicle at 4.8 miles.

MASSACHUSETTS

Mount Greylock

DISTANCE & CONFIGURATION 8.8-mile circuit using the Money Brook Trail and the Hopper Trail

DIFFICULTY Strenuous

HIGHLIGHTS A hike through old-growth forests, crossing mountain streams and passing waterfalls, to reach a grand 360-degree view of the Berkshire Hills and Green Mountains from the summit of Mount Greylock, the highest point in Massachusetts

TRAILHEAD DIRECTIONS Because overnight parking is permitted only at the parking lots on the summit of Mount Greylock and at Sperry Road Campground, this hike begins at the summit in case you wish to make this more than a day hike. The summit is reached via Notch Road off MA 2 in North Adams. From North Adams, take MA 2 west about 1 mile and turn left onto Notch Road. After about 7.5 miles, take a hard left to stay on Notch Road, and continue about 1.5 miles to the summit. (Be aware that the road system on Mount Greylock is closed to the general public from about the first of December to mid-May.)

TRAILHEAD GPS COORDINATES N42° 38.283' W73° 09.937'

FOLLOW THE AT NORTH from the monument tower, cross Summit Road, and bypass Thunderbolt and Bellows Pipe Ski Trails coming in from the right. After skirting just beneath the summit of Mount Fitch at 1.4 miles, the trail climbs to the top of Mount Williams at 2.4 miles, where you can take in the views of the mountains in southern Vermont and sign the register. Continuing, you cross Notch Road at 3.3 miles, walk through an open meadow, and come to a trail junction at 3.4 miles, where you turn left onto Money Brook Trail. Passing by a spring and staying at basically the same

Monument at Mount Greylock

elevation, you reach Wilbur Clearing AT Lean-To in a dense forest of red spruce. Soon, just after passing a side pathway to Notch Road on the left, you begin a steep descent into old-growth hemlocks and cross Money Brook for the first time at 4.4 miles. Descending through the narrow gorge, the pathway parallels Money Brook and passes by Mount Prospect Trail coming in from the right at 5.2 miles. Cross a tributary, then Money Brook, and you'll come to the Short-Cut Trail to Hopper Trail, which you'll follow as it ascends steeply left.

When you reach another junction at 6.1 miles, bear left and continue to ascend steeply via the Hopper Trail, soon passing by a reliable spring. Coming into the Mount Greylock/Sperry Road Campground at 7.0 miles, follow the road to the contact station, bearing left onto the steep pathway and passing a waterfall on your right. Keep left as the Deer Hill Trail comes in from the right at 7.3 miles, and then bear right when the Overlook Trail takes off to the left at 7.8 miles.

Upon encountering the AT at 8.2 miles, turn left, begin following white blazes, and continue to ascend. Crossing the paved junction of Notch/Rockwell and Summit Roads, the AT returns you to the summit of Mount Greylock at 8.8 miles.

Little Rock Pond

VERMONT

Little Rock Pond

DISTANCE & CONFIGURATION 5.7-mile round-trip, or 7.5-mile circuit using the Green Mountain Trail

DIFFICULTY Easy for the round-trip walk; moderately strenuous for the circuit hike

HIGHLIGHTS The ripples and short cascades of Little Black Branch; Little Rock Pond; a traverse of the full length of Green Mountain.

TRAILHEAD DIRECTIONS From US 7 in Danby, take the Danby-Landgrove Road east 3.5 miles to the trailhead parking area.

TRAILHEAD GPS COORDINATES N43° 22.376' W72° 57.751'

FOLLOWING AN OLD LOGGING ROAD, take the AT north into the woods, soon crossing and recrossing Little Black Branch, which you then parallel most of the way to the pond. (The side route to the right at 1.8 miles leads to Little Rock Pond Shelter.) Continuing on the AT, you come to the southern end of Little Rock Pond, one of the most idyllic spots on the entire AT, at 2.0 miles. On a clear day the sun dapples the surface of the pond, whose blue waters should not be resisted for a swim. In the fall, the maples, beeches, and birches of the northern hardwood forest put on a dazzling display of colors. Continuing to follow white blazes, swing around the eastern shore, soon passing by Little Rock Pond Campsite.

Reaching the northern end of the pond at 2.4 miles, leave the AT and turn left to continue along the western shore on Green Mountain Trail. Those doing the round-trip hike will soon bear left onto the Little Rock Pond Loop Trail, walk along the southern shoreline, and return to follow the AT back to the starting point. If you wish to complete the circuit hike, keep right on Green Mountain Trail at its junction with the loop trail. You'll soon ascend the hillside to reach the summit at 3.4 miles. Following the height of the mountain, with the usual minor ups and downs associated with ridge walks, you will have occasional chances to peer west into Otter Creek Valley and east across the main crest of Vermont's Green Mountains.

A little over 6.0 miles into the journey, you'll begin a descent that will take you from over 2,200 feet to close to 1,400 feet in elevation—in only 1.0 mile. Swinging around to the eastern side of the ridge, Green Mountain Trail delivers you back to the Danby-Landgrove Road at 7.5 miles. Turn left and go 300 feet to return to the starting point.

NEW HAMPSHIRE

White Mountains

DISTANCE & CONFIGURATION 25.7-mile circuit using Avalon, A–Z, Zealand, Ethan Pond, Webster Cliff, and Crawford Path Trails

DIFFICULTY Strenuous; do not underestimate the difficulty of negotiating the rugged White Mountains.

HIGHLIGHTS Zealand Falls; Ethan Pond; and many, many great views

COMMENTS Regulations on camping and fires in the White Mountains change from time to time. Obtain the latest information from Appalachian Mountain Club's Highland Center, or, to be on the safe side, just plan on camping at shelters or designated tent sites.

TRAILHEAD DIRECTIONS Trailhead parking is available at the Crawford Path trailhead parking area, directly across from Appalachian Mountain Club's Highland Center on US 302, 27 miles north of the intersection of US 302 and NH 16A in Intervale.

TRAILHEAD GPS COORDINATES N44° 13.080' W71° 24.660'

View of Ethan Pond Trail from Zeacliff in the White Mountains

FROM THE CRAWFORD PATH TRAILHEAD PARKING AREA, cross US 302, walk by the Highland Center, and take the Avalon Trail west to gain about 900 feet elevation in 1.4 miles to the junction with the A–Z Trail, which you then follow. After a bit of a descent and a short, steep climb, most of the route on this pathway has very little change in elevation, so it is a pleasant walk through what is predominantly a northern hardwood forest. At 5.1 miles, turn left onto Zealand Trail, passing by attractive Zealand Pond to intersect the AT at 5.4 miles. Bear right and make the quick ascent to Zealand Falls Hut at 5.6 miles. The hut is perched dramatically on a rock face with Zealand Falls right next to it. The view from here is equally dramatic, looking onto the ragged peaks of the southern White Mountains.

When you're ready to leave, take the trail back to its junction with Zealand Trail, and bear right to follow the white blazes of the AT (called the Ethan Pond Trail through this section) along the gentle grade of an old railroad bed. Keep left at 7.3 miles, when Zeacliff Trail comes in from the right. If you're feeling energetic, you might want to take a short jaunt to the falls on the Thoreau Falls Trail to the right at 8.1 miles.

Continuing along the AT/Ethan Pond Trail, keep left as Shoal Pond Trail comes in from the right at 8.6 miles. Soon the trail leaves the railroad grade but continues with a gradual descent. At 10.6 miles, it is worthwhile to take the short side pathway to the left to appreciate the serene setting of Ethan Pond and its accompanying shelter. One mile beyond here, the AT bypasses Willey Range Trail coming in from the left and begins a nearly 2,000-foot descent. Along the way it also bypasses Kendrum Flume Trail, coming in from the left at 14.4 miles, and Arethusa-Ripley Falls Trail, going off to the right at 16.0 miles.

Arrive at US 302 at 16.5 miles, cross the road, and steeply start to make up all that elevation you just lost (and more); follow the white blazes of the AT/Webster Cliff Trail. Eventually coming to a viewpoint, the trail stays along the cliffs, steadily gaining elevation. Cross over the top of Mount Webster at 19.8 miles, bypass Webster-Jackson Trail coming in from the left, and after a series of ups and downs, attain the summit of Mount Jackson, where you'll go by another section of the Webster-Jackson Trail at 21.2 miles. There are impressive views from here out across the Presidential Range to Mount Washington.

Going through several alpine meadows, reach Mizpah Spring Hut and Nauman Tentsite at 22.9 miles. So as to experience a bit of the terrain above treeline, continue following the AT to the summit of Mount Pierce (4,310') for a grand view of the Presidential Range, the sloping expanse of the Dry River drainage system, and the mountains to the north and west.

Just beyond, at 23.8 miles, the Webster Path comes to an end and you'll leave white blazes to bear left and descend along Crawford Path. At 24.9 miles, Mizpah Cutoff Trail comes in from the left; stay right and continue on a fairly comfortable grade. Reach your vehicle and the end of the hike at 25.7 miles.

MAINE

Bemis Mountain and Stream

DISTANCE & CONFIGURATION 13.9-mile circuit using Bemis Stream Trail

DIFFICULTY Strenuous

HIGHLIGHTS More than 4.0 miles of walking in and out of sections of trail above the treeline; numerous 360-degree views; and a chance to walk a former route of the AT

TRAILHEAD DIRECTIONS From the intersection of US 2 and ME 17 in Rumford, follow ME 17 north about 26 miles. Look for the small parking pulloff on the right. (This is about 0.5 mile south of where the AT intersects the road.)

TRAILHEAD GPS COORDINATES N44° 50.162' W70° 42.596'

WALK NORTH ALONG ME 17 for 0.5 mile to a highway turnout overlooking the Bemis Range and Mooselookmeguntic Lake. Here you will turn left onto the AT and steeply descend. At 1.3 miles, ford Bemis Stream. Be careful in periods of high water. Walk along the nearly flat valley floor and cross over a gravel road—the former railbed of the Rumford Falls and Rangely Lakes Railroad—at 1.5 miles.

The easy, first portion of the hike is over as you begin the long, 2,000-foot gain in elevation to the highest point of the Bemis Range. The first of many views opens up as you top a knob at 2.0 miles, and another at 2.2 miles. Crossing the First Peak of the Bemis Range at 2.7 miles, you might want to enjoy the abundant blueberries as you gaze down into the deep notch from which you've just climbed.

The views seem to get progressively better as you cross the open ledges of the Second Peak of the Bemis Range at 3.6 miles. Take a break at Bemis Mountain Lean-To (which has a nearby spring) at 5.1 miles before climbing up, over, and down Third and East Peaks. Also be sure to take in the sites from the lofty perch atop the highest point of the journey, West Peak, at 6.8 miles.

At 7.8 miles, leave the AT, turn left, and begin the return trip along Bemis Stream Trail, the route of the AT before a 1957–1958 relocation. After dropping quite steeply, the grade mellows upon reaching the stream. You will cross it twice before coming to the old railroad grade at 12.7 miles. Climbing up the long, steep embankment, turn left onto ME 17 and return to your car at 13.9 miles.

Trees of the Appalachian Trail and Fall Leaf Color Guide

Unless otherwise noted, these trees are found—at least in isolated spots—throughout the Appalachian Trail.

Common Name	Scientific Name	Red	Orange	Yellow	Brown	Notes
FAMILY SALICACEAE *Willow*						
Balsam poplar	*Populus balsamifera*					New England; isolated to VA
Balsam willow	*Salix pyrifolia*					mostly ME
Bebb willow	*Salix bebbiana*					MD to ME
Bigtooth aspen	*Populus grandidentata*	X				
Black willow	*Salix nigra*					
Eastern cottonwood	*Populus deltoides*			X		isolated GA to NH
Pussy willow	*Salix discolor*					VA to ME
Quaking aspen	*Populus tremuloides*			X		VA to ME
FAMILY JUGLANDACEAE *Walnut*						
Bitternut hickory	*Carya cordiformis*			X		GA to NH
Black walnut	*Juglans nigra*			X		GA to New England
Butternut	*Juglans cinerea*			X	X	
Mockernut hickory	*Carya tomentosa*			X		GA to S. New England
Pignut hickory	*Carya glabra*			X		GA to S. New England
Shagbark hickory	*Carya ovata*			X		
FAMILY BETULACEAE *Birch*						
American hornbeam	*Carpinus caroliniana*		X		X	
Eastern hophornbeam	*Ostrya virginiana*			X		
Gray birch	*Betula populifolia*		X		X	PA to ME
Hazel alder	*Alnus serrulata*	X			X	
Paper birch	*Betula papyrifera*				X	NY to ME; high elev. in NC
Speckled alder	*Alnus rugosa*		X			VA/WV to ME
Sweet birch	*Betula lenta*				X	
Yellow birch	*Betula alleghaniensis*				X	
FAMILY FAGACEAE *Beech*						
Allegheny chinkapin	*Castanea pumila*		X			GA to PA
American beech	*Fagus grandifolia*		X	X	X	
American chestnut	*Castanea dentata*			X		
Bear oak	*Quercus ilicifolia*		X		X	
Blackjack oak	*Quercus marilandica*	X				GA to mid-Atlantic
Chinkapin oak	*Quercus muehlenbergii*	X			X	GA to VT
Pin oak	*Quercus marilandica*	X				VA to VT
Scarlet oak	*Quercus coccinea*	X				
Shingle oak	*Quercus imbricaria*		X		X	isolated NC to PA
White oak	*Quercus alba*	X	X	X	X	

Common Name	Scientific Name	Red	Orange	Yellow	Brown	Notes
FAMILY FAGACEAE *Beech* **(continued)**						
Black oak	*Quercus velutina*	X				GA to VT
Chestnut oak	*Quercus prinus*		X	X	X	
Northern red oak	*Quercus rubra*	X		X	X	
Post oak	*Quercus stellata*				X	GA to MA
FAMILY ULMACEAE *Elm*						
American elm	*Ulmus americana*			X		
Hackberry	*Celtis occidentalis*			X		
Rock elm	*Ulmus thomasii*			X		
Slippery elm	*Ulmus rubra*			X		
FAMILY MORACEAE *Mulberry*						
Red mulberry	*Morus rubra*			X		GA to S. New England
FAMILY MAGNOLIACEAE *Magnolia*						
Cucumbertree	*Magnolia acuminata*			X		GA to PA
Fraser magnolia	*Magnolia fraseri*			X		GA to VA/WV
Yellow poplar	*Liriodendron tulipifera*			X		GA to VT
Umbrella magnolia	*Magnolia tripetala*			X		GA to PA
FAMILY ANNONACEAE *Custard Apple*						
Pawpaw	*Asimina triloba*			X		GA to PA
FAMILY LAURACEAE *Laurel*						
Sassafras	*Sassafras albidum*	X	X	X		
FAMILY HAMAMELIDACEAE *Witch Hazel*						
Sweetgum	*Liquidambar styraciflua*			X		isolated GA to VA
Witch-hazel	*Hamamelis virginiana*			X		
FAMILY PLATANACEAE *Sycamore*						
Sycamore	*Platanus occidentalis*			X		
FAMILY ROSACEAE *Rose*						
American mountain-ash	*Sorbus americana*	X	X			
Black cherry	*Prunus serotina*	X	X			
Broadleaf hawthorn	*Crataegus dilatata*					NY to ME
Canada plum	*Prunus nigra*	X	X			CT to ME
Cockspur hawthorn	*Cratae guscrus-galli*	X	X			
Common chokecherry	*Prunus virginiana*	X	X			
Dotted hawthorn	*Crataegus punctata*	X	X			
Downy serviceberry	*Amelanchier arborea*	X	X	X	X	
Fanleaf hawthorn	*Crataegus flabellata*			X		
Fireberry hawthorn	*Crataegus chrysocarpa*	X	X			VA to ME
Fleshy hawthorn	*Crataegus succulenta*	X	X			
Frosted hawthorn	*Crataegus pruinosa*	X	X			
Littlehip hawthorn	*Crataegus spathulata*	X	X			GA to VA
Pear hawthorn	*Crataegus calpodendron*	X	X			GA to NY
Pin cherry	*Prunus pensylvanica*	X	X			
Roundleaf serviceberry	*Amelanchier sanguinea*					
Scarlet hawthorn	*Crataegus coccinea*	X	X			
Showy mountain-ash	*Sorbus decora*	X	X			CT to ME

Common Name	Scientific Name	Red	Orange	Yellow	Brown	Notes
FAMILY ROSACEAE *Rose (continued)*						
Southern crab apple	*Malus angustifolia*	X	X			GA to VA
Sweet crab apple	*Malus coronaria*	X	X			GA to NY
Yellow hawthorn	*Crataegus flava*					GA to S. VA
Washington hawthorn	*Crataegus phaenopyrum*	X	X			GA to VA; isolated to S. New England
FAMILY LEGUMINOSAE *Legume*						
Black locust	*Robina pseudoacacia*				X	GA to PA
Redbud	*Cercis canadensis*			X		GA to PA
FAMILY ANACARDIACEAE *Cashew*						
Shining sumac	*Rhus copallina*	X				
Smooth sumac	*Rhus glabra*	X				
Staghorn sumac	*Rhus typhina*	X	X			
FAMILY AQUIFOLIACEAE *Holly*						
American holly	*Ilex opaca*					GA to S. New England
Mountain holly	*Ilex montana*			X		GA to S. New England
FAMILY STAPHYLEACEAE *Bladdernut*						
American bladdernut	*Staphylea trifolia*	X	X			isolated GA to NH
FAMILY ACERACEAE *Maple*						
Boxelder	*Acer negundo*	X		X		
Mountain maple	*Acer spicatum*	X	X			
Red maple	*Acer rubrum*	X	X	X		
Silver maple	*Acer saccharinum*		X	X	X	
Striped maple	*Acer pennsylvanicum*			X		
Sugar maple	*Acer saccharum*	X	X	X		
FAMILY HIPPOCASTANACEAE *Buckeye*						
Yellow buckeye	*Aesculus octandra*	X	X			GA to PA
FAMILY TILIACEAE *Basswood*						
American basswood	*Tilia americana*			X	X	
White basswood	*Tilia heterophylla*			X	X	GA to PA
FAMILY ARALIACEAE *Ginseng*						
Devils-walkingstick	*Aralia spinosa*			X		isolated GA to PA
FAMILY CORNACEAE *Dogwood*						
Alternate-leaf dogwood	*Cornus alternifolia*	X		X		
Black tupelo	*Nyssa sylvatica*	X				
Flowering dogwood	*Cornus florida*	X				
FAMILY ERICACEAE *Heath*						
Sourwood	*Oxydendrum arboreum*	X				GA to PA
FAMILY EBENACEAE *Ebony*						
Common persimmon	*Diospyros virginiana*			X		GA to CT
FAMILY STYRACECEAE *Snowbell*						
Bigleaf snowbell	*Styrax grandifolius*					GA to VA
Carolina silverbell	*Halesia carolina*			X		GA to S. VA
FAMILY OLEACEAE *Olive*						
Black ash	*Fraxinus nigra*			X		VA/WV to ME
Fringetree	*Chionanthus virginicus*			X		GA to PA
Green ash	*Fraxinus pennsylvanica*			X		

Common Name	Scientific Name	Red	Orange	Yellow	Brown	Notes
FAMILY OLEACEAE *Olive (continued)*						
White ash	*Fraxinus americana*	X	X	X	X	
FAMILY RUBICEAE *Madder*						
Buttonbush	*Cephalanthus occidentalis*					
FAMILY CAPRIFOLIACEAE *Honeysuckle*						
American elder	*Samucus canandensis*					
Arrowwood	*Viburnum dentatum*	X				
Blackhaw	*Viburnum prunifolium*	X				GA to CT
Nannyberry	*Viburnum lentago*	X	X			VA/WV to ME
FAMILY PINACEAE *Pine*						
Balsam fir	*Abies balsamea*					isolated VA; PA to ME
Black spruce	*Picea mariana*					NJ to ME
Carolina hemlock	*Tsuga caroliniana*					NC/TN to VA
Eastern hemlock	*Tsuga canadensis*					
Eastern white pine	*Pinus strobus*					
Fraser fir	*Abies fraseri*					NC/TN to VA
Jack pine	*Pinus banksiana*					mostly ME
Pitch pine	*Pinus rigida*					
Red pine	*Pinus resinosa*					New England; isolated to WV
Red spruce	*Picea rubens*					Georgia to VA/WV; again in New England
Shortleaf pine	*Pinus echinata*					GA to PA
Table mountain pine	*Pinus pungens*					GA to PA
Tamarack	*Larix laricina*					NJ to ME; isolated south
Virginia pine	*Pinus virginiana*					GA to NJ
White spruce	*Picea glauca*					mostly ME
FAMILY CUPRESSACEAE *Cypress*						
Common juniper	*Juniperus communis*					
Eastern redcedar	*Juniperus virginiana*					
Northern white-cedar	*Thuja occidentalis*					mostly New England; isolated to NC

Average Blooming Season for Some Appalachian Trail Flowers

Unless otherwise noted, these flowers are found—at least in isolated spots—throughout the Appalachian Trail.

Common Name	Scientific Name	FEB	MAR	APR	MAY	JUN	JUL	AUG	SEP	OCT	Notes
Asters	Aster spp.							X	X	X	
Azalea	Rhododendron nudiflorum			X	X	X					
Bee balm	Monarda didyma						X	X	X		GA to NY
Bellwort	Uvularia spp.			X	X	X					
Black cohosh	Actaea racemosa						X	X	X	X	
Bleeding heart	Dicentra eximi				X	X	X	X	X		
Bloodroot	Sanguinaria canadensis	X	X	X							
Blue cohosh	Caulophyllum thalictroides			X	X	X					
Bowman's root	Gillenia trifoliata						X	X	X		GA to NY
Bunchberry	Cornus canadensis				X	X	X				PA to ME
Butter-and-eggs	Linaria vulgaris					X	X	X	X	X	
Buttercup	Ranunculus spp.			X	X	X	X	X			
Canada lily	Lilium canadense						X	X	X		
Cardinal flower	Lobelia cardinalis						X	X	X		
Catawba rhododendron	Rhododendron catawbiense				X	X					GA to N. VA
Cinquefoil	Potentilla simplex			X	X	X					
Climbing fumitory	Adlumia fungosa					X	X	X	X	X	Fumitory Rock, PA, only
Columbine	Aquilegia canadensis			X	X	X	X				
Corn lily	Clintonia borealis				X	X	X				
Cow parsnip	Heracleum lanatum					X	X	X			
Daisies	Bellis spp.							X	X	X	
Daylily	Hemerocallis spp.					X	X	X			
Deptford pink	Dianthus armeria				X	X	X				
Diapensia	Diapensia lapponica					X	X				NY to ME
Dogtooth violet	Erythronium americanum	X	X	X							
Dutchman's-breeches	Dicentra cucullaria			X	X						
Dwarf iris	Iris cristata	X	X	X							GA to S. PA
Early saxifrage	Saxifraga or Micranthes virginiensis	X	X	X							
False hellebore	Veratrum viride				X	X	X				
Fire pink	Silene virginica			X	X	X					GA to NY
Foxglove (false)	Aureolaria spp.						X	X	X		
Fringed phacelia	Phacelia spp.			X	X						GA to VA/WV
Gaywings	Polygala paucifolia				X	X					
Goat's rue	Tephrosia virginiana				X	X	X	X			GA to mid–New England

Common Name	Scientific Name	FEB	MAR	APR	MAY	JUN	JUL	AUG	SEP	OCT	Notes
Goldenrods	Solidago spp.							X	X	X	
Gray's lily	Lilium grayi					X	X				almost exclusively NC/TN
Hepatica	Hepatica spp.		X	X	X						
Indian cucumber root	Medeola virginiana					X	X				
Indian pipe	Monotropa uniflora					X	X	X	X		
Jack-in-the-pulpit	Arisaema triphyllum			X	X	X					
Jewelweed	Impatiens capensis					X	X	X			
Joe-pye weed	Eupatorium fistulosum					X	X	X			
Labrador tea	Ledum or Rhododendron groenlandicum					X	X				mostly N. New England
Lily of the valley	Convallaria majuscula					X	X	X			
Marsh marigold	Caltha palustris			X	X	X					
Marsh pink	Sabatia stellaris						X	X	X		VA to MA
Mayapple	Podophyllum peltatum			X	X	X					
Meadow rue	Thalictrum dioicum			X	X						
Milkweed	Asclepias syriaca					X	X	X			
Monkshood	Aconitum uncinatum							X	X	X	GA to S. PA
Mountain cranberry	Vaccinium vitis-idaea					X	X				N. New England
Mountain laurel	Kalmia latifolia					X	X	X			GA to New England
Oxeye daisy	Chrysanthemum leucanthemum					X	X	X			
Pale laurel	Kalmia polifolia					X	X	X			PA to ME
Partridgeberry	Mitchella repens					X	X				
Pasture rose	Rosa carolina					X	X				
Periwinkle	Vinca major; Vinca minor		X	X	X	X					
Pink lady's slipper	Cypripedium acaule					X	X				
Pitcher plant	Sarracenia purpurea					X	X	X			mostly in New England bogs
Pokeweed	Phytolacca americana						X	X	X		
Prickly pear cactus	Opuntia humifusa					X	X	X			GA to MA
Pussytoes	Antennaria plantaginifolia			X	X	X					
Queen Anne's lace	Daucus carota					X	X	X	X	X	X	
Ragwort	Jacobaea vulgaris			X	X	X	X	X			
Rattlesnake plantain	Goodyera pubescens						X	X			
Rue anemone	Anemonella thalictroides		X	X	X						
Sarsaparilla	Aralia nudicaulis					X	X	X			
Serviceberry	Amelanchier arborea			X	X						
Sheep laurel	Kalmia angustifolia					X	X				
Skullcap	Scutellaria spp.				X	X	X	X	X		
Skunk cabbage	Symplocarpus foetidus	X	X	X							
Solomon's seal	Polygonatum biflorum			X	X	X					GA to S. New England
Spiderwort	Tradescantia virginiana			X	X	X	X				
Spotted wintergreen	Chimaphila maculata					X	X	X			

Common Name	Scientific Name	FEB	MAR	APR	MAY	JUN	JUL	AUG	SEP	OCT	Notes
Spring beauty	Claytonia virginica		X	X	X						
Squawroot	Conopholis americana				X	X					
Star chickweed	Stellaria pubera		X	X	X						GA to NJ
Starflower	Trientalis borealis				X	X					VA to ME
Star grass	Hypoxis hirsuta				X	X	X	X			
Starry campion	Silene stellata						X	X	X		GA to MA
Sundew	Drosera rotundifolia					X	X	X			mostly in New England bogs
Sundrops	Oenothera fruticosa					X	X	X			
Sweet cicely	Osmorhiza claytonii				X	X					
Tall meadow rue	Thalictrum pubescens					X	X	X			
Trailing arbutus	Epigaea repens		X	X	X	X					
Trillium	Trillium spp.			X	X	X					
Turkeybeard	Xerophyllum asphodeloides				X	X	X				GA to VA
Turk's-cap lily	Lilium superbum						X	X			GA to MA
Viper's bugloss	Echium vulgare					X	X	X	X		
White clintonia	Clintonia umbellulata				X	X	X				GA to NY
Whorled pogonia	Isotria medeoloides				X	X					
Wild geranium	Geranium maculatum			X	X	X					
Wild ginger	Asarum canadense			X	X						
Wild pink	Silene cariliniana			X	X	X					GA to S. New England
Wild oats	Uvularia sessilifolia				X	X					
Wintergreen	Gaultheria procumbens						X	X			
Wood lily	Lilium philadelphicum					X	X				
Wood sorrel	Oxalis montana				X	X	X	X	X	X	
Yellow lady's slipper	Cypripedium calceolus				X	X	X				

APPENDIX C

Birds of Shenandoah National Park

THIS LIST IS BASED on one published by the National Park Service and is used by permission of Creative Commons–Attribution ShareAlike License/Wikipedia (creativecommons.org/licenses/by-sa/3.0).

Common Name	Scientific Name	Common	Uncommon	Rare	Occasional
DUCKS, GEESE, AND WATERFOWL					
American black duck	*Anas rubripes*				X
Blue-winged teal	*Anas discors*				X
Canada goose	*Branta canadensis*				X
Green-winged teal	*Anas crecca*				X
Mallard	*Anas platyrhynchos*				X
Tundra swan	*Cygnus columbianus*				X
Wood duck	*Aix sponsa*		X		
NEW WORLD QUAIL					
Northern bobwhite	*Colinus virginianus*			X	
PHEASANTS, GROUSE, AND ALLIES					
Ring-necked pheasant*	*Phasianus colchicus*				X
Ruffed grouse	*Bonasa umbellus*				X
Wild turkey	*Meleagris gallopavo*				X
GREBES					
Pied-billed grebe	*Podilymbus podiceps*				X
PIGEONS AND DOVES					
Mourning dove	*Zenaida macroura*	X			
Rock pigeon*	*Columba livia*		X		
CUCKOOS					
Black-billed cuckoo	*Coccyzus erythropthalmus*		X		
Yellow-billed cuckoo	*Coccyzus americanus*		X		
NIGHTJARS AND ALLIES					
Common nighthawk	*Chordeiles minor*		X		
Eastern whip-poor-will	*Antrostomus vociferus*		X		
SWIFTS					
Chimney swift	*Chaetura pelagic*	X			
HUMMINGBIRDS					
Ruby-throated hummingbird	*Archilochus colubris*	X			
RAILS, GALLINULES, AND COOTS					
Virginia rail	*Rallus limicola*	X			
PLOVERS AND LAPWINGS					
American woodcock	*Scolopax minor*			X	
Common snipe	*Gallinago gallinago*				X
Killdeer	*Charadrius vociferus*				X

*Introduced to North America by the actions of humans, either directly or indirectly

Common Name	Scientific Name	Common	Uncommon	Rare	Occasional
PLOVERS AND LAPWINGS (*continued*)					
Solitary sandpiper	*Tringa solitaria*			X	
Spotted sandpiper	*Actitis macularius*			X	
Upland sandpiper	*Bartramia longicauda*		X		
Wilson's snipe	*Gallinago delicata*				X
GULLS, TERNS, AND SKIMMERS					
Caspian tern	*Hydroprogne caspia*				X
Herring gull	*Larus argentatus*				X
Ring-billed gull	*Larus delawarensis*				X
CORMORANTS AND SHAGS					
Double-crested cormorant	*Phalacrocorax auritus*				X
HERONS, EGRETS, AND BITTERNS					
American bittern	*Botaurus lentiginosus*				X
Black-crowned night heron	*Nycticorax nycticorax*				X
Cattle egret	*Bubulcus ibis*				X
Great blue heron	*Ardea herodias*				X
Great egret	*Ardea alba*				X
Green heron	*Butorides virescens*				X
NEW WORLD VULTURES					
Black vulture	*Coragyps atratus*	X			
Turkey vulture	*Cathartes aura*	X			
OSPREY					
Osprey	*Pandion haliaetus*				X
HAWKS, EAGLES, AND KITES					
Bald eagle	*Haliaeetus leucocephalus*				X
Broad-winged hawk	*Buteo platypterus*	X			
Cooper's hawk	*Accipiter cooperii*		X		
Golden eagle	*Aquila chrysaetos*	X			
Northern goshawk	*Accipiter gentilis*				X
Northern harrier	*Circus husonius*				X
Red-shouldered hawk	*Buteo lineatus*		X		
Red-tailed hawk	*Buteo jamaicensis*	X			
Rough-legged hawk	*Buteo lagopus*				X
Sharp-shinned hawk	*Accipiter striatus*		X		
OWLS					
Barred owl	*Strix varia*	X			
Eastern screech owl	*Megascops asio*		X		
Great horned owl	*Bubo virginianus*		X		

Common	Common residents, migrants, or seasonal visitors
Uncommon	Likely to be seen monthly in appropriate habitat and season; may be locally common
Rare	Present but usually seen only a few times each year
Occasional	Occurs in the park at least once every few years, varying in numbers, but not necessarily every year

Common Name	Scientific Name	Common	Uncommon	Rare	Occasional
OWLS (*continued*)					
Long-eared owl	*Asio otus*				X
Northern saw-whet owl	*Aegolius acadicus*			X	
Short-eared owl	*Asio flammeus*				X
KINGFISHERS					
Belted kingfisher	*Megaceryle alcyon*				X
WOODPECKERS					
Downy woodpecker	*Dryobates pubescens*	X			
Hairy woodpecker	*Dryobates villosus*		X		
Northern flicker	*Colaptes auratus*	X			
Pileated woodpecker	*Dryocopus pileatus*		X		
Red-bellied woodpecker	*Melanerpes carolinus*	X			
Red-headed woodpecker	*Melanerpes erythrocephalus*			X	
Yellow-bellied sapsucker	*Sphyrapicus varius*		X		
FALCONS AND CARACARAS					
American kestrel	*Falco sparverius*			X	
Merlin	*Falco columbarius*		X		
Peregrine falcon	*Falco peregrines*	X			
TYRANT FLYCATCHERS					
Acadian flycatcher	*Empidonax virescens*	X			
Alder flycatcher	*Empidonax alnorum*				X
Eastern kingbird	*Tyrannus tyrannus*				X
Eastern phoebe	*Sayornis phoebe*	X			
Eastern wood pewee	*Contopus virens*	X			
Great crested flycatcher	*Myiarchus crinitus*	X			
Least flycatcher	*Empidonax minimus*				X
Olive-sided flycatcher	*Contopus cooperi*				X
Willow flycatcher	*Empidonax traillii*				X
Yellow-bellied flycatcher	*Empidonax flaviventris*		X		
SHRIKES					
Northern shrike	*Lanius borealis*				X
VIREOS, SHRIKE-BABBLERS, AND ERPORNIS					
Blue-headed vireo	*Vireo solitaries*	X			
Philadelphia vireo	*Vireo philadelphicus*	X			
Solitary vireo	*Vireo solitaries*	X			
White-eyed vireo	*Vireo griseus*		X		
Yellow-throated vireo	*Vireo flavifrons*		X		
Red-eyed vireo	*Vireo olivaceus*	X			
Warbling vireo	*Vireo gilvus*			X	

Common	Common residents, migrants, or seasonal visitors
Uncommon	Likely to be seen monthly in appropriate habitat and season; may be locally common
Rare	Present but usually seen only a few times each year
Occasional	Occurs in the park at least once every few years, varying in numbers, but not necessarily every year

Common Name	Scientific Name	Common	Uncommon	Rare	Occasional
CROWS, JAYS, AND MAGPIES					
American crow	Corvus brachyrhynchos	X			
Blue jay	Cyanocitta cristata	X			
Common raven	Corvus corax	X			
Fish crow	Corvus ossifragus				X
LARKS					
Horned lark	Eremophila alpestris			X	
SWALLOWS					
Bank swallow	Riparia riparia			X	
Barn swallow	Hirundo rustica		X		
Cliff swallow	Petrochelidon pyrrhonota				X
Northern rough-winged swallow	Stelgidopteryx serripennis		X		
Purple martin	Progne subis			X	
Tree swallow	Tachycineta bicolor			X	
TITS, CHICKADEES, AND TITMICE					
Black-capped chickadee	Poecile atricapilla		X		
Carolina chickadee	Poecile carolinensis	X			
Tufted titmouse	Baeolophus bicolor	X			
NUTHATCHES					
Red-breasted nuthatch	Sitta canadensis				X
White-breasted nuthatch	Sitta carolinensis	X			
TREECREEPERS					
Brown creeper	Certhia americana		X		
WRENS					
Carolina wren	Thryothorus ludovicianus	X			
House wren	Troglodytes aedon		X		
Winter wren	Troglodytes hiemalis			X	
GNATCATCHERS					
Blue-gray gnatcatcher	Polioptila caerulea	X			
KINGLETS					
Golden-crowned kinglet	Regulus satrapa	X			
Ruby-crowned kinglet	Regulus calendula	X			
THRUSHES AND ALLIES					
American robin	Turdus migratorius	X			
Eastern bluebird	Sialia sialis	X			
Gray-cheeked thrush	Catharus minimus			X	
Hermit thrush	Catharus guttatus		X		
Swainson's thrush	Catharus ustulatus		X		
Veery	Catharus fuscescens	X			
Wood thrush	Hylocichla mustelina	X			
MOCKINGBIRDS AND THRASHERS					
Brown thrasher	Toxostoma rufum		X		
Gray catbird	Dumetella carolinensis	X			
Northern mockingbird	Mimus polyglottos				X
STARLINGS					
European starling*	Sturnus vulgaris		X		
WAXWINGS					
Cedar waxwing	Bombycilla cedrorum		X		

*Introduced to North America by the actions of humans, either directly or indirectly

Common Name	Scientific Name	Common	Uncommon	Rare	Occasional
OLD WORLD SPARROWS					
House sparrow*	Passer domesticus		X		
WAGTAILS AND PIPITS					
American pipit	Anthus rubescens			X	
FINCHES, EUPHONIAS, AND ALLIES					
American goldfinch	Spinus tristis	X			
Common redpoll	Acanthis flammea			X	
Evening grosbeak	Coccothraustes vespertinus				X
House finch	Haemorhous mexicanus		X		
Pine grosbeak	Pinicola enucleator				X
Pine siskin	Spinus pinus		X		
Purple finch	Haemorhous purpureus				X
Red crossbill	Loxia curvirostra			X	
White-winged crossbill	Loxia leucoptera				X
LONGSPURS AND SNOW BUNTINGS					
Lapland longspur	Calcarius lapponicus			X	
Snow bunting	Plectrophenax nivalis			X	
NEW WORLD SPARROWS					
American tree sparrow	Spizelloides arborea			X	
Chipping sparrow	Spizella passerine	X			
Dark-eyed junco	Junco hyemalis	X			
Eastern towhee	Pipilo erythrophthalmus	X			
Field sparrow	Spizella pusilla	X			
Fox sparrow	Passerella iliaca	X			
Grasshopper sparrow	Ammodramus savannarum			X	
Henslow's sparrow	Centronyx henslowii				X
Lincoln's sparrow	Melospiza lincolnii			X	
Savannah sparrow	Passerculus sandwichensis				X
Song sparrow	Melospiza melodia	X			
Swamp sparrow	Melospiza georgiana		X		
Vesper sparrow	Pooecetes gramineus			X	
White-crowned sparrow	Zonotrichia leucophrys	X			
White-throated sparrow	Zonotrichia albicollis				X
Yellow-breasted chat	Icteria virens				X
TROUPIALS AND ALLIES					
Baltimore oriole	Icterus galbula			X	
Bobolink	Dolichonyx oryzivorus			X	
Brown-headed cowbird	Molothrus ater	X			
Common grackle	Quiscalus quiscula	X			
Eastern meadowlark	Sturnella magna			X	
Orchard oriole	Icterus spurius			X	
Red-winged blackbird	Agelaius phoeniceus		X		
Rusty blackbird	Euphagus carolinus			X	
NEW WORLD WARBLERS					
American redstart	Setophaga ruticilla	X			
Bay-breasted warbler	Setophaga castanea				X
Black-and-white warbler	Mniotilta varia		X		
Blackburnian warbler	Setophaga fusca		X		

*Introduced to North America by the actions of humans, either directly or indirectly

Common Name	Scientific Name	Common	Uncommon	Rare	Occasional
NEW WORLD WARBLERS (*continued*)					
Blackpoll warbler	*Setophaga striata*				X
Black-throated blue warbler	*Setophaga caerulescens*		X		
Black-throated green warbler	*Setophaga virens*		X		
Blue-winged warbler	*Vermivora cyanoptera*		X		
Canada warbler	*Cardellina canadensis*				X
Cape May warbler	*Setophaga tigrina*		X		
Cerulean warbler	*Setophaga cerulea*		X		
Chestnut-sided warbler	*Setophaga pensylvanica*	X			
Common yellowthroat	*Geothlypis trichas*				X
Connecticut warbler	*Oporornis agilis*				X
Golden-winged warble	*Vermivora chrysoptera*		X		
Hooded warbler	*Setophaga citrine*	X			
Kentucky warbler	*Geothlypis formosa*		X		
Louisiana waterthrush	*Parkesia motacilla*		X		
Magnolia warbler	*Setophaga magnolia*		X		
Mourning warbler	*Geothlypis philadelphia*				X
Nashville warbler	*Leiothlypis ruficapilla*			X	
Northern parula	*Setophaga Americana*	X			
Northern waterthrush	*Parkesia noveboracensis*				X
Orange-crowned warbler	*Leiothlypis celata*			X	
Ovenbird	*Ovenbird, Seiurus aurocapilla*	X			
Palm warbler	*Setophaga palmarum*				X
Pine warbler	*Setophaga pinus*		X		
Prairie warbler	*Setophaga discolor*		X		
Prothonotary warbler	*Protonotaria citrea*				X
Tennessee warbler	*Leiothlypis peregrina*		X		
Wilson's warbler	*Cardellina pusilla*				X
Worm-eating warbler	*Helmitheros vermivorum*		X		
Yellow-rumped warbler	*Setophaga coronata*		X		
Yellow-throated warbler	*Setophaga dominica*				X
Yellow warbler	*Setophaga petechia*				X
CARDINALS AND ALLIES					
Blue grosbeak	*Passerina caerulea*				X
Indigo bunting	*Passerina cyanea*	X			
Northern cardinal	*Cardinalis cardinalis*	X			
Rose-breasted grosbeak	*Pheucticus ludovicianus*	X			
Scarlet tanager	*Piranga olivacea*	X			
Summer tanager	*Piranga rubra*			X	

Common	Common residents, migrants, or seasonal visitors
Uncommon	Likely to be seen monthly in appropriate habitat and season; may be locally common
Rare	Present but usually seen only a few times each year
Occasional	Occurs in the park at least once every few years, varying in numbers, but not necessarily every year

Birds of the White Mountain National Forest

THIS LIST INCLUDES birds sighted within a quarter-mile radius of Appalachian Mountain Club's (AMC) huts in New Hampshire's White Mountain National Forest during the hut season from May to October. The huts are listed in order by distance from the AT's northern terminus at Mount Katahdin. Distance is noted in miles. The Birds of the White Mountain National Forest list is courtesy of Janet Williams, Michael Greenwald, and Robert Williams.

Common Name	Scientific Name	Carter Hut Notch (313.5)	Pinkham Notch Visitor Center (319.4)	Madison Hut (327.2)	Lake of the Clouds Hut (334.3)	Mizpah Spring Hut (339.0)	Zealand Falls Hut (353.1)	Galehead Hut (360.1)	Greenleaf Hut (366.7)	Lonesome Lake Hut (376.0)
HERONS, GEESE, DUCKS										
American black duck	*Anas rubripes*			U			U			U
Black-crowned night heron	*Nycticorax nycticorax*						R			
Canada goose	*Branta canadensis*								R	
Common merganser	*Mergus merganser*						R			
Great blue heron	*Ardea herodias*	R					R			R
Ring-necked duck	*Aythya collaris*									U
Wood duck	*Aix sponsa*						R			
HAWKS										
American kestrel	*Falco sparverius*								R	
Broad-winged hawk	*Buteo platypterus*		U	U	U	U		R	U	U
Peregrine falcon	*Falco peregrinus*					U	R	R	R	
Red-tailed hawk	*Buteo jamaicensis*								R	
Sharp-shinned hawk	*Accipiter striatus*				R					
GROUSE										
Ruffed grouse	*Bonasa umbellus*		U				U			
Spruce grouse	*Falcipennis canadensis*	U					F	U		
SHOREBIRDS, GULLS										
American woodcock	*Scolopax minor*									
Ring-billed gull	*Larus delawarensis*				R					

A = Abundant | C = Common | F = Fairly Common | U = Uncommon | R = Rare

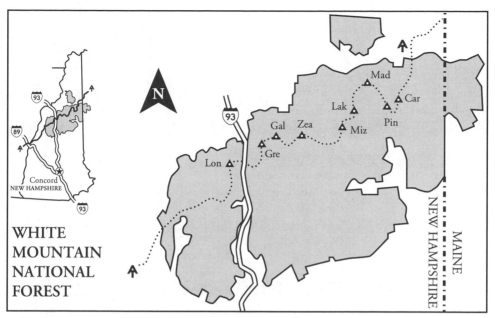

HUT NAME AND LOCATION (*Miles from AT Northern Terminus*)	
CAR = Carter Notch Hut (313.5)	**ZEA** = Zealand Falls Hut (353.1)
PIN = Pinkham Notch Visitor Center (319.4)	**GAL** = Galehead Hut (360.1)
MAD = Madison Hut (327.2)	**GRE** = Greenleaf Hut (366.7)
LAK = Lakes of the Clouds Hut (334.3)	**LON** = Lonesome Lake Hut (376.0)
MIZ = Mizpah Spring Hut (339.0)	

Common Name	Scientific Name	Carter Hut Notch (313.5)	Pinkham Notch Visitor Center (319.4)	Madison Hut (327.2)	Lake of the Clouds Hut (334.3)	Mizpah Spring Hut (339.0)	Zealand Falls Hut (353.1)	Galehead Hut (360.1)	Greenleaf Hut (366.7)	Lonesome Lake Hut (376.0)
SHOREBIRDS, GULLS *(continued)*										
Spotted sandpiper	*Actitis macularius*		F							F
Upland sandpiper	*Bartramia longicauda*				R					
DOVES, OWLS										
Barred owl	*Strix varia*		U			R				
Mourning dove	*Zenaida macroura*		C			U				
Northern saw-whet owl	*Aegolius acadicus*				R					
SWIFTS, HUMMINGBIRDS										
Chimney swift	*Chaetura pelagica*		F			F				
Ruby-throated hummingbird	*Archilochus colubris*		F			R		R		

Common Name	Scientific Name	Carter Hut Notch (313.5)	Pinkham Notch Visitor Center (319.4)	Madison Hut (327.2)	Lake of the Clouds Hut (334.3)	Mizpah Spring Hut (339.0)	Zealand Falls Hut (353.1)	Galehead Hut (360.1)	Greenleaf Hut (366.7)	Lonesome Lake Hut (376.0)
KINGFISHERS										
Belted kingfisher	Megaceryle alcyon	U	F							
WOODPECKERS										
Black-backed woodpecker	Picoides arcticus					R			R	
Downy woodpecker	Dryobates pubescens	U	F				U			
Hairy woodpecker	Dryobates villosus	U	F				U		F	
Northern flicker	Colaptes auratus		U				R		R	
Pileated woodpecker	Dryocopus pileatus		R							
Three-toed woodpecker	Picoides dorsalis								R	
Yellow-bellied sapsucker	Sphyrapicus varius		R							
FLYCATCHERS										
Alder flycatcher	Empidonax alnorum		U				F			
Eastern phoebe	Sayornis phoebe		C				U			
Eastern wood pewee	Contopus virens		F							
Least flycatcher	Empidonax minimus		C				C			
Olive-sided flycatcher	Contopus cooperi						R			
Yellow-bellied flycatcher	Empidonax flaviventris					F		F	U	U
SWALLOWS, JAYS, CROWS										
American crow	Corvus brachyrhynchos		C							
Barn swallow	Hirundo rustica		C							
Blue jay	Cyanocitta cristata		C				U		U	U
Common raven	Corvus corax	F	R	F	F	U	U	F	F	
Gray jay	Perisoreus canadensis					F		U		
Northern rough-winged swallow	Stelgidopteryx serripennis									
Tree swallow	Tachycineta bicolor		C					C		U
CHICKADEES, NUTHATCHES										
Black-capped chickadee	Poecile atricapillus		C	R			F		U	C
Boreal chickadee	Poecile hudsonicus	F		U		C		C	C	
Red-breasted nuthatch	Sitta canadensis	F	U	U	U	F		F	F	C
White-breasted nuthatch	Sitta carolinensis			F						U
WRENS, KINGLETS										
Golden-crowned kinglet	Regulus satrapa	F		U	U	F	U	F	C	F
Ruby-crowned kinglet	Regulus calendula					F	U	U	F	
Winter wren	Troglodytes hiemalis	C	C	C	C	C	C	C	C	C
THRUSHES, PIPITS										
American robin	Turdus migratorius		A			U		U	F	F
American pipit	Anthus rubescens					F			R	
Bicknell's thrush	Catharus bicknelli	F		F	U	C		C	F	U

Common Name	Scientific Name	Carter Hut Notch (313.5)	Pinkham Notch Visitor Center (319.4)	Madison Hut (327.2)	Lake of the Clouds Hut (334.3)	Mizpah Spring Hut (339.0)	Zealand Falls Hut (353.1)	Galehead Hut (360.1)	Greenleaf Hut (366.7)	Lonesome Lake Hut (376.0)
THRUSHES, PIPITS *(continued)*										
Hermit thrush	*Catharus guttatus*	U					U			F
Swainson's thrush	*Catharus ustulatus*	C	F	F		C	C	C	F	C
Veery	*Catharus fuscescens*					U				
WAXWINGS, VIREOS										
Cedar waxwing	*Bombycilla cedrorum*	U	C				C		F	A
Philadelphia vireo	*Vireo philadelphicus*		R							
Red-eyed Vireo	*Vireo olivaceus*		C				C	R		C
Solitary vireo	*Vireo solitarius*	F	U			F	C	F		F
Warbling vireo	*Vireo gilvus*		U							
WOOD WARBLERS										
American restart	*Setophaga ruticilla*		F				C			C
Bay-breasted warbler	*Setophaga castanea*						R			
Black-and-white warbler	*Mniotilta varia*						U			R
Blackburnian warbler	*Setophaga fusca*		F				F		R	F
Blackpoll warbler	*Setophaga striata*	U		C	C	C	U	C	C	U
Black-throated blue warbler	*Setophaga caerulescens*		F				C		R	F
Black-throated green warbler	*Setophaga virens*	C	C				C	R	R	C
Canada warbler	*Cardellina canadensis*						F			U
Chestnut-sided Warbler	*Setophaga pensylvanica*									U
Common yellowthroat	*Geothlypis trichas*		C				C			C
Magnolia warbler	*Setophaga magnolia*				U	F		F	F	F
Ovenbird	*Seiurus aurocapilla*		C				F			
Nashville warbler	*Leiothlypis ruficapilla*					F	F	U		F
Palm warbler	*Setophaga palmarum*								R	
Tennessee warbler	*Leiothlypis peregrina*						R			
Yellow-rumped warbler	*Setophaga coronata*	C	C	C	F	C	C	C	C	C
Yellow warbler	*Setophaga petechia*						U			
TANAGERS, BUNTINGS										
Indigo bunting	*Passerina cyanea*									
Scarlet tanager	*Piranga olivacea*		F							
SPARROWS										
Chipping sparrow	*Spizella passerina*									U
Dark-eyed junco	*Junco hyemalis*	C	C	C	C	A	F	A	C	C
Song sparrow	*Melospiza melodia*						F			R

A = Abundant | C = Common | F = Fairly Common | U = Uncommon | R = Rare

Common Name	Scientific Name	Carter Hut Notch (313.5)	Pinkham Notch Visitor Center (319.4)	Madison Hut (327.2)	Lake of the Clouds Hut (334.3)	Mizpah Spring Hut (339.0)	Zealand Falls Hut (353.1)	Galehead Hut (360.1)	Greenleaf Hut (366.7)	Lonesome Lake Hut (376.0)
SPARROWS (*continued*)										
Swamp sparrow	*Melospiza georgiana*		F				F			
White-crowned sparrow	*Zonotrichia leucophrys*						F		R	
White-throated sparrow	*Zonotrichia albicollis*	C	C	C	C	C	C	C	C	C
BLACKBIRDS										
Common grackle	*Quiscalus quiscula*		C				F			
Red-winged blackbird	*Agelaius phoeniceus*		A				C			
Rusty blackbird	*Euphagus carolinus*									U
FINCHES, GROSBEAKS										
American goldfinch	*Spinus tristis*	U	F	R	R		U		R	
Evening grosbeak	*Coccothraustes vespertinus*		C							
Pine siskin	*Spinus pinus*	F	A		R	F	F	F	R	U
Purple finch	*Haemorhous purpureus*	U	C	F		F	F	F	F	U

A = Abundant | C = Common | F = Fairly Common | U = Uncommon | R = Rare

The Appalachian Trail Conservancy and Member Trail-Maintaining Clubs

And, what is the Trail? . . .

It always was a place for people.

People who care for land and tend a simple footpath

as if it were their garden.

~ *Appalachian Trail Conservancy Member Handbook*

APPALACHIAN TRAIL CONSERVANCY
PO Box 807
Harpers Ferry, WV 25425
304-535-6331; appalachiantrail.org

GEORGIA APPALACHIAN TRAIL CLUB
PO Box 654
Atlanta, GA 30301
404-494-0968; georgia-atclub.org
Maintains 78.3 miles, from Springer Mountain, Georgia, to Bly Gap near the Georgia–North Carolina border

NANTAHALA HIKING CLUB
173 Carl Slagle Road
Franklin, NC 28734
nantahalahikingclub.org
Maintains 58.6 miles, from Bly Gap near the Georgia–North Carolina border to Nantahala River, North Carolina

SMOKY MOUNTAINS HIKING CLUB
PO Box 51592
Knoxville, TN 37950; smhclub.org
Maintains 102.4 miles, from Nantahala River, North Carolina, to Davenport Gap (TN 32)

CAROLINA MOUNTAIN CLUB
PO Box 68
Asheville, NC 28802
carolinamountainclub.org
Maintains 94 miles, from Davenport Gap (TN 32), to Spivey Gap (US 19W)

TENNESSEE EASTMAN HIKING AND CANOEING CLUB
PO Box 511
Kingsport, TN 37662; tehcc.org
Maintains 133.8 miles, from Spivey Gap (US 19W) to Damascus, Virginia

MOUNT ROGERS APPALACHIAN TRAIL CLUB
PO Box 789
Damascus, VA 24236; mratc.org
Maintains 56 miles, from Damascus, Virginia, to South Fork of the Holston River, Virginia (VA 670)

PIEDMONT APPALACHIAN TRAIL HIKERS
PO Box 4423
Greensboro, NC 27404; path-at.org
Maintains 65.4 miles, from South Fork of the Holston River, Virginia (VA 670), to US 52

OUTING CLUB OF VIRGINIA TECH
PO Box 538
Blacksburg, VA 24060; ocvt.club
Maintains from US 52 to VA 611 (8.8 miles) and from US 460 to Pine Swamp Branch Shelter (18.9 miles)

ROANOKE APPALACHIAN TRAIL CLUB
PO Box 12282
Roanoke, VA 24024; ratc.org
Maintains from VA 611 to US 460 (36.9 miles) and from Pine Swamp Branch Shelter to Black Horse Gap, Virginia (87 miles)

NATURAL BRIDGE APPALACHIAN TRAIL CLUB
PO Box 3012
Lynchburg, VA 24503; nbatc.org
Maintains 90.7 miles, from Black Horse Gap, Virginia, to Tye River, Virginia (VA 56)

TIDEWATER APPALACHIAN TRAIL CLUB
PO Box 8246
Norfolk, VA 23503; tidewateratc.com
Maintains 11 miles, from Tye River, Virginia (VA 56), to Reids Gap, Virginia (VA 664)

OLD DOMINION APPALACHIAN TRAIL CLUB
PO Box 25283
Richmond, VA 23260
olddominiontrailclub.onefireplace.org
Maintains 19.1 miles, from Reids Gap, Virginia (VA 664), to Rockfish Gap, Virginia (US 250)

POTOMAC APPALACHIAN TRAIL CLUB
118 Park St. SE
Vienna, VA 22180
703-242-0693; patc.net
Maintains 240.5 miles, from Rockfish Gap, Virginia (US 250), to Pine Grove Furnace State Park, Pennsylvania

MOUNTAIN CLUB OF MARYLAND
17340 Oster Farm Road
West Friendship, MD 21794; mcomd.org
*Maintains from Pine Grove Furnace State Park,
Pennsylvania, to Center Point Knob, Pennsylvania
(16.2 miles), and from Darlington Trail, Pennsylvania, to Susquehanna River, Pennsylvania
(12.6 miles)*

CUMBERLAND VALLEY APPALACHIAN TRAIL MANAGEMENT ASSOCIATION
PO Box 395
Boiling Springs, PA 17007
cvatclub.org
*Maintains 17.2 miles, from Center Point Knob,
Pennsylvania, to Darlington Trail, Pennsylvania*

YORK HIKING CLUB
2684 Forest Road
York, PA 17402
717-244-6769; yorkhikingclub.com
*Maintains 6.9 miles, from Susquehanna River,
Pennsylvania, to PA 225*

SUSQUEHANNA APPALACHIAN TRAIL CLUB
Box 610001
Harrisburg, PA 17106-1001; satc-hike.org
*Maintains 20.8 miles, from PA 225 to Rausch
Creek, Pennsylvania (PA 325)*

BLUE MOUNTAIN EAGLE CLIMBING CLUB
PO Box 14982
Reading, PA 19612; bmecc.org
*Maintains from Rausch Creek, Pennsylvania, to
Tri-County Corner, Pennsylvania (62 miles), and
from Bake Oven Knob, Pennsylvania, to Lehigh
Furnace Gap, Pennsylvania (3 miles)*

ALLENTOWN HIKING CLUB
PO Box 1542
Allentown, PA 18105-1542
allentownhikingclub.org
*Maintains 10.7 miles, from Tri-County Corner,
Pennsylvania, to Bake Oven Knob,
Pennsylvania*

KEYSTONE TRAILS ASSOCIATION
46 E. Main St.
Mechanicsburg, PA 17055
717-766-9690; kta-hike.org
*Maintains 10.3 miles, from Lehigh Furnace Gap,
Pennsylvania, to Little Gap, Pennsylvania*

APPALACHIAN MOUNTAIN CLUB, DELAWARE VALLEY CHAPTER
1180 Greenleaf Drive
Bethlehem, PA 18017-9319; amcdv.org
*Maintains 15.4 miles, from Little Gap,
Pennsylvania, to Wind Gap, Pennsylvania (PA 33)*

BATONA HIKING CLUB
6651 Eastwood St.
Philadelphia, PA 19149
batona.wildapricot.org
*Maintains 8.5 miles, from Wind Gap,
Pennsylvania (PA 33), to Fox Gap, Pennsylvania
(PA 191)*

WILMINGTON TRAIL CLUB
PO Box 526
Hokessin, DE 19707
wilmingtontrailclub.org
*Maintains 7.2 miles, from Fox Gap,
Pennsylvania (PA 191), to Delaware River Bridge,
Pennsylvania–New Jersey border*

NEW YORK–NEW JERSEY TRAIL CONFERENCE
600 Ramapo Valley Road
Mahwah, NJ 07430
201-512-0348; nynjtc.org
*Maintains 162.4 miles, from Delaware River
Bridge, Pennsylvania–New Jersey border, to
Hoyt Road, New York–Connecticut border*

APPALACHIAN MOUNTAIN CLUB, CONNECTICUT CHAPTER
71 Noble St.
Stamford, CT 06902
413-528-6333; ct-amc.org
*Maintains 51.2 miles, from Hoyt Road, New
York–Connecticut border, to Sages Ravine,
Massachusetts*

APPALACHIAN MOUNTAIN CLUB, BERKSHIRE CHAPTER
PO Box 2281
Pittsfield, MA 01202; amcberkshire.org
Maintains 89.7 miles, from Sages Ravine, Massachusetts, to Massachusetts–Vermont border

GREEN MOUNTAIN CLUB
4711 Waterbury-Stowe Road
Waterbury Center, VT 05677
802-244-7037; greenmountainclub.org
Maintains 150.8 miles, from the Massachusetts–Vermont border to the Vermont–New Hampshire border

DARTMOUTH OUTING CLUB
PO Box 9
Hanover, NH 03755
603-646-2428; outdoors.dartmouth.edu
Maintains 53.3 miles, from the Vermont–New Hampshire border to Kinsman Notch, New Hampshire (NH 112)

APPALACHIAN MOUNTAIN CLUB
10 City Square
Boston, MA 02129; 617-523-0655
Maintains 120 miles, from Kinsman Notch, New Hampshire (NH 112), to Grafton Notch, Maine (ME 26), with the exception of 2.2 miles maintained by the Randolph Mountain Club (see below)

RANDOLPH MOUNTAIN CLUB
PO Box 279
Gorham, NH 03581
randolphmountainclub.org
Maintains 2.2 miles, from Edmands Col, New Hampshire (north of Mount Washington), to Madison Spring Hut, New Hampshire

MAINE APPALACHIAN TRAIL CLUB
PO Box 283
Augusta, ME 04330; matc.org
Maintains 267.2 miles, from Grafton Notch, Maine (ME 26), to Mount Katahdin, Maine

Bibliography and Suggested Readings and Field Guides

There is no frigate like a book to take us lands away.

~ Emily Dickinson

Adkins, Leonard M. *All About the Appalachian Trail* (for ages 9–13). Indianapolis, IN: Blue River Press, 2020.

———. *Hiking and Traveling the Blue Ridge Parkway: The Only Guide You Will Ever Need, Including GPS, Detailed Maps, and More.* Chapel Hill: University of North Carolina Press, 2018.

———. *Images of America: Along the Appalachian Trail: Georgia, North Carolina, and Tennessee.* Charleston, SC: Arcadia Publishing, 2012.

———. *Images of America: Along the Appalachian Trail: Massachusetts, Vermont, and New Hampshire.* Charleston, SC: Arcadia Publishing, 2016.

———. *Images of America: Along the Appalachian Trail: New Jersey, New York, and Connecticut.* Charleston, SC: Arcadia Publishing, 2014.

———. *Images of America: Along the Appalachian Trail: West Virginia, Maryland, and Pennsylvania.* Charleston, SC: Arcadia Publishing, 2015.

———. *Postcards of America: Along Virginia's Appalachian Trail.* Charleston, SC: Arcadia Publishing, 2009.

———. *The Appalachian Trail: A Visitor's Companion.* Birmingham, AL: Menasha Ridge Press, 2000.

———. *Wildflowers of the Appalachian Trail.* Birmingham, AL: Menasha Ridge Press, 2017.

———. *Wildflowers of the Blue Ridge and Great Smoky Mountains.* Birmingham, AL Menasha Ridge Press, 2005.

Beane, Jeffrey C., Alvin L. Braswell, Joseph C. Mitchell, William M. Palmer, and Julian R. Harrison. *Amphibians and Reptiles of the Carolinas and Virginia.* Chapel Hill, NC: University of North Carolina Press, 2010.

Behler, John L., and Wayne F. King. *National Audubon Society Field Guide to North American Reptiles and Amphibians.* New York: Penguin Random House, 1995.

Brill, David. *As Far as the Eye Can See: Reflections of an Appalachian Trail Hiker.* Knoxville, TN: University of Tennessee Press, 2013.

Brooks, Maurice. *The Appalachians.* Morgantown, WV: Seneca Books, 1995.

Burn, Barbara. *North American Trees.* Avenel, NJ: Gramercy Books, 1992.

Byrd, Nathan, ed. *A Forester's Guide to Observing Animal Use of Forest Habitat in the South.* Atlanta: U.S. Department of Agriculture, Forest Service, 1981.

Catlin, David T. *A Naturalist's Blue Ridge Parkway.* Knoxville, TN: University of Tennessee Press, 1984.

Chew, V. Collins. *Underfoot: A Geologic Guide to the Appalachian Trail.* Harpers Ferry, WV: Appalachian Trail Conservancy, 1993.

Coats, Alice. *Flowers and Their Histories.* New York: McGraw Hill, 1971.

Constanz, George. *Hollows, Peepers, and Highlanders: An Appalachian Mountain Ecology.* Missoula, MT: Mountain Press Publishing, 2004.

Dana, Mrs. William S. *How to Know the Wildflowers.* Boston: Houghton Mifflin, 1991.

Douglas, William O. *My Wilderness: East to Katahdin.* San Francisco: Comstock Editions, 1989.

Eastman, John. *The Book of Forest and Thicket: Trees, Shrubs, and Wildflowers of Eastern North America.* Mechanicsburg, PA: Stackpole Books, 1992.

Fisher, Ronald M. *The Appalachian Trail.* Washington, DC: National Geographic Society, 1994.

———. *Mountain Adventure: Exploring the Appalachian Trail.* Washington, DC: National Geographic Society, 1988.

Grimm, William C., and John T. Kartesz. *The Illustrated Book of Trees: The Comprehensive Field Guide to More Than 250 Trees of Eastern North America.* Mechanicsburg, PA: Stackpole Books, 2001.

Gupton, Oscar W., and Fred C. Swope. *Wildflowers of Tidewater Virginia.* Charlottesville, VA: University of Virginia Press, 1982.

Halliday, Tim, and Kraig Adler, eds. *The Encyclopedia of Reptiles and Amphibians.* New York: Facts on File, 1994.

Handley, Charles O., and Clyde P. Patton. *Wild Mammals of Virginia.* Richmond, VA: Virginia Commission of Game and Inland Fisheries, 1947.

Hare, James R., ed. *From Katahdin to Springer: The Best of Hiking the Appalachian Trail.* Emmaus, PA: Rodale Press, 1977.

Irwin, Bill. *Blind Courage.* Waco, TX: WRS Publishing, 1992.

Johnson, Charles W. *Bogs of the Northeast.* Hanover, NH: University Press of New England, 1985.

Justice, William S., and C. Ritchie Bell. *Wildflowers of North Carolina.* Chapel Hill, NC: University of North Carolina Press, 2005.

Kephart, Horace. *Our Southern Highlanders: A Narrative of Adventure in the Southern Appalachians and a Study of the Life Among the Mountaineers.* Knoxville, TN: University of Tennessee Press, 1987.

Little, Elbert L. *National Audubon Society Field Guide to North American Trees: Eastern Region.* New York: Knopf, 1994.

Logue, Victoria and Frank. *The Appalachian Trail Hiker: Trail-Proven Advice for Hikes of Any Length.* Birmingham, AL: Menasha Ridge Press, 2004.

Logue, Victoria and Frank, and Leonard M. Adkins. *The Best of the Appalachian Trail Day Hikes.* Birmingham, AL: Menasha Ridge Press, 2018.

Logue, Victoria and Frank, and Leonard M. Adkins. *The Best of the Appalachian Trail Overnight Hikes.* Birmingham, AL: Menasha Ridge Press, 2018.

Luxenberg, Larry. *Walking the Appalachian Trail.* Mechanicsburg, PA: Stackpole Books, 1994.

Murie, Olaus J. *A Field Guide to Animal Tracks.* Boston: Houghton Mifflin Harcourt, 2005.

Sylvester, Robert, ed. *The Appalachian Long Distance Hikers Association's Appalachian Trail Thru-Hikers' Companion.* Harpers Ferry, WV: Appalachian Trail Conservancy, 2020.

Peterson, Roger Torey. *A Field Guide to the Birds of Eastern and Central North America.* Boston: Houghton Mifflin Harcourt, 2010.

Peterson, Roger T., and Margaret McKenny. *A Field Guide to Wildflowers of Northeastern and North-Central North America.* Boston: Houghton Mifflin Harcourt, 1998.

Petrides, George A. *A Field Guide to Trees and Shrubs.* Boston: Houghton Mifflin Harcourt, 1998.

Reid, Fiona. *Peterson Field Guide to Mammals of North America.* Boston: Houghton Mifflin Harcourt, 2006.

Rue III, Leonard Lee. *Pictorial Guide to Mammals of North America.* New York: Thomas Y. Crowell Company, 1967.

Shaffer, Earl V. *Walking with Spring: The First Thru-Hike of the Appalachian Trail.* Harpers Ferry, WV: Appalachian Trail Conservancy, 2004.

Simpson Jr., Marcus B. *Birds of the Blue Ridge Mountains.* Chapel Hill: University of North Carolina Press, 1992.

Stokes, Donald. *Stokes Field Guide to Birds: Eastern Region.* Boston: Little, Brown and Company, 2013.

Sutton, Ann and Myron. *The Appalachian Trail: Wilderness on the Doorstep.* Philadelphia: Lippincott, 1967.

Waterman, Laura and Guy. *The Green Guide to Low-Impact Hiking and Camping.* New York, NY: Countryman Press, 2016.

Webster, William David, James F. Parnell, and Walter C. Biggs Jr. *Mammals of the Carolinas, Virginia, and Maryland.* Chapel Hill, NC: University of North Carolina Press, 2004.

Weidensaul, Scott. *Mountains of the Heart: A Natural History of the Appalachians.* Golden, CO: Fulcrum Publishing, 2016.

Whitaker Jr., John O. *The Audubon Society Field Guide to North American Mammals.* New York: Knopf, 1980.

————. *Appalachian Trail Guides* (a series of books available from the Appalachian Trail Conservancy, Harpers Ferry, WV).

Index

DEAR CUSTOMERS AND FRIENDS,

SUPPORTING YOUR INTEREST IN OUTDOOR ADVENTURE, travel, and an active lifestyle is central to our operations, from the authors we choose to the locations we detail to the way we design our books. Menasha Ridge Press was incorporated in 1982 by a group of veteran outdoorsmen and professional outfitters. For many years now, we've specialized in creating books that benefit the outdoors enthusiast.

Almost immediately, Menasha Ridge Press earned a reputation for revolutionizing outdoors- and travel-guidebook publishing. For such activities as canoeing, kayaking, hiking, backpacking, and mountain biking, we established new standards of quality that transformed the whole genre, resulting in outdoor-recreation guides of great sophistication and solid content. Menasha Ridge Press continues to be outdoor publishing's greatest innovator.

The folks at Menasha Ridge Press are as at home on a whitewater river or mountain trail as they are editing a manuscript. The books we build for you are the best they can be, because we're responding to your needs. Plus, we use and depend on them ourselves.

We look forward to seeing you on the river or the trail. If you'd like to contact us directly, visit us at menasharidge.com. We thank you for your interest in our books and the natural world around us all.

SAFE TRAVELS,

Bob Sehlinger

**BOB SEHLINGER
PUBLISHER**

Check out these great titles from
Menasha Ridge Press!

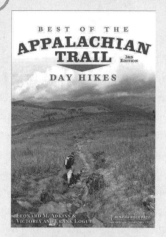

Best of the Appalachian Trail: Day Hikes

By Leonard M. Adkins, Victoria Logue, and Frank Logue
ISBN: 978-1-63404-145-4 • $18.95, 3rd Edition

From Maine to Georgia, the nearly 2,200-mile Appalachian National Scenic Trail is an iconic destination. Whether you want a short walk or a daylong adventure, let *Best of the Appalachian Trail: Day Hikes* inspire you. Appalachian Trail experts Leonard M. Adkins and Victoria and Frank Logue have selected their top 144 day hikes. Trailhead maps and driving directions get you where you need to go, and point-by-point descriptions help prepare you for what's ahead.

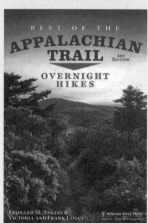

Best of the Appalachian Trail: Overnight Hikes

By Leonard M. Adkins, Victoria Logue, and Frank Logue
ISBN: 978-1-63404-147-8 • $18.95, 3rd Edition

In *Best of the Appalachian Trail: Overnight Hikes,* the same authors present 64 of their favorite hikes for an overnight trip on the beloved long trail. Ranging from 10 to 30 miles, the hikes offer options for experienced backpackers and casual explorers alike. Difficulty ratings, maps, and trail descriptions help you plan your trip, while fascinating flora, fauna, and history tidbits entertain and educate you about the 14 states traversed by the AT.

Wildflowers of the Appalachian Trail

By Leonard M. Adkins
ISBN: 978-1-63404-090-7 • $16.95, 3rd Edition

Wildflowers of the Appalachian Trail, a National Outdoor Book Award winner, is the go-to resource for anyone interested in the wildflowers found along the AT. Stunning full-page color photos by Joe Cook and Monica Sheppard accompany the detailed descriptions by author Leonard M. Adkins.

  MENASHA RIDGE PRESS
menasharidge.com

About the Author

Photo: Laurie Adkins

LEONARD M. ADKINS has walked the entire length of the Appalachian Trail five times and lacks less than 600 miles of completing it for a sixth. In all, Leonard has hiked more than 20,000 miles exploring the back-country areas of the United States, Canada, Europe, New Zealand, and the Caribbean. Among other long-distance trails, he has traversed the Continental Divide Trail from Canada to Mexico; followed the Pacific Northwest Trail through Montana, Idaho, and Washington; walked several hundred miles of Canada's Great Divide; and traipsed the mid-Atlantic's Tuscarora Trail. He has also trekked the full length of the Pyrenees High Route from the Atlantic to the Mediterranean and explored the interior of Iceland. He and his wife, Laurie, were the first people to hike the full length of West Virginia's Allegheny Trail. They have also tramped New Zealand's Milford Track and a number of that country's other Great Walks.

Jobs as an interpreter for the Virginia State Parks system and as an assistant direc-tor for George Mason University's Outdoor Education Center have helped increase Leonard's appreciation for and knowledge of the natural world. He is the author of more than 200 articles on the outdoors, nature, and travel; is the walking columnist for *Blue Ridge Country* magazine; and has written more than 20 books. His *Wildflowers of the Appalachian Trail* received the National Outdoor Book Award, and the previous version of this book, titled *The Appalachian Trail: A Visitor's Companion,* received the Society of American Travel Writers Foundation's Lowell Thomas Travel Journalism Award.

Leonard has also been a Natural Heritage Monitor for the Appalachian Trail Con-servancy, helping to observe and protect rare and endangered plants; a volunteer main-tainer of the McAfee Knob section of the trail in Central Virginia; and on the board of directors of two Appalachian Trail–maintaining clubs.

He and Laurie currently live in Virginia, just a short drive from the AT.